IN THE SHADOW OF THE CROSS

Jewish–Christian Relations Through the Ages

BOOKS OF RELATED INTEREST

IN THE SHADOW OF THE CROSS

Jewish–Christian Relations Through the Ages

LEON SHELEFF
Tel Aviv University

VALLENTINE MITCHELL
LONDON • PORTLAND, OR

First published in 2004 in Great Britain by
VALLENTINE MITCHELL
Crown House, 47 Chase Side, Southgate
London N14 5BP

and in the United States of America by
VALLENTINE MITCHELL
c/o ISBS, 920 NE 58th Avenue, Suite 300
Portland, Oregon, 97213-3786

Website: www.vmbooks.com

British Library Cataloguing in Publication Data

Sheleff, Leon Shaskolsky
  In the shadow of the cross: a theology of generational
  relations and a sociology of Jewish–Christian interactions
  1. Christianity and other religions – Judaism 2. Judaism –
  Relations – Christianity 3. Intergenerational relations –
  Religious aspects 4. Religion and sociology
  I. Title
  306.6'6126

ISBN 0-85303-497-4 (cloth)
ISBN 0-85303-499-0 (paper)

Library of Congress Cataloging-in-Publication Data

Sheleff, Leon Shaskolsky
The shadow of the cross: Jewish–Christian relations through the ages
/ Leon Sheleff.
    p. cm.
Includes bibliographical references and index.
ISBN 0-85303-497-4
1. Christianity and other religions–Judaism. 2. Judaism–Relations–
Christianity. 3. Antisemitism–Psychological aspects. 4. Isaac (Biblical
patriarch)–Sacrifice–Comparative studies 5. Jesus Christ–Crucifixion–
Comparative studies. 6. Complexes (Psychology) I. Title.

BM535.S39 2004
296.3'96–dc21

2003051220

Typeset in 10.5/12pt Classical Garamond by Vallentine Mitchell Books
Printed in Great Britain by MPG Books Ltd., Bodmin, Cornwall

To Yoav and Aliza Tibon

Wonderful listeners, wonderful friends

Leon S. Sheleff

Leon S. Sheleff, who died suddenly while *In The Shadow of the Cross* was still in press, was Professor Emeritus in Law and Sociology at Tel Aviv University, Israel. During his rich academic career, he published eight books, in both English and Hebrew, covering a wide range of subjects, including: capital punishment and life imprisonment, civil disobedience, bystander studies, customary law and legal pluralism, the rule of law, generational conflict, a critique of sociological theory, and a commentary on selected biblical texts and their relevance to modern Israeli society.

Sheleff was an active member of several human rights organizations and wrote numerous articles in popular and academic journals, warning of the consequences of Israeli governmental policies with respect to the Occupied Territories and of judicial decisions approving such policies. He was also critical of the religious establishment in Israel and sought to highlight the democratic and socially conscious elements in Judaism.

Sheleff's last books were *The Thin Green Line: From Intractable Problems to Feasible Solutions in the Israel–Palestinian Conflict* (Xlibris) and *Drowning One's Sorrow: A Socio-Legal Study of Alcoholism Among Indigenous Peoples* (in press). He was also founding editor of two Israeli journals in criminology and sociology.

More information about Leon Sheleff and his research is available at www. sheleff.com

Contents

Preface

The basic thesis of this book was originally a chapter in my book, *Generations Apart*, published a quarter of a century ago. For a number of reasons, at the last moment, I decided to remove this chapter, mainly because I realized that the argument being presented was too complex and controversial to be encompassed within the limited framework of a chapter. I decided then that one day I would return to the theme, with the intention of devoting more time and thought to the research required. In the intervening years, I have published several books, in English and Hebrew, dealing mainly with the sociology of law and related topics. In a way this book, too, is connected to the sociology of law, as its starting point is one of the most important trials in the history of the world – the trial of Jesus.

However, the legal issues were not of its essence (even though they have some relevance for understanding the process that took place nearly 2,000 years ago). Its overriding importance is embedded in its theological interpretation and historical impact. I must stress, though, that I am neither a theologian nor a historian, though some of my earlier works do refer to religious themes and past events. This book is basically a combination of a sociology of religion and a sociology of generational relations. It is written from the perspective of the sociology of knowledge, which acknowledges the influence of personal, social and political factors in the nature of one's research. Thus, some of the chapters deal with the text of the New Testament, which I read as a Jew who does not accept two of the basic tenets of Christianity, which are also two of the major claimed facts of Jesus' life – that is, the nature of his birth and his resurrection. I am aware that, in recent years, Christian scholars have become engaged in a deep and revealing debate as to the full extent of the factual truth of their holy book, and I have utilized some aspects of their arguments to clarify my own musings as to the accuracy of the descriptions, and the pertinence of the meanings assigned to them. The existence of this clash of opinions among

Christian writers has undoubtedly facilitated my own entry, as an outsider, into this delicate area of research – but my own ideas were developed independently and, for the most part, prior to the recent research.

In prefaces of earlier books, I have thanked colleagues and friends who have read and helped me to revise earlier versions of the manuscript. In this book I have deliberately refrained from showing the written version to anyone (except for my diligent typists, Sylvia Weinberg and Daniela Korem, whom I thank most profusely). I have however discussed the thesis with many people over the years, and, in more formal manner, presented parts of the book at seminars of the Department of Sociology and Anthropology and the Faculty of Law at Tel Aviv University, as well as to students in academic courses. My gratitude for helpful comments made on these occasions. Naturally, my own immediate family has been amply exposed to my ideas and has always provided the necessary critique and encouragement. I also thank my daughter, Kinor, for designing the cover. On several occasions I have had lengthy discussions about the book with Yoav and Aliza Tivon, and, partly for this reason, but especially for many other reasons, of which they are well aware, I dedicate this book to them.

TWO TESTAMENTS

1
Bible

Perhaps the most amazing fact about the Bible is the manner in which it retains its vitality and impact over the years, despite the blatant discrepancy between much of what is contained therein and modern knowledge as to physical reality. The Bible was originally written for people who presumed that basic facts of physical reality were as they perceived them – namely that the earth, flat in its dimension, was the center of the universe; that the sun revolved around it; that the stars were no more than flickering lights; that the moon was to provide, at various times, some minimum modicum of light in the night hours; and that God himself reposed, in His Heaven, somewhere in that celestial setting directly above.

On the other hand, there are other aspects of the Bible that, within the framework of legitimate interpretation, bear a striking resemblance to the accumulated findings of scientific research. Indeed, one of the major inroads into biblical authenticity – the nineteenth-century theory of evolution – is, in many respects, and within the realm of reasonable exegesis, quite compatible with the biblical account of Creation. The story of Creation follows the broad contours of evolutionary theory – with life starting in an aquatic environment and human beings appearing only at the end of the biblical account, preceded by all other forms of life. A purely homo-centric description could well have started with the arrival of human beings on a deserted planet, which would then have been developed – with flora and fauna – to serve the needs of those who were to have dominion over it.

In any event, some biological and psychological research carried out on persons deliberately isolated for lengthy periods from all contact with the outside world, and deprived of any artificial time mechanism, indicates that there is no full synchronization between the human biological clock and the routine of nature. The human being apparently functions on a 25-hour basis, and thus in a non-artificial environment is perforce obliged to adapt his body to a world of nature that is attuned to a shorter (24-hour) day. The upshot of this gap is that a rest day is needed after a sequence of about six days in order to allow the body to recoup the accumulated hours that are lost during those six days – in fact, a week of seven days is the only universal measure of time that has no direct relation with nature (in contrast to days, months, years), as the seven-day week is a direct outcome only of biblical injunction.

The above are no more than idle thoughts on the role that the Bible plays in the lives of most people on Planet Earth, certainly those in the western world who have been exposed for the last two millennia to its teachings, and those in the many outposts of the former colonial world where the Bible was introduced together with the flag, trade and the gun (missionary activity being an integral part of military, political and commercial operations).

But, if physical and biological sciences pose a constant challenge (and even threat) to the validity of biblical writing, there can be no gainsaying the value of the Bible in presenting stories and themes that deal with everyday living, with characters of all kinds who are so easy to identify with in terms of their passions and pains, their struggles and achievements, their loves and their envies, their human frailties and their personal dilemmas.

In referring to the Bible, I am using it in its broadest meaning as referring to both the Old Testament (known in the original Hebrew as *Tanuch* – from the acronym of its three parts, *Torah, Neveim and Ketuvim* – that is, Pentateuch, Prophets and Other Writings) and the New Testament, which is sacred to Christians and also recognized by Muslims, but which forms no part of Jewish tradition. Indeed, parallel to some of the early Christian writings are books in the Apocrypha and then later internal Jewish exegetical writings, compiled into the Talmud in 300–500 CE.

One of the major differences between the Old Testament and the New Testament is that the former contains a varied host of characters, involved in all the intricacies of social life (and often, in fact, its intrigues), both within the immediate range of family life and on the larger political stage, whereas the latter focuses almost exclusively around the life of Jesus, his actions and his sayings, his parthogenetic birth, his death on the Cross and his subsequent resurrection, his closest disciples and the larger following that he attracted, and the accounts of his supernatural power and his ethical beliefs as expounded in many of the parables. The figures that stand out in the New Testament (such as Lazarus, risen from the dead by Jesus' intervention) have no independent status but are of consequence only due to their interactions with Jesus.

In the Old Testament, there is indeed a dominant figure – that of Moses, the Lawgiver – and the Pentateuch is often referred to as the Five Books of Moses (even though he only appears for the first time in the second book), but his prominence does not make for exclusivity. The first book of the Pentateuch deals extensively with those considered to be the Fathers and Mothers of the Children of Israel, and who are still referred to as such in Jewish prayers – Abraham, Isaac and Jacob in the patriarchal form of Jewish traditional liturgy (with the addition of Sarah, Rebecca, Leah and Rachel in some more modern prayers.) These three founding generations present an ongoing family saga, with all the overtones of generational conflict, familial favoritism and sibling rivalry; the kinds of contacts and conflict that exist in real life, that are the core of good literature, and the essence of perceptive social science research.

Even before the advent of the Children of Israel, the opening theme deals with the clash between Cain and Abel, which provides a basis to this day for serious social issues framed both in the naive question, 'Am I my brother's keeper?', with its implications for issues of altruism or fraternity, and in the stigmata of the 'Mark of Cain', with its implications for criminological and sociological theorizing in the modern world.

Similarly, after the first three founding generations, the fourth generation provides the basis for the nation of 12 tribes that emerges from the dozen sons of Jacob with his two wives and two mistresses (or handmaidens). Here too, sibling rivalry leads to one of the most vicious actions in the Bible when the ten older brothers decide to be rid of Joseph, their father's favorite, and after contemplating even his very demise, they sell him into slavery. This culminates, many years later, in a happy ending, as Joseph becomes the provider who saves his family (as he had done the Egyptians) from the consequences of prolonged drought.

Much later, the Bible, a holy book, does not spare the details of all the evil actions committed by some of its leading figures, such as the initial adulterous liaison of King David with Bat-Sheva, and the related betrayal of her husband, a faithful soldier, who was deliberately sent on a doomed and fatal mission so that the King could marry his widow.

These and other stories – because of the problematic nature of the personal and political behavior of so many of its major figures – have sometimes served to fan the flames of anti-Semitism. But there is something ruthlessly honest and appealingly genuine in these exposés, in this willingness, in sacred writings, to divulge not just the beauty that is often present, but also the nether side of life.

This is one of the major differences between the two testaments. In the New Testament, there is certainly a climactic tragedy in the arrest, trial and crucifixion of Jesus, as well as a few dubious stories, but for the most part, the dominant personality is devoid of human failings. Even his failure to avoid crucifixion, and the apparent desertion by his Divine

Father at this critical moment, is turned into a positive achievement, as it is presented not as a failure but as an act of redemption; a willingness by God to sacrifice his only begotten son to expurgate the sins of humankind, both those committed in the past, and those yet to be committed in the future.

This is an essential part of Christian theology. It inevitably raises the nagging question as to how humanity would have been redeemed if no such sacrifice had been forthcoming. In this sense, just as Jesus was acting out an inevitable denouement (which, according to the Gospels, he had actually foreseen), so those who carried out the Crucifixion were playing a pre-destined role that was essential for the very fulfillment of some divine plan – which involved a divine sacrifice for the benefit of countless past and future generations. After all, even without the Crucifixion, Jesus had, according to the New Testament, achieved much in his short life – his acts of medical and spiritual ministration to the sick, the lame and the needy had all been duly and fully noted, his eloquent Sermon on the Mount had been precisely recorded, and his immediate disciples were at hand to spread the message of his words and deeds. Surely here was the basis – especially if he had survived – for making a major impact on the Jewish people; or, alternatively, for laying down the basis, as indeed later happened, for a new religion, which could reach out, using his words and his actions, to the Gentiles, to make them also aware of the concept of one God who cared for and about his children on earth.

Was the incident of the killing of God's son really necessary (as Christian theology holds) for this message to be heard and accepted? In any event, the Crucifixion became the central moment of Christianity. It is the basis for one of its two major holidays (commemorating the birth on Christmas and the death at Easter of Jesus), and provides the symbol, the Cross, which has been associated ever since with the Church.

The Cross is indeed a dominant feature of Christianity, but for those considered responsible for the execution of Jesus – the Jewish people throughout all generations – the Cross is a problematic sign: the touchstone of so much of their oppression and suffering. The Cross may well shine out for Christians as a sign of God's love for humanity, but for Jews it is far more a reminder of their own humiliation because of the accusations hurled at them of having committed deicide. For them, the shining Cross has thrown an awesome shadow over their subsequent history.

That is the issue in terms of historical memory. But, for Jews, there is also a deep theological issue which, given the close interaction between the two religions, cannot be avoided – namely the question as to why a loving God would have to sacrifice his son in order to save humanity. This is a burning issue that deeply divides Judaism and Christianity. It is an issue which I, as a Jew, intend to probe, drawing on modern social science research in order to understand, if possible, the underlying message contained in the belief in a divine being who wishes to sacrifice his son for a larger good. Of course, the Old Testament itself has a similar story, in which this same divine being wishes, according to traditional interpretation – Jewish, Christian and Muslim – to test the depth of belief and the degree of loyalty of the first person to freely and fully acknowledge God's existence. In one of the most moving passages of the Bible, a detailed description is provided of the Father of the Jewish people, Abraham, being required to sacrifice his son at God's command in order, so it is explained, to prove his unequivocal belief in God. At the ultimate moment, divine intervention, through the voice of an angel, causes him to desist; instead of his son, he sacrifices a ram that had by chance become entangled in some nearby bushes. This story also raises many awkward questions as to the nature of a God who makes such demands on those who believe in Him, even if only as a test, with no intention of its consummation. This is not a minor episode in the Bible, but a story that is not only well-known but read every year in synagogues during the New Year services, with the additional blowing of a *shofar* (a ram's horn) as a further reminder of what took place between Abraham and Isaac.

Interestingly, the episode is not referred to in Hebrew as the Sacrifice of Isaac, but the Binding of Isaac (the *Akedah*). This is obviously more accurate, as Isaac was indeed bound but not actually sacrificed. This difference in nomenclature, as also in perception of the event, is very significant, as will be explained in later chapters. This is also not a minor episode in Christianity, for there are many references in its theology to Isaac's narrow scrape with death, and a direct connection is made between the Sacrifice of Isaac and the Crucifixion of Jesus – between the test of Abraham's willingness to sacrifice his son at God's behest, and God's willingness to sacrifice his own son for the sake of humanity.

Behind these two stories are not only theological inferences, but hints at larger social themes. This book will examine those larger themes in the process of attempting to understand the hidden messages about social life that are reflected in these stories, and attempting to explain their popularity in religious terms. In doing so, I shall attempt to remain as close as possible to the original text of the *Akedah* in the Old Testament, and the Crucifixion in the New, while taking into account both traditional religious interpretations of the stories and social science knowledge (based on research and theories) concerning generational contacts.

Note will be made in particular of the fact that these stories of sacrificing a son are by no means exceptional: historical incidents, popular myths and legends and world literature all contain many similar accounts of extreme paternal (or parental) actions taken against the younger generation. The connection of such stories with the biblical episodes will be examined. At the same time, it must be noted that there are also alternative themes in which it is the younger generation that carries out a harmful act against its progenitors. The Oedipus theme is the most significant story of this type, especially so since it has been adumbrated into a major psychological theory by Freud in the form of the Oedipus Complex. These insights by Freud, based on the use of Greek mythology to clarify modern social life, are of extreme importance, but his overall thesis must also be carefully analyzed. Several alternative approaches (in stories and themes) will be juxtaposed to Freud's idea – in particular, a theme that I have used as the basis for what I have termed the Rustum Complex. This is based on a Persian myth and an epic poem by the English poet Matthew Arnold, in which a father, Rustum, inadvertently kills his son, Sohrab, in a chance encounter (this is the precise opposite of the Oedipus theme). Stories (in myths, legends, literature) similar to that of the Rustum–Sohrab story seem to be far more prevalent than the Oedipus–Laius alternative – Laius being the less well-known father of Oedipus; also, incidentally, a father who had initially attempted to rid himself of his infant son by abandoning him in the woods.

Thus, there are three superficially similar, but diverse, stories: of Rustum, who kills his son accidentally; of Laius, who tries to kill his son by abandoning him but fails, and is subsequently accidentally killed by him; and of Abraham, who intends to kill his son in fulfillment of a divine command, but at the last moment desists. The theme of paternal violence being inflicted on one's own progeny is prevalent in different cultures and in different periods; in a secular age, when religion is nevertheless still a dominant factor of life, these basic and simple facts are in need of critical, but simultaneously sympathetic, analysis.

Modern fundamentalist religion does not allow for such questioning – neither did the medieval priesthood or rabbinate. In fact, some of the basic empirical knowledge (as to human behavior, motivations and machinations) was not available. Modern social science (and to a certain extent, critical studies in the humanities) has only emerged in modern times, into what is a basically secular world. Social science research is not restricted in the same manner as the pioneers of modern physical science (such as Copernicus and Galileo), of the biological sciences (such as Darwin), or of geology, which challenged the accepted age of the earth, putting it aeons earlier than the few thousand years of the biblical account. However, to this day, the biblical narrative is still used as the basis for the Jewish calendar (the world, from the moment of creation, now being presumably near the end of its sixth millennium).

But, paradoxically, the very freedom of social science from religious fetters has also led to a certain disinterest in religious ideas, despite some excellent studies in the sociology, anthropology and psychology of religion in the work of Durkheim, Weber and Freud, and other modern authors. What is also sometimes lacking is a sufficient degree of seriousness towards the original text. Since it is, as already noted, transparently incorrect in some of its basic data (out by billions of years in terms of the creation, lacking archaeological substance for significant parts of its presentation), the preference of social science research is to ignore it – or alternatively, to categorically, often cynically, totally undermine its validity. My own approach is to offer utmost respect for written material that is considered sacred by so many people, but – specifically because of its undoubted importance – to present a critical analysis of the text, and most particularly, to challenge dubious interpretations that have been made, whether by social scientists in the present era, or by religious authorities in the past.

Religion deals with eternal themes – the creation and the cosmos; life and death; heaven and earth; possible afterlife or a potential resurrection; the human life-cycle and nature's seasonal variations; familial relations and generational memories; inner faith and normative conduct; mysticism and mystery; holy rites and sacred sites. But these eternal themes are in need of constant examination, in terms of developing knowledge and updated insights. A divine being is, for religious people, eternal, but understanding must inevitably develop in line with increasing knowledge of nature and of ourselves.

Over the years, the Bible has been exposed to constant interpretation and explanation by religious leaders and others, based not just on belief, but also wisdom. It is still the most widely published and translated book in the world, and probably also the most widely read. Social life cannot be fully understood without due consideration being accorded to the role of religion. The recent millenium celebrations were basically a secular event, but they stemmed from a religious event – the birth of Jesus. Admittedly, they lacked the same pregnant expectations of a second coming of the Messiah that had accompanied the ending of the first millenium. But that is precisely the point – times have changed, and perceptions of changing phenomena have also fluctuated. This is indeed part of the difference between fundamentalist sects in any religion and the mainstream movements.

Amongst some Christian fundamentalist groups, there are still expectations of a cataclysmic clash between Gog and Magog – near Megiddo in Central Israel – which will culminate in a new Messianic Age. Amongst Jewish fundamentalist groups, plans are under way to prepare for the re-building of the Temple on the Temple Mount, where today stand two magnificent mosques that can be seen in all their splendor from many parts of the city. A Christian tourist once set fire to one of these; and at least three Jewish underground groups have been apprehended for planning to damage one of the mosques, or while actually in the process of attempting to do so.

This site has historical and religious significance for both Islam and Judaism. For Jews, it plays a dual role – as the place where the Temple once stood (or both temples, the first destroyed by Nebuchadnezer, the second by Titus), and as the presumed site of Mount Moriah, where Abraham intended to sacrifice his son. It is possible (though not clearly stated in the Bible) that the site of the Temple was specially chosen because of this connection with the intended sacrificial act of the venerable Jewish patriarch.

The Palestinian uprising of October 2000 was presumably triggered by the decision of the then Leader of the Opposition, Arik Sharon, to enter the Muslim compound in the company of several fellow parliamentarians from his party and under the protection of several hundred Israeli policemen. In this manner, and in a myriad of other ways, ancient biblical themes intrude on modern political and social happenings.

The Jews – specifically known as the 'People of the Book' – more than any other people are most acutely aware of this fact. Internally aware because, through the years of exile, they remembered vividly their contact with the Holy Land through prayers and rituals . Externally aware because they have been constantly exposed to the full measure of Christian wrath due to their (presumed) role in the death of Jesus, in the claimed cruel crucifixion of the Messiah, in the rejection by God's 'Chosen People' of God's only-begotten son. This is an essential part of the history of the western world, of the story of Christendom, of the chronicles of the Jewish people.

There is a deep underlying difference between a modern reading of the Old Testament and the New Testament. First, the Old Testament is clearly incapable of specific proofs of its authenticity – there is no Garden of Eden, and there were human beings well before the biblical story of Adam and Eve, which is set in a period only some six thousand years ago. However, the later stories, from Abraham onwards, do provide a stronger basis for meaningful understanding, although the conversations recorded can only represent an infinitesimal part of the overall dialogue, and the events described only represent an iota of the total social interaction; the New Testament refers to a time where human memory is more reliable, and the happenings themselves were set down within several decades of their occurrence. They therefore appear to have the immediacy that today we might associate with journalistic accounts – however, they often elicit the same skepticism due to their biases, selectiveness, and unavoidable human limitations, made even more tenuous because a significant amount of time had elapsed. Indeed, this provides partial explanation for the very discrepancies that exist between the different accounts of the four gospel narratives, but all historians and social scientists have to struggle with such problems.

In any event, there are probably more biographies of Jesus than of any other historical figure; they number in the thousands, and perhaps even tens of thousands, and include fictional lives or accounts oriented towards the needs of children.

Second, interpretations of the Old Testament – including possible misinterpretations – are far less pertinent for modern society than the New Testament (even given the admitted biblical background to much of the present confrontation between Israel and the Palestinians, or even the larger world of Arab society or of Islam). This is because the major focus of Christianity – the act of crucifixion and the ensuing symbol of the Cross – has a direct link with the Jewish people because of their supposed role in the death of Christ. There are many reasons for classical anti-Semitism – including the unfortunately ever-present phenomenon of xenophobia: the dislike of the different, the plight of minorities – but the Crucifixion is undoubtedly of major importance, and it relates directly to much of the essence of Christian theology.

Over the years, the Jewish people have borne the brunt of the message ensconced in the existence of the Cross: not the Romans, but the Jews bear responsibility for the suffering imposed on the Messiah, the Son of God. Indeed, Rome itself became the center for Christianity, even though the seat of the Holy See, the site of the new eternal city, is the very place where the early Christians were most subjected to the sort of tortures and indignities never imposed on them by their former co-religionists in Palestine. There might well have been anti-Semitism without the Crucifixion, given that the Jews were almost the prototype of a minority group; this very problem – of how to relate to minorities – confronts modern democracies all over the world. But the Cross was the ever-present symbol, the constant reminder not just of Jesus' death, but of those who were assumed to bear responsibility for the deed.

In a secular age, within a welcome atmosphere of ecumenical contacts, it is time to probe more deeply into biblical themes that have accompanied us through the generations – more specifically into the fuller and deeper meaning of the Crucifixion, of the subtle message contained in the ubiquitous Cross. The Cross appears to be so simple (two lines), so inspiring (a Messiah suffers on behalf of all humanity), and so beckoning (as is indicated by the very success of Christianity in spreading throughout the world). But for those who live in its shadow, for Jews, it is a menacing reminder of past oppression, of present tensions, of future dangers. In Israel, children are taught a truncated letter 't' as a sign for addition instead of a '+'; intersections are denoted by a multiplication sign (used elsewhere to denote railway tracks, which in Israel have another sign); all this in order to avoid having to make a cross. So deep are the wounds of Christianity, so powerful is the symbol of the Cross. In Israel, the equivalent of the international Red Cross Movement is the Red Magen David (the Shield of David, which appears also on its flag). However, the undoubtedly benevolent Red Cross Movement, which works in close liaison with the Red Magen David, has refused to grant this Jewish symbol (which is only marginally religious) the same recognition that it has given to the Red Sahar, used by many Islamic countries.

For the Christian, the Cross is protective and inspiring; for the Jew, the Cross is an antagonist, literally almost a sword, against which the Shield of David provides little protection.

In this book, I shall try to throw some light on the shadow of the Cross. What I write will not be pleasant for Christians, but I shall try not to be offensive. In any event, the Christian quest for the historical Jesus also raises doubts about many traditional beliefs. For that matter, aspects of my analysis will also possibly offend Orthodox Jews, and certainly Ultra-Orthodox Jews, particularly my re-interpretation of the story of the *Akedah*, which is essential as the foundation of the ensuing theoretical presentation.

Without the *Akedah*, there would possibly have been no Cross – that is, Jesus may still have been crucified, but the meaning and impact of his execution would have been vastly different. Furthermore, the site of the *Akedah*, as already noted, was the site where, some 40 years after the death of Jesus, the Jews experienced their greatest tragedy to that point – the destruction of the Second Temple. It was also about this time that the oral memories of the birth, trial and execution of Jesus started being transposed into written form, initially by the Evangelist, Mark, and then by Luke and Matthew in the other two synoptic Gospels, some time before John provided his slightly different version. This juxtaposition of the tragedy of Jesus and the Jewish tragedy is not, I submit, fortuitous. Mount Moriah, site of the *Akedah* and of the Temple, stands close to

Golgotha, the Hill of Skulls, also known as Calvary, where Jesus was crucified.

In much of Christian theology, the destruction of the Temple was the inevitable, and deserved, punishment inflicted on the Jews because of the sin they had committed in rejecting the Messiah and insisting on his execution. A parallel to this kind of thinking may be discerned in the modern world of Judaism, where some Ultra-Orthodox leaders have claimed that the Holocaust was divine punishment for the sins of secular Jews, in particular those within the Zionist movement who sought redemption for the Jewish people from the scourge of anti-Semitism not through penitent prayers and pedantic ritual, but through political action. Whereas redemption is supposed to come only with the advent of the 'real' Messiah, whom the Ultra-Orthodox patiently and expectantly await.

The followers of Jesus, including the Evangelists, faced within their own lifetime with the humiliation of his crucifixion, and then with the catastrophe of the destruction of the Temple, resolved their cognitive dissonance by linking the two events inextricably together. The crucial catalyst in this historical interpretation was the *Akedah* – Isaac saved by fortunate fate, Jesus by resurrection, both of them playing the role of sacrificial son to a loving father.

2
Akedah

The story of the *Akedah* begins with God calling out to Abraham by name, and Abraham responding with one word (in Hebrew): '*Hineni*' – 'Here I am'. This is an archaic form no longer in use in the modern language, but it is understood to contain an inner message beyond the mere declaration of one's presence: namely a prior readiness, in the course of the ensuing dialogue, to fulfill God's wish. Abraham is requested to take his son to a place, Moriah, a three-day journey from Beer-Sheba, where Abraham lived, and on arriving there, to sacrifice his son, his only son, his beloved son. The Bible elucidates that God's purpose was to test Abraham.[1]

Shalom Spiegel, in a fascinating book, describes this test as the last test; the ultimate test in a series of contacts between God and Abraham.[2] The Bible tells us directly only that God tests Abraham. What the test related to is not spelled out specifically. It is presumed, in Jewish and Christian interpretations of the Bible, that the test was of Abraham's willingness to sacrifice his son, but this is at no stage made clear. Other possibilities suggest themselves and will be examined.

Traditional Jewish and Christian interpretations have seen Abraham's willingness to sacrifice his son as the ultimate proof of his absolute and unswerving belief in God, and of his determination to obey all of His commands without reservation. However, from what is known of Abraham's behavior till then, from accounts of several earlier events in Abraham's life, it would seem that this is a simplistic approach to the momentous story of the *Akedah*.

On the one hand, we know that Abraham does not always implicitly accept God's plans. On being informed of the impending destruction of the cities of Sodom and Gomorrah because of the wickedness of their citizens, Abraham spares no effort in his attempt to convince God to avert the harsh decree. In an inspiring and fascinating dialogue, Abraham bargains with God, desperately seeking arguments to placate God's anger, focusing on the possibility of saving all the wicked people because of the virtuous behavior of a dwindling number of righteous people. In the end, the final smallest number of such people that is agreed upon is apparently not to be found, and God's original plan is executed.[3]

Yet, when Abraham is told to sacrifice his son, there is no similar desperate insistence on his part to seek a different outcome. On the contrary, Abraham meekly and immediately submits to God's command, and obediently and suppliantly sets out to consummate God's request. For this obedience, he has been widely and warmly commended as a model of true faith, to be emulated by others eager to fulfill God's will.[4] Religious thought does not even try to compare the contradiction between Abraham's response to the imminent fate of the people of Sodom and Gomorrah and the fate awaiting his own son, except, perhaps, to stress even more Abraham's implicit faith.

On the other hand, Abraham had, only a short while before – in terms of biblical chronology, a few paragraphs preceding the story of the *Akedah* – already proved his willingness to sacrifice a son. On this occasion, it was not God's original idea, but certainly carried out with his specific approval. Because of family tensions between his wife, Sarah, and the handmaiden, Hagar, the former had requested Abraham to have the latter and her son, Ishmael, sent away. Abraham was reluctant to do so, since he felt genuine love for his eldest child, a son with whom he had entered into a covenant with God by their simultaneously undergoing circumcision. On seeing Abraham's reluctance, God intervenes to tell Abraham to hearken unto the voice of his wife; only then, after the divine intervention, does Abraham accede to Sarah's demands. He then sends Hagar and Ishmael out into the desert with only minimal preparations, provisions and equipment, with every likelihood of their succumbing in the heat of the desert to their lack of sufficient food and water. As to how problematic this incident is in terms of Abraham's qualities, we may learn from a series of stories (*midrashim*) related in later Jewish legends of Abraham making several attempts to re-establish contact with Ishmael in the desert, but to no avail.[5]

So, even before Abraham received the direct order to sacrifice Isaac, he had already heard God command, in a slightly different context, that he should commit an act that would directly endanger another son's life. The background to these two instances is certainly very different, but Abraham's earlier dismissal of a son tends to undermine the significance that religious leaders attach to his later obedience in performing what is, in essence, a similar act (certainly in its potential outcome).

In any event, despite the fact that the Bible tells the reader that Ishmael does not die, and even provides a basic description of his subsequent marriage in Egypt and the birth of 12 children – thereby confirming part of God's promise to Abraham regarding the people that would emerge from his progeny – Abraham himself, from the biblical account, had no knowledge of these fortunate developments. For all practical purposes, on the personal level, he was left to grieve alone over the loss of this son.

Ishmael later returns to the Land of Canaan to participate with his half-brother, Isaac, in the burial of Abraham next to his wife, Sarah, at the 'Cave of the Patriarchs' in Hebron. No explanation is provided, no hint is even offered, as to how Ishmael even knew of his father's death in order to participate at the funeral, but it is symbolic of the strength of the family bond, in particular, perhaps, of Ishmael's filial fidelity.[6]

A number of writers have noted this juxtaposition of the two incidents: the actual expulsion of Ishmael and the intended sacrifice of Isaac. For them, the demand being made on Abraham is a divine punishment for the earlier action – in a sense, if you will, an inverted (or perhaps a perverted?) application of the *lex talionis* – a son for a son. David Polish actually poses this possibility. He writes that, 'Abraham cannot get Ishmael out of his mind. He is answering with Isaac because of Ishmael – "Take (Isaac) as you once took Ishmael whom you still love".' But he then goes on to explain that in the outcome of the incident, Abraham is enabled to discover 'a new and more compassionate God.'[7]

In the first incident, God had exhorted Abraham to acquiesce in Sarah's demand, that is, Abraham was acting against his better judgment only because of God's directive. On this basis, there is a distinct possibility that, having chosen Abraham as his messenger, God now has doubts as to his capacity to fulfill this mission, as his meekness in surrendering to Sarah, after God's intervention, suggests an underlying weakness. Where, one may surmise, is the courage and the humanity once displayed in pleading the cause of the people of Sodom and Gomorrah?

Perhaps, then, the last test imposed by God is not one of faith and belief, but of Abraham's spirit of humanity, his independence of mind, his courage at heart. The Bible does no more than tell us that God tested Abraham,: what specifically was at stake is left open to interpretation. Was the test to see if Abraham would immediately and implicitly obey (as he had done with the divine command to listen to Sarah's voice when she was seeking to be rid of her rival and her rival's son); or was it to see if Abraham had the inner resources (as he had displayed in the Sodom and Gomorrah incident) to challenge God's words? Was God looking for a pliant, blind believer, or for an independent, courageous personality?

For religious thinkers, Jewish and Christian, it is the former. In a secular age, while respecting religious traditions and acknowledging the Bible's persistent and perpetual power, the possibility exists of the latter.

Having, by indirect means, endangered the life of his eldest son, would Abraham now, in a more direct fashion, be prepared to eliminate his youngest son? Would filicide be the pattern of his behavior?

The Hebrew Bible describes mainly direct action, even to the extent of placing God in a human setting, where His precise words are quoted. At this stage, it is not spiritual enlightenment that is being described, but a God who takes on the attributes of humans by engaging them directly in dialogue. It is left to interpretation to make deeper and larger sense out of the drama being played out. In a religious age, it is perhaps understandable that the test to which Abraham was submitted would be considered one of faith. In a secular age – in which generational tensions have been the focus of research, treatment and theory – alternative explanations emerge.

This is the approach that I shall adopt. In doing so, I add a caveat – that the suppositions presented are biased toward Abraham and his possessing special qualities that enabled him to perceive human reality in a manner that is no less worthy of admiration than his ability, from a religious perspective, to understand and accept the novel idea of monotheism. Furthermore, it is presumed that his battle on behalf of Sodom and Gomorrah is a truer reflection of his qualities, and that these qualities – unique and special – are present also during the *Akedah* incident.

According to modern understanding, based on the accumulated findings of social science, a key factor of social life is the well-nigh inevitable clash of generations. This is expressed in modern times, on the one hand, through the prism of psychoanalysis (for example, the Oedipus Complex[8]), and on the other hand, through increasing evidence, especially in recent decades, of child abuse in the home and elsewhere, expressed through violence and sexual exploitation.[9]

Abraham is by no means, by biblical account, a person without blemish, but his positive attributes are undoubted. Whatever the depth of his belief in one God, one may presume that there was no less a depth of love for his children, for both of his sons; one may also presume that the spirituality that enabled him to perceive of the idea of monotheism was matched by his humanistic capacity to appreciate the complexities of family life: of the rivalry between Sarah and Hagar, of the impact this had on his sons, Ishmael and Isaac, of his own feelings towards them, and of his interaction with them.

If this is correct, after having in a moment of weakness acceded to Sarah's demand, without displaying any opposition to the divine intervention in favor of Sarah, he was bluntly and abruptly confronted with the full complexities of family life, and with the invariable ambivalence that accompanies it. Having expelled Ishmael (and religious interpretations agree on his reluctance to do so and his subsequent regrets[10]), he now had, on his own – without the kind of psychological support that might be available in modern times – to confront this ugly reality, to contemplate the nature of human nature.

And then comes the command: take your son, your other son, your remaining son, and sacrifice him to your God. To the modern age, and even earlier ages, this has been an outrageous demand and has caused much embarrassment to religious thinkers. But, to a certain extent (and not completely, as we shall see), it is mitigated by the fact that the story has a happy ending. Isaac is saved. However, it must be remembered that at the time that the demand for sacrifice was made, there was nothing unusual about such a practice. According to the Bible itself, and to archaeological and historical evidence, filicidal practices were prevalent at that time throughout the region. Those who believed in idols, those who worshipped Baal and Moloch, were ever eager to sacrifice their sons.[11] Even some modern apologetics for such actions – such as it being an attempt to limit over-population, which placed strains on the common resources – fails to convince, as normally it was the eldest child (generally the eldest son) who was the victim of these practices, and not the younger ones.[12]

Filicide (or infanticide), then, is part of the overall human experience. In universal terms, it appears to be only one aspect – if admittedly an extreme one – of patterns of hostility (including non-violent). It has not been practiced by everyone, but has been sufficiently common to make it a social phenomenon worthy of note.[13] The killing of a son is filicide, even if carried out in biblical times – and in biblical terms.

In any event, for Abraham, the divine command to sacrifice his son must clearly have been an ambiguous statement: on the one hand, this appears to be a total denial of the earlier promise of the great nation that was to emerge (especially given the loss of Ishmael); on the other hand, the demand itself was not specifically monotheistic, since child sacrifice was part of the normative practices of that time and in that area amongst the heathens. To do precisely what his neighbors were doing would be to diminish the very uniqueness of the monotheistic concept that Abraham was struggling to conceptualize and appreciate.

From this perspective, we may begin to understand why the sacrifice had to be carried out at Moriah – not on a nearby hillock or mountain (of which there is no shortage in the desert terrain near Beer-Sheba), but in an area with which Abraham had, till then, had little contact, a full three days' journey away. These three days are crucial. They indicate no rush to act, but a prolonged period of expectation, allowing time for reflection, allowing time for regret, allowing time for introspection, allowing time for insight.

On this score, the Bible provides us with little assistance. We only know of the length of time it took to walk from Beer-Sheba to Moriah; we also know that the father and son were accompanied by two young people, but nothing is known of what transpired during this journey, what they spoke about, what emotions were sensed, how father and son interacted with each other. The Bible sometimes provides extensive descriptions (such as the meeting between Jacob and Esau at the River Jabbock, or that between Joseph and his brothers in Egypt),[14] on other occasions it provides only a bare outline. In this case, it is possible, given the gravity of the occasion, that little was said, but even so, the concerned and curious would want to know what transpired between father and son; whether there was physical contact between them, the former aware of the impending tragedy awaiting them at their destination, the latter perhaps sensitive enough to be aware of the tension emanating from his father, from the manner of his walk, from the tenderness of their physical touching, in their eye contact.[15]

In fact, rabbinical exegesis has shown no lack of creativity in attempting to fill in the gaps. However, much of these additions serve only to further complicate the problematics of the story. Intent on proving Abraham's utter faith, they allow for evil attempts by hostile forces to dissuade Abraham from his intended action. Satan, according to some of these additions, accosts Abraham and suggests to him that he should disobey God's will, that he should forego the sacrifice. But, according to these stories, Abraham is steadfast in his intention, steadfast in his faith. And so, rabbinical explanation unabashedly allows for a God who wishes to sacrifice a human being, and a Satan that wishes to forestall this act! More than this, and worse than this, other *midrashim* (rabbinical exegesis), which Spiegel describes in detail, actually change the climax of the story – referring to the consummation of the sacrifice, with a subsequent resurrection (which allows, of course, for the later emergence of the Jewish people).[16]

For those who adopt this approach, there is apparently a desperate need to prove Abraham's faith beyond any doubt. The doubt apparently arises from the fact that, in the end, the sacrifice is not performed. This, it seems, leads to the gnawing feeling that, perhaps, Abraham, from the beginning did not intend to sacrifice Isaac, that his three-day journey to the site was only a charade: an attempt to outwit God.

This possibility poses problems not only for the story *per se,* but for the very destiny of the Jewish people as, through years of persecution and suffering, much succor has been gained from this story, which has been etched deeply in the collective memory.[17] For it has been believed that God will remember Abraham's complete faith as well as His later intervention to save Isaac, and will in a similar fashion allow for the redemption of God's people, who are the descendents of Abraham. Given this close connection between Abraham, the father of the Jewish people, and their ongoing fate through the generations, it becomes of supreme importance to allay any doubts as to the sincerity and purity of Abraham's intentions. While being grateful for the deliverance of Isaac from his fate, there must nevertheless be a firm conviction that Abraham had no reservations as to the outcome, not even, one presumes, a sneaking hope that somehow, at the end of the three-day journey, his son would yet be saved. Any such hope would detract from the fullness of his faith and would simultaneously perhaps deny his people salvation at crucial times in later generations because of his diminished faith. Their fate is intimately bound up with his faith.

In this kind of interpretation, there are obvious overlaps with the Christian approach to the meaning of the Crucifixion; this is not surprising, given the fact that the early Christians were themselves mostly Jews, who were amenable to the redemption aspect of the event at Golgotha due to the similar implications of the event at Moriah. The differences between the two – Jesus was sacrificed, Isaac was saved – are also, however, of major theological and sociological import, as will be explained in later chapters.

The possible alternative explanation for the three days that constitute the *Akedah* story is that Abraham experienced a period of deep soul-searching as he desperately tried, on his own perhaps, or in communion with his God, to understand one of the basic facts of social life: the ambivalence, so often expressed within the family setting, of love and concern and pride, mingled, on occasion, with hostility, indifference and anger. Abraham, being uniquely capable of interaction through belief with a divine being, was surely no less capable of sensitive perception of his immediate surroundings within his family. The trauma of Ishmael's expulsion with Hagar was a catalyst for understanding the complexities of his relations with his remaining son. In order to come to terms with this disturbing situation, he embarked, through an interaction with God, on a three-day trek that allowed him to reflect both on his relationship with his son and his capacity as a father to harm him (even unto death), and also on his desire to protect and guide him.

In modern terms, Abraham was undergoing a mimesis: that is, acting out an event in order to fully appreciate its meaning.[18] The negative aspect of generational contacts is expressed in the binding of Isaac prior to his imminent demise through sacrifice; the closer the actor (Abraham) came to actually performing the deed, the more precisely would the problem confronting him (of the relationship between fathers and sons) be clarified. This is what happened on Mount Moriah – or, to be more exact and fair – this is *possibly* what happened on Mount Moriah. Abraham was creatively setting up a situation that would enable him to better comprehend and cope with his own confused feelings by exposing them to symbolic reality.

A further conundrum remains. The voice that called out to Abraham to desist was not that of God, but an angel acting for God. Indeed, never again was God to engage in a dialogue with Abraham, as he had so often done until then. In fact, Abraham himself responds with a second *Hineni*, on hearing his name being called, and willingly foregoes the sacrifice of his son by supplanting him with a ram. Again, religious interpretation ignores this key transformation. It is now not the voice of God calling out, but only an angel as an emissary. Why? Is God now angry with Abraham for going so far, almost to the point of no return (on the assumption that the test was to see if Abraham would understand the horror of what was being asked of him)? Does He refuse any further conversation because Abraham was so close to failure?[19]

Or alternatively, does God understand, watching from celestial heights, what thoughts and emotions are churning within Abraham's very being? Does He then send only an emissary to prevent the action, in a continuation of the test, in order to allow Abraham this final degree of flexibility, of independence? For, perhaps, from Abraham's perspective, this is not God's emissary; perhaps, drawing on rabbinical exegesis, it may be asked if this is one last attempt by Satan to undermine Abraham's faith.[20] Why should Abraham, responding initially to God's voice directly, now allow an emissary to cancel the project?

But, as the Bible explains, Abraham is quite willing to trust this new voice, one he has never encountered before; by now, it seems, the mimesis has been acted out to the end. Isaac has been bound, the fatal instrument is at hand, and then Abraham immediately responds to this new, strange voice calling out to him, and once again he says '*Hineni*', perhaps anticipating the countermanding order to stay his hand. Having proved himself in this final, ultimate test, by pulling back from the brink, he may now be relied upon to act with sensitivity and wisdom. Having understood the depths of possible depravity, he may now soar to greater spirituality on his own.

And so Abraham is, at the end of the biblical account, rewarded by God for listening to the voice, for obeying what presumably was God's command, by a renewed promise of the future power and plenty of his progeny. But which command: the initial directive to take the son for sacrifice, or the last-minute intervention to desist? For the text puts into the mouth of the emissary the command to obey 'my' word. Is this a reference to the actual words of God at the beginning of the story, or to the words of the emissary at its conclusion? Let me suggest the latter. At this moment, according to Erich Wellisch, a critical juncture in world history was reached.[21] There is no room for human sacrifice on the altar of a monotheistic God. Human life is precious, filicide is an abomination. Religious rituals, important for social life, may instead focus on the sacrifice of animals (*vide* the nearby ram). Many generations later, the site of the *Akedah* was to become the presumed site of the Temple, where animals were indeed sacrificed to the honor and glory of God. But to establish a ban on human sacrifice, given generational frictions and the prevalent surrounding norms that sanctioned it, words alone are not sufficient: the drama had to be acted out in vivid reality. The only question remaining is whether (given generational tensions) the message will be understood.

This type of explanation for Abraham's role in the *Akedah* also provides an explanation for the contrasting behavior of Abraham in the Sodom–Gomorrah incident. On that occasion, the harm about to be wrought was beyond Abraham's direct control. The fate of the inhabitants was in God's hands, and Abraham could do no more than plead their case, which he did so eloquently and almost effectively. However, in the case of Isaac, it was he, Abraham, who bore direct responsibility for what would transpire at Moriah. Abraham was in control of what was happening; he could comply with God's directive, or he could refuse. Passionate debate with God was a distinct possibility, but it would tend only to blunt the issue at stake which – beyond the divine issues of faith and obedience – was a human one of familial relations. The issue was not his capacity to plead on behalf of others, but his capacity to probe within himself the essence of a key problem in social life – generational conflict. Abraham, if he is to be given due credit based on modern understanding, was willing to struggle with the full import of generational relations on his own. Confronted with the sacrifice of his son, he finally understood the full extent of his dilemma: a universal dilemma not confined to any period or place, a dilemma of parental power *vis-à-vis* the vulnerable young – a dilemma not concerned with killing alone (or even mainly), but with harm inflicted, even unwittingly, even in error, and not necessarily in anger.

Religious thinking holds that by his action, Abraham assured God's compassionate protection of his people. Secular thinking suggests that by his action, Abraham exposed the problematics of parenthood and provided a message that may well resound through the generations: a warning about parental power, but also an example of parental devotion. The test was not about love of God (for Abraham had already proved that in manifold ways), but love of progeny, despite the dilemmas and difficulties of parenthood (facts which are so much easier to ignore or deny).

The story of the *Akedah* is a superb one, in its wording it is a literary masterpiece; it grips the reader, it speaks magnificently to people of different times and different climes. But, as with all good literature, it is open to varying understandings and interpretations. For hundreds of years, the emphasis was on the religious understanding of faith in God. In recent years, other possibilities have been probed, drawing on the findings of social science research. Some of the above descriptions fit in well with much of this modern writing.[22] It is now necessary to examine separately some of these more modern ideas. The story remains constant as a short, succinct episode in a sacred text; the understandings must be adapted to the broader perceptions, perhaps even more perceptive wisdom, that developed by virtue of increased knowledge. To do so is not to diminish the text or desecrate it; on the contrary, it is to accord it due respect, and to perhaps reinvigorate its overall appeal.

Indeed, it is only with the wisdom of hindsight that the inner message of biblical themes may be ascertained; only with the accumulated knowledge of modern social science that deeper understanding may be achieved. In a series of books and articles, David Bakan suggests that, in general, the underlying theme of the Bible – both Old and New Testaments – is to warn against the dangers of child sacrifice.[23] More specifically, he states that:

> The essence of Judaism and Christianity is the management of the infanticidal impulse ... and a binding of the father against acting out the impulse. One of the main historical functions of the Judeo-Christian tradition has been to counteract the infanticidal impulses which arise as a dialectical antithesis to the assumption of paternal responsibility on the part of men.[24]

Symbolic support for Bakan's approach is found in the final book of the second part of the *Tanakh* (containing all the prophetic books), which concludes with a statement of almost messianic proportions, especially since it incorporates a reference to Elijah, the prophet, who is traditionally considered to be a forerunner of the Messiah. As Malachi, the prophet, exclaims:

> Behold, I will send you Elijah the prophet before the coming of the great and terrible day of the Lord. And he shall turn the heart of

the fathers to the children, and the hearts of the children to their fathers; lest I come and smite the land with utter destruction.[25]

Bakan's use of the word 'binding', in the context of preventing the father from acting out any negative impulse, is of some interest. For the direct translation of the Hebrew word *Akedah* is 'binding'. Bakan himself refers elsewhere to an act of binding that is part of religious ritual – namely the practice of religious Jews at morning prayers on an ordinary weekday, of putting on *tefillin* (phylacteries). This is in fulfill-ment of a biblical command. In practice, it involves, amongst other actions, the binding of a leather strap seven times around the forearm. Bakan, himself a practising Jew, writing from a professional psychologi-cal perspective, suggests that in this physical action (a sort of mimesis, if you will) the hand, with its potential capacity to harm, is restrained: a constant reminder of the need to be aware of paternal power, to avoid its possible damaging manifestations.[26]

But Bakan himself is fully aware of the limitations of symbolic acts: plain and simple, they may be easily misinterpreted. This is indeed, according to Bakan, what happened with the *Akedah*. Its real message, of avoiding doing harm to children, was not understood. Thus, as already noted, the reference to the incident on Mount Moriah is generally made in terms of 'sacrifice', even though no sacrifice was consummated. Thus, according to Bakan, a more direct action is required, and this is precisely what happened several generations later when Jesus, considered by many as the son of God, was sacrificed – and, of course, Christian theology considers this as an act of redemption. (To which I would add that this message too, despite its directness, was also misunderstood, as will be explained in later chapters.) Indeed, for Bakan, the interconnections between the two incidents may be noted in the overlap between the Jewish festival of Passover and the Christian holiday of Easter.[27] The very name of Passover is a reference to the saving of the first-born of the Israelites in Egypt when, in the final plague, the first-born of the Egyptians were killed, but in this methodical slaughter, the houses of the Israelites, clearly designated by the blood of a lamb smeared on the doorposts, were passed over; in the harsh biblical description:

> And the blood shall be to you for a token upon the houses where ye are; and when I see the blood, I will pass over you, and there shall no plague be upon you to destroy you, when I smite the land of Egypt.[28]

As Isaac was saved at the last moment and replaced by a ram, so, several generations later, all the first-born of the Israelites are spared the fate of their Egyptian neighbors. As Moses explained to the people:

> For the Lord will pass through to smite the Egyptians; and when
> He seeth the blood upon the lintel, and on the two side-posts, the
> Lord will pass over the door, and will not suffer the destroyer to
> come in unto your houses to smite you.[29]

This is then, by Jewish tradition, one of the first examples of redemption granted because of the proven faith, through the *Akedah*, of Abraham.

Of course, the harm inflicted on the Egyptians is also problematical: the first-born children were, after all, not responsible for the unfortunate fate of the Israelites; it was Pharaoh who displayed obstinacy in refusing to release the Israelites. Yet, this tenth plague is only one more example of the manner in which the fate of children, as noted by Bakan, is a dominant theme in the Bible. In later chapters, we shall deal with the theme of the interconnection between Passover and Easter. For the moment, we must return to the theme of the initial attempt to sacrifice a son in the *Akedah* story revolving around Isaac.

The story has evoked many different reactions: of puzzlement, of inspiration, of embarrassment, of rejection, of fear. Of puzzlement as to why God should even conceive of a test as extreme and cruel as this; of inspiration for those eager to accord Abraham the capacity for expressing utter faith; of embarrassment as to how to relate to a story so sinister in its intended consequences; of rejection by those who want no part of a religion whose patriarchal figure is capable of committing (or almost committing) such a despicable act; of fear, which has been specifically used by Kierkegaard in the title of his book, *Fear and Trembling*, which deals philosophically with the meaning of this sacrifice.[30]

A useful summary of these varying approaches is provided by Louis Berman, who deals comprehensively with many of the myriad responses to the story of the *Akedah*.[31] In any event, as extensive as this presentation is, it can by no means be exhaustive, as for every written exposition there must surely be several oral analyses – more particularly since many New Year sermons must inevitably focus on the story, given the fact that it is read in the synagogue on the second day of Rosh Hashana (the Jewish New Year).

Furthermore, almost nothing is known about how the story is perceived by young people when they are exposed to it for the first time. For instance, in Israel, where the Bible is taught in all schools, the story is included in the curriculum for the third grade, that is, for children at the age of eight. Little is known of the emotions that grip the child as he follows the unfolding of a story about a father who is willing to kill his son. What possible fears does it instill in him? Sigmund Freud related that one of his patients – from one of his seminal case studies – explained his loss of religious faith as a rejection of a God who was capable of making such a demand; Freud himself did not attempt to probe the story at greater depth, or the emotions of his patient.[32] Freud himself – who was otherwise so involved with generational conflict (such as in the Oedipus Complex) and ever ready to draw on biblical themes (for instance, in his book, *Moses and Monotheism*[33]) – never related to the *Akedah*, a story that is in its bare essence, as we shall explore later, the very opposite of the Oedipus theme.

Possibly the most troublesome explanations given over the years are those that attempt to explain Abraham's action in terms of the normative procedures of that period. A leading American-Jewish scholar, Robert Gordis, in a book entitled *Judaic Ethics for a Lawless World,* provides perhaps the most succinct and pertinent example of this approach. He writes:

> The sacrifice of a child was an all-but-universal practice in ancient Semitic religion and beyond ... Abraham, living ... in a world permeated by pagan religion, did not feel himself confronted by a moral crisis when he was commanded by God to sacrifice Isaac, and he proceeded to obey ... In the patriarchal age, this horror of child sacrifice, an attitude in which Judaism was unique in the ancient world, still lay in the distant future.[34]

In discussing the work of Gordis, Berman comments that, 'The error of presentism flaws any attempt to evaluate the event from another era as if it were occurring in our time. When you attempt to put yourself in Abraham's shoes, first ask yourself, "Did he wear shoes?"'[35] Such an approach seems to me to denigrate whatever contribution Abraham made to Judaism and to universal influence, for it ignores the fact that his greatness lay precisely in his being able to rise above the prevailing tide of custom and opinion, to acknowledge the very idea of monotheism in an environment of idol-worship. Apologetics for Abraham's action diminish his stature. In any event, modern life provides us with ample evidence of child abuse in various forms – in one of extreme instance, a father explained in court that the murder he committed was in response to a divine command, just like Abraham. Carol Delaney[36] uses this incident as a basis for an interesting, but still problematic, analysis of Abraham's action, as she remains troubled till the end by the violence endemic in the story.

Abraham's action cannot be understood in terms of normative values and customary practices of that time; such an approach is to deny his innovative creativity. Certainly today, it must be understood in universal terms, which is perhaps easier to do because of the twin facts of it being a secular age (not bound by rabbinical and priestly interpretations), and a scientific age (allowing the use of sociological and psychological knowledge). In these terms, Abraham's last-minute withdrawal from completing the sacrifice of his son is the mark of his positive qualities, of his passing of the test, and the real lesson to be learned by others, the true message ensconced in the story.

The most significant opposition to such a positive approach comes from a thoughtful book by Jon Levenson on the *Death and Resurrection of the Beloved Son.*[37] His opening gambit is that, whatever reservations were expressed by several of the prophets in the Bible regarding the contemporary practice of child sacrifice to pagan gods (a practice that some of the Israelites seemed to have adopted), the Bible itself makes reference on several occasions to the handing over of a first-born son to God; like the first fruits and first born animals, they belong to God. Thus, Levenson refers to a passage in Exodus (coincidentally in chapter 22, the same number as the story of the *Akedah* in Genesis). Exodus 22:28 states: 'You shall give Me the first-born among your sons.' To this day, religious Jews still perform a ceremony of redemption for a first-born son 30 days after birth (known in Hebrew as *Pidyan ha-Ben*). Levenson contrasts the differing approaches of two prophets to this issue of child sacrifice. Both Jeremiah and Ezekiel condemned the practice but, whereas the former indicated that the practice was clearly idolatrous and not part of God's will, the latter suggests that at some stage it had been acceptable. Thus, Levenson writes:

> Whereas Jeremiah vociferously denied the origin of the practice in the will of YHWH, Ezekiel affirmed it: YHWH gave Israel 'laws that were not good' in order to desolate them, for only as they were desolated, only as they were brought to humiliation, could they come to recognize YHWH and obey His sovereign will. Here, as often in the Hebrew Bible, God's goodness conflicts with His providential designs; He wills evil in order to accomplish good. The evil that He once willed is the law that requires the sacrifice of the first-born. The good toward which this aims is Israel's ultimate recognition and exaltation of Him as their God.[38]

What Levenson ignores is the uncertainty as to the intention behind the giving of the first-born to God. Is this intended for sacrifice or for service, the actual killing of a son, or his dedication to the service of God? The reference concerning the son contains no intrinsic meaning of sacrifice. Indeed, in the same passage, reference is made to the offering up not just of the first-born of animals, but 'the fullness of thy harvest, and outflow of thy presses'.[39] Clearly, no killing was involved in such products. Why then presume that such was indeed God's intent for children? And, if this was indeed the intent, why was it not specifically stated? On the contrary, a later passage, where a clear distinction is made between animals and humans, clarifies this dilemma – whereas the first-born of the former are to be sacrificed, the first-born of the latter are to be redeemed. As written in the Bible, 'The first-born of man shalt thou surely redeem ... And their redemption money – from a month old shalt thou redeem them – shall be, according to the valuation, five shekels of silver.'[40] Indeed, this process of first declaring the need to make an offering, and then describing how it was to be avoided by the payment of redemption money, may have been done specifically so as to undermine – in a measured process – the prevalent customs of contemporary society. The very juxtaposition of the two contrasting references would enhance the norm (of child protection) that was being established.

Indeed, if child sacrifice really was incumbent on the Israelites, then this would, from a different perspective, make the story of the *Akedah* – whatever interpretation is placed on it – totally redundant. If everybody was obliged to sacrifice a son, as Abraham had been asked to do, how would the test imposed on Abraham be unique? Where would be the wonderful proof of his firm belief in God? On the contrary, the idea of offering the first fruits or the first son may easily be perceived as a ceremonial thanksgiving for a new expression of creative power. (Parenthetically, it may be noted that, to this day, observant Jews do not eat the first fruits of a young tree but wait for the next season, as an expression of thanksgiving for the abundance of God's creation.)

Levenson, however, turns this rather obvious argument upside down. Lacking a direct reference to the actual practice of child sacrifice at God's command, he reminds us, in the opening chapter, that:

> There is one text in the Hebrew Bible in which an Israelite father – indeed, the father of all Israel, the Patriarch Abraham – is commanded to offer his son Isaac ... Whatever the ambiguities of the legal and prophetic materials on child sacrifice, Gen. 22:1–19 is frighteningly unequivocal about YHWH's ordering a father to offer up his son as a sacrifice ... For here it is not the wayward people but the faithful God who demands the immolation of the favored son, and not as a punishment in the manner of the

hardening of Pharaoh's heart either, but *as a test of true devotion.*
Were the practice of child sacrifice always so alien to YHWH …
would there have survived a text in which it is this act and no other
that constitutes YHWH's greatest test of his servant Abraham?[41]

Noting that some scholars, including Spiegel,[42] have claimed that the real
message (found in the story's ending) is not to encourage child sacrifice
but to abolish it, Levenson then goes on to argue that, 'As an etiology of
the redemption of the first-born son through the death of the sheep,
however, the *Agedah* [*sic*] is, it seems to me, most ineffective.' He
suggests that,

> It is passing strange to condemn child sacrifice through a narrative
> in which a father is richly rewarded for his willingness to carry out
> that very practice. If the point of the agedah is 'abolish human
> sacrifice, substitute animals instead', then Abraham cannot be
> regarded as having passed the test.[43]

It may be difficult to determine if Abraham actually passed the test with
flying colors because of the ambivalence evident during his journey of
mimesis, but that does not affect the issue of what the nature of that test
is, namely the abolition of filicide, as I and others have suggested.

However, Levenson – having completely ignored any such possible
explanation of the *Akedah* – is then insistent that there can only be one
explanation for the text in Exodus, namely that 'You shall give Me the
first-born among your sons.' He notes that 'Most fathers did not have to
carry out this hideous demand. But some did.'[44]

A possible reason for this very focused approach by Levenson is that it
is not the sacrifice of the son (or, from the title, the death) that solely
interests him, but two further themes: the resurrection of the son and the
implications that these stories have for Jewish–Christian relations. This is
spelled out specifically in the opening sentence of a chapter entitled 'The
Displacement of Isaac and the Birth of a Church.' He writes:

> The identification of Jesus of Nazareth with 'the beloved son' on
> which our discussion has focused comes early in the Synoptic
> Gospels. It is first made through a heavenly announcement, during
> Jesus' ablution at the hands of John the Baptist: 'You are my
> beloved son. With you I am well pleased.' A quote that is based on
> sayings of all four of the evangelists.[45]

Levenson also writes that:

Alongside the depiction of Jesus ... as the archetypical Christian, as the first-born, and as the eschatological Adam lies the typology most pertinent to our topic. This is, once again, Jesus in the role of Isaac, the son brought to the point of death by his loving father.[46]

A few pages later he admittedly writes that:

No claim is here made that the Jewish theme of the near-loss and miraculous return of the beloved son accounts for the Christian interpretation of the reported resurrection of Jesus as the pivotal moment of all history.[47]

Yet, constantly returning to the cryptic sentence, 'You shall give Me the first-born among your sons,' Levenson sees the saving of Isaac from the planned sacrifice in terms of a resurrection – indeed, almost a prototype of the idea of resurrection – and certainly as a forerunner of the Crucifixion. Thus he writes:

In Abraham's greatest test, his preference for the love of God over the love of his favored son enables him to have both: Abraham remains absolutely faithful yet Isaac lives. All things work out for Abraham not because, hedging his bets, he finds a middle way between his two great loves, but because God respects and rewards the uncompromising obedience – obedience even unto death – that he demands from those he has chosen. In the case of the new agedah in which Paul believes, the crucifixion and resurrection of Jesus, God's willingness to hand over his son eventuates not in Jesus' death, but in his post-mortem life. Indeed, Paul maintains that such life is possible only because God the Father follows in the path of Father Abraham and refuses to spare his son from being slain and offered. God proves faithful to the hoary imperative to slay one's first-born son, yet Jesus lives. As in the first agedah and in the story of Joseph, the son can be enjoyed and the promise sustained only if he is exposed to death itself.

The most memorable statement of the role of love in the new agedah of the Christian faith appears in the Fourth Gospel: 'For God so loved the world that he gave his only Son, so that everyone who believes in him might not perish but have eternal life.'[48]

Levenson is, I would agree, entirely correct in making this close link between the *Akedah* and the Crucifixion. Indeed, I would go further and suggest that without the *Akedah*, there could have been no meaning attached, by the early Christians who were Jews, to the Crucifixion. Indeed, the New Testament itself makes several references to the *Akedah* in the context of understanding the fate of Jesus.[49] Levenson himself adds that:

> In a sense, Jesus provides those who believe in him with immortality by dying in their stead – except that, as in the cases of the beloved sons in the Hebrew Bible, Jesus' brush with death proves reversible and he is, like them, miraculously restored to those who love him but have had every reason to give up all hope for his return.[50]

This contact between the *Akedah* and the Crucifixion allows Levenson to extend his analysis by trying to understand, in this context, the relations between the two religions. However, he ends his book by suggesting that the true model is not a generational one – in which Judaism is conceptualized as the parent and Christianity as the child – but one of sibling rivalry. In referring to the 'relationship of the two traditions', he states:

> That relationship, usually characterized as one of parent and child, is better seen as a rivalry of two siblings for their father's unique blessing. Judaism and Christianity are both, in substantial measure, midrashic systems whose scriptural base is the Hebrew Bible and whose origins lie in the interpretive procedures internal to their common Scripture and in the rich legacy of the Judaism of the late Second Temple period. The competition of these two rival midrashic systems for their common biblical legacy re-enacts the sibling rivalry at the core of ancient Israel's account of its own tortured origins.[51]

Levenson ends his book with the quizzical statement that, 'The two traditions lose definition and fade when that universalistic affirmation overwhelms the ancient, protean, and strangely resilient story of the death and the resurrection of the beloved son.'[52]

It is true that some rabbinical exegeses refer to Isaac as having been killed and then resurrected. These additions were made, as already described, in order to emphasize even more strongly Abraham's faith. But they are not consistent with the biblical text, which refers only to the saving of Isaac, and not to his actual sacrifice. In this sense, the two stories are not completely symmetrical: the idea of the willingness of a father to sacrifice his son is indeed common to them, but their outcomes are totally different. Isaac is not killed, and therefore his 'resurrection' is irrelevant. Jesus is killed, and therefore, for Christian theology, his resurrection becomes essential: one of the pillars of its subsequent theology.

This is where Judaism and Christianity differ. This is the basis of the historical rivalry between them. In the final analysis, the issue of sonhood is crucial. To understand this theological debate – which is carried out not at some celestial level but between human beings, all of whom were at one stage children, most of whom were later parents (though not those who, because of the rule of celibacy, were leaders of the Catholic Church) – it is important to understand the nature of generational contacts and generational conflicts. What is needed is a sociology of theology. This theme will be pursued, but first, the full ramifications of the crucifixion of Jesus must be examined, both as a continuation of the *Akedah* of Isaac, and also as a deviation from it.

NOTES

1. Genesis, 22:1–19.
2. Shalom Spiegel, *The Last Trial* (Philadelphia, PA: Jewish Publication Society, 1967).
3. Genesis, 17:16–33.
4. For a recent example of the traditional Jewish approach to the story *see*, for instance, Aharon Agus, *The Binding of Isaac and Messiah: Law, Martyrdom, and the Deliverance in Early Rabbinic Religiosity* (Albany, NY: State University of New York, 1988). He specifically links Abraham's willingness to martyrdom, which he sees as being 'The ultimate love of man for God.' For an example of a widely known and respected Christian approach, *see* Soren Kierkegaard, *Fear and Trembling* (New York: Doubleday Anchor, 1953). This work will be discussed in more detail in chapter 10.
5. *See* Spiegel, *The Last Trial*, for accounts of these stories.
6. Genesis, 25:8–9: 'And Abraham expired, and died in a good old age, an old man, and full of years; and was gathered to his people. And Isaac and Ishmael his sons buried him in the cave of Machpelah.'
7. David Polish, 'Akedat Yitzhak: The Binding of Isaac', *Judaism*, 6 (1957), p. 20. Elsewhere, Polish writes: 'To understand what happened to Isaac we must first comprehend what happened to Ishmael and collaterally with Abraham.' *The Eternal Dissent: A Search for Meaning in Jewish History* (London: Abelard-Schuman, 1961), p. 35.
8. *See*, for instance, Erich Fromm, 'The Oedipus Complex and the Oedipus Myth', in Ruth Nanda Anshen (ed.), *The Family: Its Functions and Destiny* (New York: Harper and Row, 1959), p. 426; and A.J. Levin, 'The Oedipus Myth in History and Psychiatry', *Psychiatry*, 2 (1948), p. 287.
9. *See*, in general, articles in the *History of Childhood Quarterly*; also Lloyd de Mause, *The History of Childhood* (New York: Harper Torchbooks, 1975).
10. *See*, for instance, the comment by Louis Ginzberg, *Legends of the Bible* (Philadelphia, PA: The Jewish Publication Society, 1968). On p. 122 he writes: 'Of all the trials Abraham had to undergo, none was so hard to bear as this, for it grieved him sorely to separate himself from his son.' He adds: 'Abraham said to Sarah, his wife, "I will go and see my son Ishmael; I yearn to look upon him, for I have not seen him for a long time"' (p. 124). Later, a story is told about Abraham not finding Ishmael, but leaving a message for him with his wife.
11. *See*, for instance, Nahum Sarna, *Understanding Genesis* (New York: Schocken, 1966). He writes (p. 158):

There is much archaeological evidence to show that human sacrifice was more in vogue here than elsewhere, from very early times until far into the second millenium. The biblical sources furnish additional abundant testimony. The *Torah* legislation lists child-sacrifice among the abominations of the Canaanites and other texts consistently attribute its presence in Israel to the importation of foreign practice.

For instance, 'the story of the King of Moab who, in desperation, offered up his first-born son at a critical moment in battle'. *See also* Martin Bergman, *In the Shadow of Moloch: The Sacrifice of Children and its Impact on Western Religions* (New York: Columbia University Press, 1992).

12. *See*, for instance, Marvin Harris, *Cannibals and Kings: The Origins of Cultures* (New York: Random House, 1977).

13. *See,* for instance, the work of an Argentinian psychoanalyst, Arnoldo Rascovsky, who founded a society in South America in the 1970s for the study of this problem; for example, *El Filicido* (Buenos Aires: Ediciones Orion, n.d.).

14. I have discussed these meetings extensively in a recently published Hebrew book, *Weeds in the Garden of Eden: Biblical Narratives and Israeli Chronicles* (Tel Aviv: Ha-Kibbutz Ha-Meuchad Publishing House, 2002).

15. *See* the sensitive analysis by Israel Charny, 'And Abraham Went to Slay Isaac: A Parable of Killer, Victim, and Bystander in the Family', *Journal of Ecumenical Studies*, 10 (1973), p. 304.

16. *See*, for instance, Spiegel, *The Last Trial*.

17. Yet it also has a contrasting impact, leading to the willingness to die '*Al Kiddush Ha-shem*' (in the Sanctification of the Name, that is, of God). *See*, for instance, Silvano Arieti, *Abraham and the Contemporary Mind* (New York: Basic Books, 1981).

18. As defined in the Random House Dictionary, mimesis is the 'imitation or reproduction of the supposed words of another, as in order to represent his character'.

19. For an interesting and original approach, see Burton Caine, 'The *Akedah*: Angel Unbound', *Conservative Judaism*, 52 (1999), p. 5; he suggests the possibility that the angel is not acting on God's authority, but has actually intervened, on his own initiative, to counter-mand God's instruction; and thereby, of course, ensure that no only will Isaac be saved, but that God's promise to Abraham of a great future nation can yet be attained.

20. *See* Spiegel, *The Last Trial*.

21. Erich Wellisch, *Isaac and Oedipus: A Study in Biblical Psychology of the Sacrifice of Isaac: the Akedah* (London: Routledge and Kegan Paul, 1954).

22. *See*, for instance, the work of Dorothy Bloch, 'Fantasy and the Fear of Infanticide', *Psychoanalytic Review*, 61 (1974), p. 5; and, *So the Witch Won't Eat Me* (Boston, MA: Houghton Mifflin, 1978).

23. *See*, for instance, David Bakan, *The Duality of Human Existence: An Essay on Psychology and Religion* (Chicago, IL: Rand McNally, 1966).

24. David Bakan, 'Paternity in the Judeo-Christian Tradition', *The Human Context*, 4 (1972), p. 354.

25. Malachi, 3:23–4.

26. *See* Bakan, 'Paternity in the Judeo-Christian Tradition', pp. 219–21, n23. He writes that the placing of the phylacteries:

> on the arm and between the eyes, can be interpreted as the binding of the agentic which would engage in infanticide. What is most significant is that they are combined with the commandment to give instruction to the son. Essentially what is involved is *the diversion of the force which would kill the son to his education*. I believe that this is a major moral imperative of the Old Testament ... [emphasis in origial – L.S.].

27. Ibid., p. 224, where Bakan writes:

> The Passover, in my interpretation, had to be the time of Jesus' crucifixion. For it was in connection with the Passover that the infanticidal tendency of God had been made very clear, at which time the first-born of the Israelites had been spared. God had withheld his arm and not killed Jesus in his infancy ... Jesus repeated in his own life the history of the Jews from the time of the Exodus.

28. Exodus, 12:13.
29. Exodus, 12:23.
30. Kierkegaard, *Fear and Trembling*.
31. Louis Berman, *The Akedah: The Binding of Isaac* (Northvale, NJ: Jason Aronson, 1997).
32. Sigmund Freud, *The Wolf-Man* (London: Hogarth Press, 1939).
33. Sigmund Freud, *Moses and Monotheism* (London: Hogarth Press, 1939).
34. Robert Gordis, *Judaic Ethics for A Lawless World* (New York: Jewish Theological Seminary, 1986), p. 108.
35. Berman, *The Akedah*, p. 41.
36. See Carol Delaney, *Abraham on Trial: The Social Legacy of the Biblical Myth* (Princeton, NJ: Princeton University Press, 1998).
37. Jon Levenson, *The Death and Resurrection of the Beloved Son: The Transformation of Child Sacrifice in Judaism and Christianity* (New Haven, CT: Yale University Press, 1993).
38. Ibid., p. 5.
39. *Exodus*, 22:28.
40. Numbers, 27:15–16.
41. Levenson, *Death and Resurrection*, p. 12.
42. Spiegel, *The Last Trial*.
43. Levenson, *Death and Resurrection*, p. 13.
44. Ibid., p. 17.
45. Ibid., p. 200.
46. Ibid., p. 221.
47. Ibid., p. 223.
48. Ibid., p. 222.
49. *See*, for example, in the New Testament, Hebrews, 11:17; and James, 2:21.
50. Levenson, *Death and Resurrection*, p. 223.
51. Ibid., p. 232.
52. Ibid.

3
Crucifixion

The most important trial in the history of the world – in terms of its subsequent impact – was undoubtedly that which ended in the execution of Jesus Christ. There is no official record of the trial, not even a reliable account by any witnesses to the proceedings. What is known of the trial is based on the four reports presented in the Gospels of Mark, Luke, Matthew and John.

Yet, while there is no first-hand report of what transpired, there are countless analyses of the Gospels' descriptions, examining minutely each stage of the forensic drama, as well as the events leading up to it and the subsequent developments. As may be expected, there is no consensus as to what actually happened, and the interpretative versions differ from those that deny that a proper trial took place, to those that claim that certainly the Jews were not involved. There are also claims that the proceedings bore a closer resemblance to a 'kangaroo court', or alternatively a precise documentation is provided of two separate trials, one by the Jewish Sanhedrin, and the other by the Roman authorities.

A fascinating anecdote reveals some of the ongoing impact of the trial. One of the main books discussing the trial is by a leading Israeli jurist, Haim Cohn,[1] who says that what aroused his initial interest in the trial was the fact that after the establishment of the State of Israel, several petitions were submitted to the legal authorities in Israel by individual Christians pleading for the opportunity, now afforded by the renewal of Jewish sovereignty, to announce a pardon for the miscarriage of justice that was perpetrated some 1,900 years earlier.

Cohn was then the Attorney-General in Israel, and as a learned scholar of Jewish law, embarked on a project to examine what was known of the trial in order to check its authenticity. He then claimed that very little of the description was compatible with Jewish law as then practiced, and as handed down through the generations: starting with the fact that the Jews never practiced crucifixion, which was a particularly cruel and prolonged mechanism used by the Romans (whereas the Jews used strangling, beheading, hanging and stoning), and including such facts as the incompatibility of a trial at a time so close to the Jewish Sabbath and the festival of Passover.

However, Jewish jurists are not the only experts who have challenged the role that history, according to the Gospels, has assigned to the Jews. In a book sub-titled *A Christian Defends the Jews Against the Charge of Deicide*, Weddig Fricke,[2] a German scholar, meticulously analyses the evidence in a manner similar to Cohn's work, and comes to similar conclusions. Indeed, he refers to the legal proceedings not as a trial, but as a court martial, in order to convey the idea that the regular formalities of a court were not observed and that basically, summary justice was handed out – but by the Romans, and not by the Jews.

Thus, the most significant trial in history is full of dubious facts and ambiguities, with attempts to resolve them often dependent not only on legal expertise but also ideological propensities. In any event, no less important than the trial – in fact, in terms of historical impact, far more important than the actual trial – are the events preceding it and subsequent to it.

Prior to the trial, at what is known as the Last Supper, Jesus is betrayed by one of his 12 closest disciples, Judas, whose name to this day is synonymous with betrayal, and whose name also subtly, perhaps unconsciously, conjures up connections, through its pronunciation, with Jews, thus adding further to the negative image of Jews. Subsequent to the trial, there are several significant incidents, the most important being the choice given to the Jewish crowd to decide which of the four condemned men are to be set free. In choosing Barabbas, they further indicate their rejection of the man believed by Christians to be the Messiah.

The actual process of crucifixion also leads to varied explanations of the manner in which Jesus was affixed to the Cross,[3] and the question of when and why his body was removed from the Cross. Finally, of course, the discovery three days later, on what was to become Easter Sunday, that his body was no longer at the burial site, and the belief that he had been seen by several people afterwards, conjoined together to lay the foundation for the claim of the Resurrection and its linked promise of eternal life.

Crucifixion, as a form of judicial execution, was foreign to the Jews, yet it was widely used in the Roman world; this was a deliberately contrived, tortuous punishment practiced by the Romans. In this sense, the suffering undergone by Jesus was no different, no worse, than that inflicted on many people at that time by the Romans. During his anguish, two common criminals were undergoing the same penalty for the offenses that they had committed. Indeed, Jesus was actually taken down from the Cross before them, apparently after about three hours, whereas others were known to have had the fatal procedure extended over many more hours, or even days.

Thus, there is special importance to this cruel means of execution only when linked to the fact that it was imposed on a divine being so that he could fully appreciate the nature of human suffering. If Jesus was merely a talented preacher, with a certain degree of charismatic power, then there is nothing particularly unusual or noteworthy about the manner in which he was killed. It is the claimed contact with God that gives meaning and significance to his crucifixion, and the symbolic value to the emblem of the Cross. These are factors that will be explored in the next chapter. For the meantime, the focus will be on the legal proceedings themselves, from arrest to execution.

While legal experts have examined the actual process, theologians have raised empirical possibilities that, given the lack of hard evidence, can only remain within the realm of hypothetical conjectures. One of the best-known essays in this area of suppositions is the work of a Jewish scholar, Hugh Schonfield,[4] who claims that Jesus and some of his disciples conspired together, in the words of the title of his book, to make a Passover plot to feign his death for reasons that would suit their interests. The plot itself failed, Jesus died, but some of the subsequent reporting is affected by these machinations.

Any discussion of the problematics of the trial in terms of hard evidence must also take account of revisionist history being undertaken by Christian scholars and theologians. The most notable is the Jesus Seminar, based in California, which constantly updates its perceptions as to what is true and what is false in the New Testament. Naturally, the facts of the trial are included in these reassessments.

A leading figure in this group is John Dominic Crossan, who argues that there is no proof that the Jews killed Jesus. His thesis is controversial, but simultaneously important and deserving of serious consideration. His work deals not only with the trial, but with an ongoing deep textual analysis of all the writings in the New Testament.[5] In one of his books, asking *Who Killed Jesus?*,[6] he takes strong issue with one of the most recent and authoritative presentations of the *Death of the Messiah*,[7] by Raymond Brown (a follow-up to an earlier book on the *Birth of the Messiah*[8]). Crossan attempts to show bias in Brown's interpretation and selective use of convenient examples. Of most significance is the theoretical perspective from which Crossan develops his thesis. He writes of:

> ... a delicate and absolutely crucial distinction between scriptural prophecies as *confirmative* or *constitutive* of historical events. Prophecy as confirmative of historical events means that the event happened, and prophecy is used to understand it, defend it, or vindicate its necessity. Prophecy as constitutive means that the

event did not happen, but prophecy has been used to imagine it, describe it, and create it. But how do you tell whether prophecy is creating history as its fulfillment, or history is selecting prophecy as its confirmation?[9]

In particular, Crossan draws a distinction between ancient prophecy as it appears in biblical texts of the Old Testament (particularly, of course, in the words of the prophets), which project conjectural happenings to some time in the future; and recent prophecies, mainly made by Jesus in the form of hints as to what is liable to happen to him, hints that are retrospectively interpreted as clear intimations of what indeed did happen. As Crossan explains:

> For something as terrible as the crucifixion, it was not enough to select ancient biblical prophecies announcing it would happen in the future. It was necessary to create more recent prophecies from Jesus himself proclaiming his knowledge and acceptance of that destiny.[10]

Discussing, in separate chapters, the various stages of the criminal proceedings, Crossan comes to the conclusion that while Jesus was undoubtedly arrested and then later executed, there is no definitive proof as to a trial – either a Jewish one or a Roman one. Drawing on this theoretical basis, he suggests that the description of the trial in the Gospels 'is based entirely on prophecy historicized rather than history remembered. It is not just the *content* of the trial(s) but the very *fact* of the trial(s) that I consider to be unhistorical.' He acknowledges that 'It is, of course, always possible that there were trial(s) whose exact details are now lost forever.' Finally, he concludes that 'there may well have been Arrest and Execution but no Trial whatsoever in between'.[11]

Such conclusion does not, of course, resolve the issue of responsibility for those aspects which Crossan does not deny: the arrest and the Crucifixion. In fact, if there were no trial, the burden of blame would be seen by their adversaries as even more intense, for there would then have been no legal justification for an act whose significance and implications were to become so far-reaching, both in theological and historical terms.

I have drawn attention to Crossan's approach in order to stress the great deal of uncertainty that surrounds the trial. This is not the work of an anti-religious scholar, but rather of a Christian deeply committed to his faith, yet determined to seek the historic truth, as well as coping with, in the words of the sub-title to the book, 'the roots of anti-Semitism'.

Crossan's difficulties with the New Testament arise for obvious reasons: there are several versions of what happened in the Four Gospels of Mark, Matthew, Luke and John, as well as other contemporary reports, not included in the New Testament (such as the Gospel of Thomas[12] and the Gospel of Peter,[13] and parts of the document known as the Q Gospel).[14] While differences are inevitable, and need not necessarily undermine the veracity of the overall picture that has been established, some of the differences are not marginal or trivial. In particular, while there is general agreement that there is a large degree of overlap between the first three Gospels, known for that reason as the Synoptic Gospels, the Gospel of John, written some time later, presents a substantially different picture: one which Crossan (as well as other writers)[15] suggests is oriented more to ideological needs than historical accuracy.

As for the similarities between the three Synoptic Gospels, even here it is not clear to what extent they based themselves on each other, or on some other unknown, common source. As Mark wrote the earliest, it is thought that Matthew and Luke based themselves mainly on him. Even so, there are some key differences: for instance, Luke claims that the second part of the legal proceedings, the 'Roman' trial, was conducted in its key phases not by Pontius Pilate but by Herod Antipas.[16] This is a major difference, perhaps an attempt to shift the blame even for the Roman trial onto the Jewish ruler (under Roman authority) of the Galilee, the area from which Jesus came. This assumes that the trial was based not in the place where the crimes were committed (Jerusalem), but in the accused's place of residence (the Galilee): not a very likely situation. But if Herod Antipas was not involved, then Luke's account becomes suspect. Conversely, of course, if Luke is correct, then the others are at fault.

Many other writers – not just those involved in the Jesus Seminar – have also struggled to reconcile all the discrepancies in the reports and a lively debate has developed, stimulated partly by Ernest Renan's work on Jesus in the nineteenth century,[17] and intensified by Albert Schweitzer's later contribution to the issue.[18] Most of these writers attempt to provide an authoritative description of the life and struggles of Jesus, clothing the minimal framework provided by the Gospels and other early accounts (for instance, the Jewish writer, Josephus[19]) with elaborations that allow for a fuller understanding of his character and motivations. Since the basic material revolves mainly around the last three years of his life, and since the Gospels themselves are fairly succinct, much remains unknown or speculative, and consequently even greater emphasis is placed on the final hours of his life, from the Last

Supper with his disciples to his suffering on the Cross.

Little is known of Jesus' early life. Some writers hypothesize about his relations with his parents; thus, some writers conjecture that he probably worked with his father, Joseph, from whom he learned the craft of carpentry. Reference is made to his younger siblings, but no stories remain as to the nature of their relationships in childhood and adolescence (though there are hints of sibling tensions, for some of them doubt his special status, whereas others are counted among his disciples).

However, these are acceptable gaps, given the desire of the Gospels to accentuate his teachings and his deeds (particularly the miracles). More problematical is the lack of agreement as to the manner of his birth[20] – mentioned in only two of the four Gospels, with different versions even then being given as to the manner in which Mary, his mother, was apprised of the unique nature of his birth – a topic that will be explored in more detail in the next chapter. A further indication of confusion is the fact that, in the Gospels, there is not even agreement as to whether the Last Supper was the Seder meal of Passover, or whether it took place the night before. Given the importance and festivity of the Seder meal, this is not a marginal factor.

Renan's book on Jesus was a pioneering work: the first time a basically academic (or, in other words, a secular) biography had been written about Jesus, unfettered by the demands of religious uniformity. Yet Renan himself wrote as a believing and practicing Christian. What gives added authority to his account is the fact that, in writing for a European audience for whom the Holy Land in Palestine was a distant Utopia, he drew extensively on his personal knowledge of the terrain gained from years spent in the area while on an official mission as a researcher. As his translator, William Hutchison notes in a biographical sketch: 'On its publication in 1863, it was soon apparent that the *Life of Jesus* was to be one of the most hotly discussed books of the century.'[21] The book received much praise (for example, 'By a very large public it was welcomed with undiscriminating applause'),[22] but detractors were also not lacking:

> Archbishops, Jesuits, priests, theological professors, and dissenting ministers joined eagerly in a heresy hunt of unprecedented dimensions, the heavens were darkened with a multitude of pamphlets and reviews, and controversial treatises; pulpits rang with indignant denunciations; Renan's private character was picturesquely defamed.[23]

Renan created the possibility of publishing works on the founding figure of Christianity without the Church imposing strict censorship, and the nature of his work may be gauged by his description of Jesus' family background:

> The family, whether it proceeded from one or many marriages, was rather numerous. Jesus had brothers and sisters, of whom he seems to have been the eldest. All have remained obscure, for it appears that the four personages who were named as his brothers and among whom ... James had acquired great importance in the earliest years of the development of Christianity, were his cousins-germane. Mary, in fact, had a sister also named Mary, who married a certain Alpheus or Cleophas (these two names appear to designate the same person) and was the mother of several sons who played a considerable part among the first disciples of Jesus. These cousins-germane who adhered to the young Master, while his own brothers opposed him, took the title of 'brothers of the Lord'. The real brothers of Jesus, like their mother, became important only after his death. Even then they do not appear to have equaled in importance their cousins, whose conversion had been more spontaneous.[24]

I have presented this non-controversial aspect (from a theological perspective) of Jesus' life in order to clarify the many dubious facts that biographers, theologians and other commentators have to deal with. This uncertainty becomes even more pertinent and crucial when dealing with controversial issues, with pregnant implications, such as those facts relating to the trial and Crucifixion.

In dealing with the trial itself, Renan is brief and definitive. Lacking a direct eyewitness, he draws on talmudic explanations of trials, explicitly footnoted. He writes, 'the narrative of the Gospels corresponds exactly with the procedure described by the Talmud'.[25] He describes how one of the priests, Hanan (known in other books as Anais), took the lead in the interrogation, but, 'Hanan, although the true author of the judicial murder about to be accomplished, had not power to pronounce the sentence upon Jesus; he sent him to his son-in-law, Kalapha, who bore the official title.'[26] Kalapha promptly proceeded to act according to his father-in-law's wish, activating the Sanhedrin in order to provide a full legal basis for the punishment. According to Renan, a key factor in the trial was Jesus' statement that he was able to destroy the temple, and re-build it in three days, a statement considered both blasphemous and a physical threat.

Renan sums up the consequences of the trial, both factually (the death sentence) and interpretatively (casually imposed). Thus, he writes:

> With one voice, the assembly declared him guilty of a capital crime. The members of the Council who secretly leaned to him, were absent or did not vote. The frivolity which characterizes old, established aristocracies, did not permit the judges to reflect long upon the consequences of the sentence they had passed. Human life was at that time very lightly sacrificed; doubtless the members of the Sanhedrin did not dream that their sons would have to render account to an angry posterity for the sentence pronounced with such careless disdain.[27]

Having pronounced sentence, the Jewish authorities were now confronted with a dilemma: they lacked the power to carry it out, and so needed authorization from the Roman authorities. In order to explain the complications of a judgment in a religious trial being sanctioned by the secular authorities of a conquering empire, Renan writes that, 'the situation was nearly that of the sacred cities of India under the English dominion, or rather that which would be the state of Damascus if Syria were conquered by a European nation'.[28]

Renan claims that relations between the procurator, Pontius Pilate, and the Jews were tense, because of the conflicts that had arisen in the past, which:

> ... had rendered him very prudent in his relations with this intractable people, which avenged itself upon its governors by compelling them to use toward it hateful severities. The procurator saw himself, with extreme displeasure, led to play a cruel part in this new affair, for the sake of a law he hated. He knew that religious fanaticism, when it has obtained the sanction of civil governments to some act of violence, is afterward the first to throw responsibility upon the government, and almost accuses them of being the author of it. Supreme injustice; for the true culprit is, in such cases, the instigator![29]

Renan then adds that Pilate 'would have liked to save Jesus'.[30] He suggests that Jesus (of whom he knew nothing prior to the trial) probably made a positive impression upon him, as also on his wife who, according to Renan, quite possibly pleaded on his behalf. Going beyond such suppositions, Renan then conjures up an intimate picture from his imagination:

She may have seen the gentle Galilean from some window of the palace, overlooking the courts of the temple. Perhaps she had seen him again in her dreams; and the idea that the blood of this beautiful young man was about to be spilt, weighed upon her mind.[31]

Thus, whereas Crossan meticulously examines each sentence in the Bible before confirming its accuracy, based on knowledge and consistency, Renan allows his imagination to conjure up a picture that involves presumptions, naturally totally unfounded, of the dreams of a minor character, in order to subtly suggest how determined Pilate was to avoid implementing the religious decrees.

The New Testament's description, of course, provides the reason for the execution. Not only did the Sanhedrin demand the demise of Jesus, but also Jewish public opinion, represented in those days by the crowd that assembled at the site of the execution. Even here, according to Renan, Pontius attempts desperately to prevent the execution. The prior scourging of Jesus, as described in the Gospels, is seen by him as a ploy to outwit the crowd; by agreeing to let the soldiers scourge Jesus (a normal preliminary to crucifixion), Renan suggests that 'Perhaps Pilate wished it to be believed that this sentence had already been pronounced, hoping that the preliminary would suffice.'[32] But his plan failed: the 'revolting' display (Renan's term) of scourging was of no avail. If Pilate hoped that by doing this he could 'turn aside the blow which threatened Jesus by conceding something to the hatred of the Jews, and by substituting for the tragic denouement a grotesque termination, to make it appear that the affair merited no other issue',[33] he was mistaken. The cry of 'crucify him, crucify him' was heard from all sides.

At this stage, Pilate becomes apprehensive that any attempt to save Jesus would likely lead to a riot. In his desperation, he even attempts to pass responsibility on to some other political figure – a potential solution suggests itself when he finds out that Jesus is from Galilee; this would enable him to transfer the judgment to the political authority in that area. Fortunately, according to Luke, Herod Antipas is in Jerusalem, perhaps to celebrate the pilgrim festival of Passover, like Jesus himself. This would be an ideal solution, as already noted, for exculpating Pilate from all responsibility and ensuring that only Jews were involved – not just the Sanhedrin, and not just the assembled crowd, but even the political authority itself: the Jew appointed by the Romans to rule over the northern part of the country.

However, whereas Renan is quite willing to imagine the dreams of Pilate's wife, he has more trouble in placing Herod conveniently in

Jerusalem at this time because of the paucity of evidence: 'According to
one tradition, he even sent Jesus to Antipas, who, it is said, was then at
Jerusalem.'[34] At this point, Renan makes a revealing statement; in a
detailed footnote he writes:

> It is probable that this is a first attempt at a 'Harmony of Gospels.'
> Luke must have had before him a narrative in which the death of
> Jesus was erroneously attributed to Herod. In order not to sacrifice
> this version entirely he must have combined the two traditions.
> What makes this more likely is that he probably had a vague
> knowledge that Jesus (as John teaches us) appeared before three
> authorities. In many other cases, Luke seems to have a remote idea
> of the facts which are peculiar to the narration of John.[35]

This footnote comment ends with a further general clarification that
Luke's Gospel 'contains in the history of the Crucifixion a series of
additions which the author appears to have drawn from a more recent
document, and which had evidently been arranged with a special view to
edification'.[36]

Here is a clear hint at the very issue that so concerns Crossan and the
other members of the Jesus Seminar: how much of the description is
accurate; how much is embellishment on raw facts; and, most
importantly, how much is oriented to theological or ideological needs
(for instance, the need to edify)?

Inasmuch as any dubious facts relate to the parables or miracles that
Jesus performed, or the precise wording of his teachings, the issue is
mainly a theological one; but when it deals with the description of the
trial and crucifixion of Jesus, it touches on ideological issues with far-
reaching implications on subsequent history, in particular the nature of
Jewish–Christian relations. Crossan deals with this issue in some detail,
but rejects the possibility that Herod Antipas, as representative of Jewish
authority, was involved in the crucifixion of Jesus; or, indeed, that the
Jewish crowd could be directly implicated. He climaxes his analysis of
this aspect by stating that:

> Even if one could imagine Herod (Antipas) in charge of a crucifix-
> ion in Pilate's Jerusalem, it would have to be soldiers or at least
> police and not 'the people' who carried it out. Stoning to death
> could be done by 'the people', but crucifixion demanded brutal
> expertise particular to executioners.[37]

In any event, Renan resolves this problem by absolving Pilate and
blaming the narrowness of the Jewish legal tradition, which lacked

flexibility and tolerance. Ignoring the fact that most of the Jewish prophets had criticized the religious and political establishment far more harshly than Jesus had – and not only had none of them been killed or even harmed, but their words had been fully incorporated into the corpus of Jewish religious writing – Renan argues that it was not Pilate 'who condemned Jesus. It was the old Jewish party; it was the Mosaic Law.'[38]

How far removed such a statement is from a mere academic analysis of a given situation, how pregnant with sociological and historical meaning, may be gauged from the manner in which Renan immediately analyzes the implications of his conclusion. Acknowledging that it is not fair to blame Jews in subsequent generations for what happened at Calvary, nevertheless:

> Nations, like individuals, have their responsibilities, and if ever a crime was the crime of a nation, it was the death of Jesus. This death was 'legal' in the sense that it was primarily caused by a law which was the very soul of the nation. The Mosaic law...pronounced the penalty of death against all attempts to change the established worship.[39]

Leading on from this explanation, Renan then notes that Judaism is not alone in the narrowness of its application of theological principles, and its intolerance of those who advocate change. Aware of historical reality, he writes that:

> Even at the present time, in countries which call themselves Christian, penalties are pronounced for religious offences. Jesus is not responsible for these errors ... Christianity has been intolerant, but intolerance is not necessarily a Christian fact. It is a Jewish fact in the sense that it was Judaism which first introduced the theory of the absolute in religion, and laid down the principle that every innovator, even if he brings miracles to support his doctrine, ought to be stoned without trial ... The Pentateuch has thus been in the world the first code of religious terrorism.[40]

These are strong words, written over a century ago. Yet, specifically within the academic and objective framework in which they were written, they provide some indication of how intensely felt is the blame associated with the Jews – and in this case, even with the very essence of Jewish belief. Given the multitudes that were put to death by the Inquisition (and not just Jews, but also heretical Christians, and perhaps more of the latter than the former), Renan's analysis is perhaps the epitome of a-historicity: a theoretical stance totally devoid of any relevance to reality. The Jewish religion – particularly in its Orthodox and Ultra-Orthodox manifestations (as also amongst the Pharisees and Sadducees of Jesus' time) – certainly has an obsessive tendency to observe the myriad of do's and don'ts in the Pentateuch (a total of 613 in all, laid down as *mitzvot*). Yet, it is pluralistic by nature and has accorded the prophets an honorable place in its tradition; indeed, the harsher the castigation, the more respected the prophet.[41]

In many respects, Jesus was a typical example of such independent thinking and of such courageous actions; as such, he was an heir to a rich tradition, of which Nathan the prophet boldly challenging the excesses of King David is a classic example.[42] However corrupt the priesthood of the time might have been, however much Jesus' words and actions might have antagonized them, there was nothing in theoretical Jewish customs or in empirical historical data that would inevitably lead to legal action against a radical and innovative preacher.

Surely it is imperative for those who wish to blame the Jews for an historical injustice to ensure that their facts are correct and, at the very least, that the surmises they make are fair. It is considerations of this type that have spawned some of the most involved research into the trial and execution of Jesus. The best example of such work is Walter Chandler's two-volume book, *The Trial of Jesus, From a Lawyer's Standpoint*, the first volume of which deals with the Jewish trial, and the second with the Roman trial.[43]

Chandler is well aware of the fact that it is necessary to allay any doubts as to the veracity of the accounts of these two trials, and so expends much effort at the beginning of his book to adduce the legal claims as to their accuracy. Being a lawyer, he relies on leading legal scholars on the law of evidence to buttress his argument. Chandler acknowledges that the basis of information is the Gospels; beyond that, there is no more than, in his words:

> A line from Philo – a dubious passage from Josephus – a mere mention by Tacitus – a few scattering fragments from the Talmud – all else is darkness, save the light that streams down through the centuries from Calvary and the Cross through the books of the Evangelists.[44]

A preliminary question that concerns Chandler is the very authenticity of the Gospel narratives themselves: is what has been handed down over the generations the original version, as written by Mark, Matthew,

Luke and John? Even more important is the credibility of what they recorded, specifically, in Chandler's words, 'did they tell the truth when they wrote and published these narratives to the world?' In order to deal with these issues adequately, 'academic reasoning and metaphysical speculation will be rejected. Well-established rules of evidence, as employed in modern courts of law, will be rigorously applied.'[45] Not religion is at stake, not the critical writings of subjective authors (such as Renan, as already specifically mentioned), but the rules of forensic inquiry.

Chandler relies on a legal authority on the modern law of evidence, Simon Greenleaf, to help examine the issue.[46] By chance, Greenleaf had discussed the evidence as to the reliability of the scriptures: being an ancient document, Greenleaf claims they must be presumed to be genuine unless proven otherwise. However, this only addresses their 'admissibility' (like that of a document presented to the court). The question of the 'truth' of what is contained therein is a different matter, far more relevant for modern discussion. Chandler presents several logical factors to be considered: for instance, given the dangers of preserving Jesus' work and continuing his ministry, it can only be assumed that the people exposing themselves to the wrath of the authorities, both Jewish and Roman, were honest people. Furthermore, they were possessed of personal qualities of observation and memory. For instance, two of them had professions that required these qualities – Matthew, a customs worker, and Luke, a physician.[47]

Chandler also raises the issue of motive. Why, he asks, would the four Evangelists, in presenting their Gospels, have endangered themselves as they attempted not just to record what had happened (perhaps an innocuous factor), but also to spread the message for which, according to them, Jesus had been crucified. Chandler suggests the need to review:

> ... the political and religious situation at the beginning of the Apostolic ministry. The Master and Savior of the First Christians had just perished as a malefactor on the cross. The religion which the Apostles began to preach was founded in the doctrine of repentance from sins, faith in the Crucified One, and belief in His resurrection from the dead. Christianity, of which these elements were the essentials, sought to destroy and supplant all other religions.[48]

For an author who is insistent, in the course of his argument, on probing for the truth, this is an extremely dubious explanation – or justification – of the clear motives of the authors of the Gospels. At the time of their writing they were, no less than Jesus himself, Jews aiming to change the direction of the Judaism of their time; and Judaism, like other religions, has known no end of such clashes. Their mission was to persuade Jews to join them. The message to others – to the Gentiles of the surrounding areas, in Greece, Rome and elsewhere – was initially spread by Paul, but he is ignored by Chandler, receiving only two passing mentions in irrelevant matters,[49] and this only in the second volume of his work dealing with what he terms 'the Roman trial'.

Even so, Chandler is obliged to concede the possibility of the Evangelists being in error. This possibility he resolves by focusing on their sincerity and the risk they were taking. Thus, he writes that:

> It is not a question at this time as to the absolute correctness of their statements. These statements might have been false, though their authors believed them to be true – it is a question of sincerity at this point; and the test of sincerity, as an element of credibility rests upon the simple basis that men are more disposed to believe the statement of a witness if it is thought that the witness himself believes it.[50]

On this point, Chandler eschews any need to substantiate his argument by a reference to Greenleaf, or any other authoritative author of a text on evidence in a court of law – for, in fact, to the best of my knowledge, there is no such rule. Courts probe, through cross-examination and other means, to ascertain the truth; in doing so, the belief of a witness in his evidence carries little or no weight.

More seriously, there is a widely accepted rule that hearsay evidence is always suspect; indeed, to such a degree that in many legal systems – including the one Greenleaf was describing, and in which Chandler himself operated – such evidence is inadmissible. Chandler does not directly discuss this aspect of evidence, but he indirectly suggests that 'it is reasonable that all of the Gospel writers were eyewitnesses of most of the events recorded by them in the Gospel histories'.[51] Yet, in substantiating this statement, Chandler discusses only general events relating to the ministry of Jesus, not the trial itself; in fact, as far as Mark is concerned, he actually suggests that he 'wrote the Gospel ascribed to him, at the dictation of Peter'.[52] If this is correct, then 'Peter is the real author'[53] of this Gospel (as a legal fact this would, of course, totally undermine its judicial credibility).

In any event, as far as the actual trial of Jesus is concerned, only John, the last of the four Gospel writers, may possibly have had some minimal access to it; but even this is unlikely. His account was written probably over a half-century later; although, for Chandler, this is irrelevant, given the importance of the events that were being recorded. Now, in a non-legal setting, this may be acceptable – for instance, oral historians are doing excellent work in this area, and have their own rules as to the credibility to be attached to the memories being related[54] – but this does not apply to the strict rules of legal evidence. However, Chandler, the immaculate jurist, has laid down – in a throwaway line – his own 'ground rules', which are simply that in considering:

> The credit that should be accorded the testimony of Matthew, Mark, Luke, and John concerning the trial and crucifixion of Jesus...at the outset it should be borne in mind that there is a legal presumption that they told the truth. This presumption operates in their favor from the very moment that their testimony is admitted in evidence.[55]

Chandler's book is admittedly not well known or widely quoted. Yet it is an outstanding example of a meticulous attempt to provide a modern, objective analysis of the data: namely the four Gospels. The arguments are carefully presented, with extensive quotations; the author obviously has a sound knowledge of the biblical text, is well versed in legal knowledge, and is eloquent in his descriptions. On occasion, he uses his extensive knowledge of talmudic jurisprudence to suggest that, in their eagerness to convict, the Jewish authorities were even prepared to deviate from the regular and recognized procedures. After discussing 'Hebrew Criminal Law: Mosaic and Talmudic' in a 100-page chapter, he then presents what he terms 'The Brief', in which he presents a list of 12 specific legal points, which could have been argued in an appeal against the decision based on procedural blemishes – from the assertion that 'the arrest of Jesus was illegal', through assorted claims that the conviction was based on 'an uncorroborated confession', to the failure to consider 'the merits of the defense'.[56] Thus, whereas Cohn argues extensively that the Gospel descriptions prove that there was no Jewish trial (because of the numerous deviations from the acknowledged procedures of Hebrew law), Chandler uses these descriptions to argue for a miscarriage of justice, thus, of course, intensifying the wrath against the perpetrators.

Chandler's book was originally published in 1908, republished in 1925, and then brought out in a reprint edition in 1983 by William Hein and Company, a publishing house that specializes in reprints of outstanding books that are no longer available. One may suggest that Crossan and the other members of his group could profit from the learned discourse of Chandler. But, learned as it is, it is also a reflection of his underlying presumptions and his personal biases. It is the erudition displayed that particularly reveals how much the discussion of this crucial historical event is subject to external influences, and even ulterior motives.

The sociology of knowledge has long warned of the need for critical – and even skeptical – readings of academic writings,[57] as social scientists are inevitably the prisoners of their personal backgrounds, social memberships, environmental influences, and – in any discussion of the life, trial, death and resurrection of Jesus – of their religious beliefs.

I write this as a Jew who denies the divinity of Jesus, his role as the Messiah, and his resurrection. I recognize the fact of his arrest, trial and execution, as well as the beauty of much of his teachings, particularly his 'Sermon on the Mount'. I believe that much of his teachings reflect the better aspects of Jewish life at that time, including parallels with the sayings of a leading contemporary, Hillel, who was known for his liberal and flexible attitude.[58] Indeed, Hillel was one of the great protagonists in the many clashes between what is known today as the House of Hillel, and the House of Shammai – the latter was an arch-conservative, perhaps even a reactionary; the kind of person Jesus himself probably railed against because of his obsessive inflexibility.

As an Israeli Jew, I find much of modern Jewish orthodoxy, and certainly ultra-orthodoxy, incompatible with modern needs, particularly in the State of Israel itself. This includes not only theological issues, but stances adopted towards the occupied territories, the peace process, and the relations with Arab citizens of Israel and the Palestinians in Gaza and the West Bank, and I have dealt with this in separate publications, mainly in Hebrew.[59]

But my interest in Jesus stems from another factor: my own work in the field of generational relations, in which initial, yet only peripheral, references were made to both the *Akedah* of Isaac and the Crucifixion of Jesus.[60] From a social scientist perspective, these ancient themes fit into the modern concept of the Oedipus Complex and its various contrasting themes, including my own suggestion of an alternative Rustum Complex.[61] In the next section of this book, I shall deal with these, as well as with the question of the messianic nature of Jesus' work.

The basic argument that I shall present is that, at the time of his death, Jesus' ministry had reached its nadir: the Crucifixion itself signified failure, and his demise could well have led to his movement being considered as insignificant as the parallel movement (in fact the earlier movement) that had developed around the figure of John the Baptist who, like Jesus, had been put to death. Jesus himself was deeply affected by the teachings and rituals of John (for instance, baptism itself) and, in light of the fate that befell John, must have been well aware that a similar fate might await him. This is partly the basis of Schonfield's thesis about a Passover plot. Realizing the dangers that his ministry (which was so similar to John the Baptist's) would encounter, Jesus prepared himself for the ultimate showdown, with the intention of evading it and outwitting his foes – whether Jewish (based on the religious challenge) or Roman (based on the political threat that he posed). Indeed, Schonfield, a Jew, is one of the few authors concentrating on the trial of Jesus who makes this strong connection between these two dominant figures of the period.[62]

Jesus was baptized by John and, according to Schonfield, 'The Gospels clearly regard the baptism of Jesus as the effective beginning of his ministry, the moment of his designation as king of Israel, when God made acknowledgment of him as his messianic son and representative.'[63] Schonfield contends that after John the Baptist had been put to death by Herod Antipas, the latter:

> ... heard with dismay that another preacher was operating in Galilee and drawing large crowds, giving out the same message as John. It was as if the Baptist had risen from the dead to mock and defeat him. Here was a new menace, and for the first time, Jesus was in danger.[64]

It was now, in his teachings and in his discussions with his disciples, that Jesus began to hint about his status as a Messiah, and about his own awareness of his impending death at the hands of the authorities. In Schonfield's words, 'Never before had (Jesus) spoken about his end, but the death of John the Baptist made it essential that he should now do so.'[65] This was the beginning, in Schonfield's understanding, of the 'Passover plot'.

The 'plot' was based on the fact that, unlike most other forms of execution, death by crucifixion was not immediate; the intention was to cause tortuous suffering before life expired. However, unlike the medieval process of execution preceded by torture through drawing and quartering, which involved constant activity by the executioner, the suffering on the Cross was caused in a passive manner. The executioner only had to tie the condemned person to the Cross: the slow agony commenced immediately and ended with the dead person's body being left on the Cross to be eaten by the birds.[66] However, in the case of Jews, it was apparently permissible to remove the dead body in order to perform a normal burial in accordance with Jewish custom.

On this basis, Schonfield explains that, 'Provided the crucifixion was not too prolonged it was possible for the life of the victim to be saved.'[67] He then immediately adds that 'first-hand information about this is furnished by Josephus', who describes an instance where '... he passed a number of prisoners who had been crucified, and recognized three of them as acquaintances ... he pleaded for them'. The commanding authority at the time was Titus, who:

> ... ordered that they should be taken down and given the best possible treatment. Two of them died, but the third recovered. The indications are that these men had been on the cross longer than was Jesus, yet even so one of them survived.[68]

Thus, Schonfield argues that Jesus realized that, even given the likelihood that action would be taken against him, he would nevertheless be able to outwit his foes. Furthermore, inasmuch as he had a conception of himself as a Messiah, he believed that:

> ... the spirit of wisdom and understanding had been conferred on him, and that it was God's will that he should employ these powers of the mind to accomplish what must come to pass. He did not expect, indeed it was alien to his nature, to sit with folded hands waiting for things to happen, whether in a natural or supernatural manner. His whole ministry was purposeful, masterful and practical. He plotted and schemed with the utmost skill and resourcefulness, sometimes making secret arrangements, taking advantage of every circumstance conducive to the attainment of his objectives.[69]

According to the Fourth Gospel (by John), Jesus was on the Cross not more than three to four hours. Schonfield then conjectures that Jesus would have known this would be the case beforehand since, it being a Friday, he could well have assumed that he would be taken off the Cross before sundown. Under these circumstances, he might well hope that he might survive the horrendous ordeal, but would then be faced with a further hurdle: those in charge of the Crucifixion might notice that he was still alive and, at that stage, take action to kill him. This would be a critical moment: could Jesus feign death?

Schonfield describes the possibility that Jesus took a drug before the Crucifixion that would give the impression, after a certain number of hours, that he had died. Here, Schonfield uses his fertile imagination to draw conclusions as to various facts that appear in the Gospels. For instance, the fact that a bystander to the Crucifixion:

> ... saturated a sponge with vinegar, impaled it on a cane and put it
> in the mouth of Jesus. He did not perform this office for either of
> the two robbers crucified with Jesus, which he might well have
> done if his intention was purely humanitarian.[70]

Furthermore, while already on the Cross, and just prior to being taken
down, Schonfield states that Jesus was given something to drink, and
says that this was possibly a drug that caused him to lapse into
unconsciousness. Now, the person in whom he had confided – and
Schonfield assays a guess that it was not one of his disciples, since none
of them seem to have been present, but somebody who was supportive
of Jesus and also had ready access to the authorities – beseeched Pilate
to allow Jesus to be taken from the Cross, as the Sabbath was approach-
ing. As further proof of differential treatment for Jesus at this stage,
Schonfield notes that Jesus was spared the final act of having his legs
broken: an act which was performed on the two robbers at his side. He
suggests that this was because it was assumed that he was already dead.

However, at this stage, the plot breaks down: one of the soldiers, as
described in the Gospels, suddenly thrusts a lance into Jesus' side. It was
this, suggests Schonfield, that ultimately caused his death. Meanwhile,
however, Jesus had allowed expectations to be raised of his surviving the
Crucifixion. This, according to Schonfield, is the basis of the subsequent
accounts of Jesus' resurrection: his followers were apparently not
expecting his resurrection, but his survival. In any event, those who were
in on the plot would have removed his body from the tomb wherein it
was placed in order for him to fully recover and then make his way back
to the Galilee. When, because of the stabbing, he fails to recover, he is
then given a full and proper burial elsewhere. Schonfield completes his
conspiratorial thesis thus:

> If, as the Fourth Gospel says, his side was pierced by a lance before
> he was taken from the cross his chances of recovery were slender.
> It was much too risky, and perhaps too late, to take the body back
> to the tomb, replace the bandages left there, roll the stone across
> the entrance, and try to create the impression that everything was
> as it had been on Friday evening. It would also have been thought
> most unseemly. Before dawn the mortal remains of Jesus were
> quickly yet reverently interred, leaving the puzzle of the empty
> tomb.[71]

I have presented Schonfield's thesis not only because it is one of the most fascinating extrapolations from the Gospels, but because of the immense interest it aroused on publication: in the first five years after publication, it went through over 20 hardback and paperback printings. Of particular interest is the fact that it preceded many of the attempts by Christians – for example, by Crossan and other members of the Jesus Seminar – to reconstruct what happened on those fateful few days almost 2,000 ago.

It is a creative attempt to make sense of sacred texts, although, as Schonfield mentions, at least two fictional accounts – by George Moore and D.H. Lawrence – explored similar themes.[72] Yet, as creative as his thesis is, as close as it is to the key texts from the Gospels, it is not really convincing. It is a possibility, derived from the text, but it is not a likelihood. Indeed, the story disintegrates because it attempts to provide an explanation, by a Jew, for the belief in the Resurrection. According to Schonfield, the basis of this story rests on the empty tomb, but it fails to explain the accounts of all those who claim to have seen Jesus over a period of several weeks, and in different places, subsequent to the Crucifixion. Most specifically, because it is based on a supposition that Jesus had believed himself to be a Messiah, and that he had confided this awareness of his role to his disciples and followers, it raises no fewer issues than it purports to resolve, especially from a Jewish perspective.

Schonfield explains that he is attempting to understand the Gospel accounts in the context of his own analysis of the Crucifixion, the immediate aftermath, and the puzzle of the empty tomb. He writes that:

> We have to allow that the Gospel accounts come to us from a time when the figure of Jesus had become larger than life, and his story had acquired in telling and retelling many legendary features. Yet we must not treat them as wholly fictitious and they have preserved valuable indications of what happened. We can almost see the process at work which transformed the deep despondency of the companions of Jesus into the joyful conviction that he had triumphed over death as he said he would.[73]

Schonfield builds his theory on two key facts: first, that a real person was indeed seen, and presumed to be Jesus; second, that 'Jesus was positive that he was the Messiah of Israel and applied himself in a remarkable manner to carrying out the predictions as he understood them.'[74]

It is precisely here that the thesis breaks down, especially when presented by someone who does not believe that Jesus was the Messiah or that he rose from the dead. In particular, the Jewish concept of the

Messiah, the Anointed One, is theologically – to this day, as it was in the past – different from the conception carved out later by the Christian Church. We shall examine this aspect in the next chapter. For the moment, it is important to note that a number of explanations for the crucifixion of Jesus, by Christian writers, challenge some of the key factors in the story of the Passion: the very factors that Schonfield relies on. Most of these authors wrote subsequent to his book, and are not necessarily part of, or party to, the Jesus Seminar. The modern world has allowed speculations that, in earlier times, would have led to the authors being tried for heresy – although the Catholic Church still uses the weapon of excommunication against those who stray too far from the official line.[75]

One of the most recent explanations is given by a German theologian, Gerd Lüdemann, who, in his preface to the translated US edition,[76] explains the furore created by the original (German) edition of his book, and the academic tradition from which he, as a professor of New Testament studies at the University of Göttingen, derives. Amongst his predecessors was Julius Wellhausen, the pioneer of the 'Higher Criticism', as well as other leading Protestant thinkers such as Emil Schürer and Ernst Troeltsch.[77] He explains the overall approach shared by so many 'German Protestant theologians ... [whose] main conviction was that religion is not something fixed; it develops and is subject to human history'.[78]

Writing in this tradition, and drawing on some of his own earlier works, Lüdemann writes revealingly – and radically – that:

> In the course of my investigation of the resurrection of Jesus, of the heretics in early Christianity, of the unholy in Holy Scripture, of the virgin birth, and finally, in the present book, of the many words and actions of Jesus which have been put into his mouth or attributed to him only at a later stage, I have come to the following conclusion. My previous faith, related to the biblical message, has become impossible, because its point of reference, above all the resurrection of Jesus, have proved invalid and because the person of Jesus himself is insufficient as a foundation of faith once most of the New Testament statements about him have proved to be later interpretations by the community. Jesus deceived himself in expecting the Kingdom of God. Instead the church came; it recklessly changed the message of Jesus and in numerous cases turned it against the mother religion of Judaism.[79]

While still retaining his position as an academic scholar of the New Testament, Lüdemann renounces his religious faith[80] – a renunciation that is a consequence of his involvement with the sacred texts. Paradoxically, Schonfield works within the text to build his thesis; Lüdemann claims the text is false. As far as the Crucifixion itself is concerned, Lüdemann discusses this within a chapter entitled 'Inauthentic Sayings of Jesus'.[81] The first statement is the oft-quoted plea, 'My God, my God, why have you forsaken me?' – a statement often quoted in the original language (probably Aramaic, but almost identical to Hebrew, even modern Hebrew:'*Eli, Eli, lamah azavtani?*').

Lüdemann notes that 'Jesus' complaint corresponds word for word with Psalm 22.2 – with the exception that there God is addressed in Hebrew as *Eli*, whereas Mark has the Aramaic *Elohi.*'[82] He goes on to claim that, 'Although Jesus spoke Aramaic, the very fact that Mark gives the cry of Jesus in its Aramaic version is an argument against its historicity.'[83] Lüdemann suggests that it would have been unlikely that the Roman soldiers standing nearby would have fully caught on to the Aramaic, and that other bystanders were too far away to hear. This contention, like Schonfield's argument, is not too convincing – the three words, '*Elohi, Elohi, lama azavtani*', are not so complicated. In any event, the next Gospel by Matthew simplifies the sentence by giving the first two repeated words in the Hebrew, '*Eli, Eli*'. He notes that it has been suggested that this is a cry to Elijah, Eli being an accepted shortened form.[84]

In any event, in his short, polemical, and admittedly superficial book, Lüdemann claims that, 'The historical judgment must be that the early Christians tailored Jesus to their wishes and interests, and in whatever way seemed to them to be most useful in the fight against deviants and those of other beliefs.'[85]

Lüdemann's book is short and, as noted, not over convincing in its confrontation with reality. Far more serious in its presentation, and deep in its analysis, is the work by another German writer, a lawyer, Weddig Fricke, based, in a similar fashion to Chandler's book, on a strict legal analysis of the New Testament text by a jurist.[86]

He opens his book by expressing surprise that few lawyers have concerned themselves with the trial of Jesus for, 'according to tradition, his trial is one of those – and indeed the most momentous – in which an innocent person was sentenced to death and executed'.[87] However, Fricke immediately encounters a problem. There is, according to him, no real trial. The Gospel accounts do not indicate that a proper criminal trial actually took place. He rejects all three major explanations of what happened, since none 'can be conclusively verified'[88] – neither the version that the 'Jewish establishment wanted to rid itself of the troublesome prophet from Galilee', nor that he was 'a zealot resistance fighter against the Roman occupation', nor that he was 'sentenced and crucified by the Romans as a suspected rebel in a military-type summary proceeding',[89] though this latter is the most probable, according to him, and hence his reference to a court martial. In a footnote comment he acknowledges the problematics of using such terminology;[90] his aim is to emphasize the 'summary' nature of the proceedings.

Despite his critical approach, Fricke assures his readers that he has no intention of undermining religious faith, and that 'Christians who may be inclined to subscribe to my arguments will be able to hold unreservedly to the central message of Christianity for the individual: that Jesus of Nazareth is the Christ who died and rose from the dead.'[91] However, Fricke is intent on ensuring that blind faith does not lead to the denial of 'the findings of historical research'.[92] His book is then to be understood, as he affirms, 'not in theological but in juridical-historical terms'.[93] The implication of his thesis is clearly stated in the sub-title of his book: *A Christian Defends the Jews Against the Charge of Deicide.*

Fricke immediately raises the question of historicity: which I personally believe to be irrelevant, since there is no doubt that Jesus existed and was crucified. There is certainly more evidence as to his existence than is available for earlier biblical characters,[94] including, as some Israeli archaeologists have pointed out, for the existence of Abraham (presumed to be buried in Hebron with five of his family – wife, son, daughter-in-law, grandchild and one of the latter's wives); or even of Moses, whose burial place is unknown (as specifically stated in the Bible). Indeed, a great modern Jewish scholar, Ahad Ha-Am, in his classic article discussing whether or not Moses really lived, or lived according to the details of his life as described in the Bible, declares that this is an irrelevant issue, for it is the impact of the narrative about his life and his works that is of significance.[95]

However, having raised the issue of proof of the existence of Jesus, Fricke resolves it by arguing that the very fact of the description of his death – humiliating in the extreme – may be seen 'as the most convincing proof of Jesus' historicity'.[96] The Evangelists:

> ... did not consider death on the cross to be an honorable martyr's death; on the contrary, it must have been seen as a scandal of the first rank, the most shameful end that could befall the Messiah. Had Jesus been stoned like the other martyrs, or beheaded like John the Baptist, it would have been much easier to bear. In Jesus' time, crucifixion was viewed as a most dishonorable punishment, as Moses had made clear: 'for one who has been hanged is accursed of God.' (Deut. 21:23)[97]

Fricke then adds that Moses clearly was not talking about crucifixion, which was unknown to him; the fact is that by the time of Jesus, 'In their unshakable loyalty to the written word and the resultant literal mode of thinking, the later Jews heaped curses and other humiliations on people who were tied or nailed to a cross for execution.'[98]

Fricke's conclusion as to the key question of where lies the responsibility for this humiliating demise of a great religious leader is given in a definitive statement, as the opening paragraph in a chapter entitled 'The Romans, Not the Jews'.[99] He writes that, in contrast to much uncertainty that relates to the person of Jesus:

> One fact that can be established with absolute certainty is that Jesus was killed not by the Jews but by the Romans. Despite all the efforts to make the Jews primarily responsible and to cast the Roman procurator in the role of an unwitting instrument of Jesus' death, the biblical accounts make it quite clear that Pontius Pilate pronounced the death sentence. The sentence was then carried out by his legionnaires, probably Syrians working for the Romans.[100]

In explaining the cruel nature of the Crucifixion, and stating that the punishment was used not only by the Romans but also by the Persians, the Greeks and the Carthaginians, Fricke refers to reports (by Josephus) that claimed that, 'during the siege of Jerusalem Titus, the Roman commander, had at least 500 Jewish refugees crucified daily'.[101]

Amongst the arguments advanced by Fricke is the fact that, although the Romans basically claimed exclusive jurisdiction in the use of the death penalty, there were known cases of Jews who were executed by the Jewish authorities – for instance, John the Baptist (beheaded at the behest of Herod), as well as Stephen (as also described in the New Testament), in addition to James, the brother of Jesus. The implication, of course, is that if the Jewish authorities had truly wished to execute Jesus, they could have done so without turning to Pilate, and without the need for a Roman form of execution. This is an argument that takes on added pertinence in the light of the Gospel by Luke, which claimed that the final authorization was given by Herod and not Pilate. If so, why the need for a crucifixion? When Herod had John the Baptist put to death, he did so by beheading. It is specifically the use of crucifixion (subsequently to become the basis of the very symbol of Christianity) that belies the major role of the Jewish authorities.

Fricke also writes of the short time that Jesus was on the Cross, mainly to argue that it was surely fortuitous that death came so quickly. Since it was shortly before the Sabbath (which comes at sundown), the inevitable question arises as to why the process would have started so close to sundown when there could be no certainty that it would be completed expeditiously. In fact, there is no evidence (and, as far as I know, no extended discussion) as to what became of the two criminals on the adjacent crosses. Were they too taken down before the advent of the Sabbath (and possibly the Passover)? Were they by then dead or alive? Nobody seems to know, nobody seems to care.

In the following chapter, Fricke refers to the 'alleged' trial before the Sanhedrin. This 'trial' is, as he specifies, 'at the heart of the Passion story in the Synoptic Gospels. It is the basis for the later break between Christians and Jews.'[102] Fricke refers to four German theologians, Catholic and Protestant, who in the decade before the publication of his work 'have called into question the historicity of a trial before the Sanhedrin'.[103]

Fricke confirms their approach, arguing also, theologically (despite his basically legal approach), that the followers of Jesus could not have believed in him as a heavenly being. He states categorically that:

> The notions that God is a Trinity, and that God would take someone to heaven and delegate to him definite functions of divine rulership, would have been as inconceivable to any Jew of two thousand years ago as it is today.[104]

Faithful to his religious belief, Fricke concludes that anyone who accepts Jesus' divinity, and his part in the Trinity, anyone:

> who understands the deed of the redemption to mean that God's 'only begotten Son' took upon himself the fate of human beings, namely birth, life, and death, does not need to accept the notion of a violent death that Jesus suffered at the hands of the Jews. The kernel of Christian faith can only be this: because death came into the world through a human being, the Son of God become a man therefore also had to die. The overcoming of death, however, the Resurrection, is the fulfillment of the act of redemption.[105]

In the end, Fricke goes beyond the 'juridical-historical terms' that he had set out as his guidelines, and ends with a typically theological statement. From a practical point of view, there is value in his concluding remark that 'the charge of deicide raised against the Jews is historically false, theologically superfluous, and ruinous from a moral point of view',[106] but it fails to resolve the underlying issue of Jewish-Christian relations – the claimed divinity of Jesus as the Messiah, as the Son of God.

NOTES

1. Haim Hermann Cohn, *The Trial and Death of Jesus* (New York: Harper and Row, 1971). The original Hebrew version was published in 1968. For an understanding of the deeper, underlying factors in Jewish–Christian relations that would understandably have led to such pleas by some Christians to the new Jewish State, see the fascinating study by Stephen R. Haynes, *Reluctant Witnesses: Jews and the Christian Imagination* (Louisville, MI: Westminster John Knox Press, 1995). He explains:

    > A thesis of this book is that Jews must always be special cases in products of the Christian imagination, because of the uniquely ambivalent place which the Jewish people inhabit there. (p. 3)

    He then explains that:

    > In the Christian imagination the existence and survival of the Jews have been invested with religious significance, even – and especially – when Jews refuse to recognize this significance ... Jews continue to function in the Christian mind as fundamental symbols in the divine alphabet. (p. 5)

    I would suggest that it is these kinds of imaginings about, and interpretations of, the actions of Jews – collectively as well as individually – that led to the requests for a delayed and posthumous pardon to be given by Jewish officialdom for its long-standing, but well-remembered, 'judicial error'.
2. Weddig Fricke, *The Court Martial of Jesus: A Christian Defends the Jews Against the Charge of Deicide* (New York: Grove Weidenfeld, 1987).
3. For instance, the Cross used in the Russian Orthodox Church has a small stand, placed at an angle, near the bottom, signifying a small platform on which Jesus could place his feet, or perhaps alternatively, to which his feet were tied, instead of nailed.
4. Hugh Schonfield, *The Passover Plot* (New York: Bantam, 1967).
5. *See*, for instance, John Dominic Crossan, *The Historical Jesus: The Life of a Mediterranean Jewish Peasant* (San Francisco, CA: Harper, 1993); *The Cross that Spoke: The Origins of the Passion Narrative* (San Francisco, CA: Harper and Row, 1988); and *Jesus: A Revolutionary Biography* (San Francisco, CA: Harper, 1994).
6. John Dominic Crossan, *Who Killed Jesus? Exposing the Roots of Anti-Semitism in the Gospel Story of the Death of Jesus* (San Francisco, CA: Harper, 1995).
7. Raymond E. Brown, *The Death of the Messiah: From Gethsemane to the Grave: A Commentary on the Passion Narratives in the Four Gospels*, 2 Vols (New York: Doubleday, 1994).
8. Raymond E. Brown, *The Birth of the Messiah: A Commentary on the Infancy Narrative in Matthew and Luke* (Garden City, NY: Doubleday Image Books, 1979).
9. Crossan, *Who Killed Jesus?*, p. 66. *See also* discussion by Larry D. Shimm, *Two Sacred Worlds: Experience and Structure in the World's Religions* (Nashville, TN: Abingdon, 1977), where he writes:

    > The core experience of the early Christians apparently occurred after Jesus' crucifixion ... Jesus' life and ministry became crucially important only *after* his death. This is noted in the disproportionate amount of oral and written tradition that focuses upon the last week of his life (nearly one-third of the Gospel accounts) and the complete absence of a birth narrative in all but two of the New Testament narratives (Matthew and Luke). Furthermore, since his ministry of approximately three years formed the abiding experience of Jesus by the early disciples, the remaining two-thirds of the Gospel accounts report those years *from the perspective of a Lord already risen*. For example, prophecies of his impending death are written back into his sacred history again and again. (pp. 40–1, emphasis in original)
10. Ibid., p. 67.
11. Ibid., p. 117.
12. Ibid., pp. 26–7.

13. Ibid., pp. 22–5.
14. Ibid., pp. 25–6.
15. *See*, for instance, C.H. Dodd, *The Interpretation of the Fourth Gospel* (Cambridge: Cambridge University Press, 1968). In an Appendix to this authoritative book he writes:

> It will have become clear that I regard the Fourth Gospel as being in its essential character a theological work, rather than a history. Nevertheless, the writer has chosen to set forth his theology under the literary form of a 'Gospel,' a form created by Christianity for its own proper purposes. A Gospel in this sense consists of a recital of the historical narrative of the sufferings, death and resurrection of Jesus Christ, prefaced by some account of His ministry in word and deed. (p. 444)

Dodd continues that 'it is important for the Evangelist that what he narrates happened'. However, immediately after this comment, Dodd states that:

> In the process, however, of bringing out the symbolic value of the facts he has used some freedom. Like many ancient writers, he has put into the mouth of his characters speeches which, since they bear not only the stamp of his own style, but also the stamp of an environment different from that in which the recorded events took place, cannot be regarded as historical...there is good reason to suspect that in some cases and in some respects the narratives which provide the setting for such speeches may have been moulded by the ideas which they are made to illustrate. (pp. 444–5)

Dodd notes that it is the historian's task not just to present the facts, but also, 'to make perceptible and intelligible the influence they in turn exert'. (p. 445)
16. 'Then said Pilate to the chief priests and to the people, "I find no fault in this man." And they were the more fierce, saying, "He stirreth up the people, teaching throughout all Jewry, beginning from Galilee to this place." When Pilate heard of Galilee, he asked whether the man were a Galilean. And as soon as he knew that he belonged unto Herod's jurisdiction, he sent him to Herod, who himself also was at Jerusalem at that time.' (Luke, 23:4–7)
17. Ernest Renan, *The Life of Jesus* (1863). The quotations later in this chapter are taken from the English version, published by A.L. Burt Company, Publishers.
18. Albert Schweitzer, *The Quest of the Historical Jesus: A Critical Study of the Progress from Reimarus to Wrede* (London: A.C. Black, 1911).
19. Crossan, *The Historical Jesus*, pp. 13–14, based on Josephus Flavius' book, *Jewish Antiquities* (Cambridge, MA: Harvard University Press, 1943).
20. *See* Matthew 2:18–20, particularly 2:20, 'the angel of the Lord appeared unto him in a dream, saying, "Joseph, thou son of David, fear not to take unto thee Mary thy wife: for that which is conceived in her is of the Holy Ghost"'; and Luke 1:26–35, particularly 34–5:

> Then said Mary unto the angel, 'How shall this be, seeing I know not a man?' And the angel answered and said unto her, 'The Holy Ghost shall come upon thee, and the power of the Highest shall overshadow thee; therefore also that holy thing which shall be born of thee shall be called the Son of God.'

21. Renan, *The Life of Jesus*, 'Biographical Sketch', by William Hutchison, p. 3.
22. Ibid., p. 3.
23. Ibid., p. 4.
24. Ibid., chapter 2, entitled 'Infancy and Youth of Jesus', pp. 84–5.
25. Ibid., p. 346.
26. Ibid., p. 347.
27. Ibid., p. 348.
28. Ibid., p. 349.
29. Ibid., p. 352.
30. Ibid.
31. Ibid.
32. Ibid., p. 355.

33. Ibid., p. 356.
34. Ibid.
35. Ibid., pp. 356–7n6.
36. Ibid.
37. Crossan, *The Historical Jesus*, p. 96.
38. Renan, *The Life of Jesus*, p. 358.
39. Ibid.
40. Ibid., p. 359.
41. *See*, for instance, the claim by Hans Kohn about the essential democracy of Judaism, because of the honored place accorded the prophets in Jewish tradition: *The Idea of Nationalism: A Study in its Origins and Background* (New York: Collier Books, 1967). He writes, 'Within the Jewish people and within humanity the Prophets had started a re-evaluation of all accepted values ... The dignity of man as such, regardless of his class, his ancestry, his abilities, was discovered' (p. 40). *See also* Abraham J. Heschel, *The Prophets* (Philadelphia, PA: The Jewish Publication Society of America, 1962).
42. Samuel i:12,1–24. This is the story of David's illicit affair with Bat-Sheva, leading to his planning the death of her warrior husband, Uriah. The prophet Nathan even predicts the death of the son that she will bear: a prediction which comes to pass.
    See also Rinah Lipis Shaskolsky, 'The Prophets as Dissenters', *Judaism*, 19 (1970), p. 15.
43. Walter M. Chandler, *The Trial of Jesus: From a Lawyer's Standpoint*, Vol. 1, *The Hebrew Trial*, Vol. 2, *The Roman Trial* (New York: The Federal Book Co., 1908; republished, Buffalo, NY: William S. Hein and Co., 1983).
44. Chandler, *The Hebrew Trial*, p. 3.
45. Ibid., p. 4.
46. Ibid., p. 5, quoting extensively from 'the celebrated treatise on the "Testimony of the Evangelists"'.
47. Ibid., p. 19.
48. Ibid., p. 16.
49. Chandler, *The Roman Trial*, pp. 284 and 299.
50. Chandler, *The Hebrew Trial*, p. 18.
51. Ibid., p. 24.
52. Ibid., p. 25.
53. Ibid.
54. There are also warnings as to the reliability of evidence related decades after the event.
55. Chandler, *The Hebrew Trial*, pp. 9–10.
56. Ibid., part 3, 'The Brief', pp. 175–366. This part of the book is partly written in the form of a modern-day argument presented to a court. As to the nature of Chandler's argument, an interesting example revolves around his contention that the verdict was illegal because it was unanimous. This rule was intended to ensure that verdicts would not be the outcome of a desire to achieve consensus among the 23 members of the Sanhedrin (a fact that sometimes plagues modern juries). After noting this rule as being strange, Chandler does concede that it is not as unreasonable as it seems at first glance. Having granted validity to the rule, he then attempts to prove that it was violated, his proof hinging on a single passing reference by one of the Evangelists. In Chandler's words (original emphasis):

> The condemnation of Jesus was illegal because the verdict of the Sanhedrin was unanimous. We learn this from Mark, who says: 'they *all* condemned him to be guilty of death'. If they *all* condemned Him, the verdict was unanimous, and therefore illegal.

However, faced with the paucity of evidence as to the issue of unanimity, Chandler then offers this additional reasoning: 'The other Evangelists do not tell us that the verdict was unanimous; neither do they deny it. Mark's testimony stands alone and uncontradicted; therefore we must assume that it is true' (p. 282).
57. *See* Karl Mannheim, *Ideology and Utopia: An Introduction to the Sociology of Knowledge* (New York: Harcourt, Brace and World, 1936).
58. Nahum N. Glatzer, *Hillel the Elder: The Emergence of Classical Judaism* (New York:

B'Nai Brith Hillel Foundations, 1957).

59. *See* especially Leon Sheleff, *Marut Ha-Mishpat ve-Mahut Ha-Mishtar (The Rule of Law and the Nature of Politics)* (Tel Aviv: Papyrus Publishing House/Tel Aviv University, 1996 – in Hebrew); and *Weeds in the Garden of Eden – Biblical Narratives and Israeli Chronicles* (Tel Aviv: Kibbutz Ha-Me'uchad, 2002 – in Hebrew); *see also The Thin Green Line: Intractable Problems and Feasible Solutions in the Israeli–Palestinian Conflict* (in press).

60. See Leon Sheleff, *Generations Apart: Adult Hostility to Youth* (New York: McGraw-Hill, 1981).

61. Ibid., Part 3, 'The Rustum Complex'.

62. Schonfield, *The Passover Plot.*

63. Ibid., p. 67.

64. Ibid., p. 84.

65. Ibid., p. 85.

66. This practice is still observed in some belief systems, for example, in Zoroastrianism.

67. Schonfield, *The Passover Plot*, p. 155.

68. Ibid.

69. Ibid.

70. Ibid., p. 160.

71. Ibid., p. 165.

72. Ibid. *See* George Moore, *The Brook Kerith*, and D.H. Lawrence, *The Man Who Died.* There have also been fictional accounts in which Jesus was replaced by a substitute figure who died on the cross instead of him. In addition, it should be noted that at least one Gnostic text makes the same point. In one of the manuscripts found in 1945 at Nag Hammadi in Egypt, the 'Second Treatise of the Great Seth', it is stated, as part of the teaching of Jesus, that:

> It was another ... who drank the gall and the vinegar; it was not I. They struck me with the reed; it was another, Simon, who bore the cross on his shoulder. It was another upon whom they placed the crown of thorns. But I was rejoicing in the height over ... their ... error ... and I was laughing at their ignorance.

As quoted in Elaine Pagels, *The Gnostic Gospels* (London: Weidenfeld and Nicolson, 1979). This book is a fascinating account of the discovery of the manuscripts and the scholarly research being undertaken, including by the author herself. The material raises many serious questions as to the history of early Christianity, and as to which of the written accounts (those in the Bible or those in the Gnostic writings) are more accurate and more authentic. But, in this book, the arguments will focus on the biblical texts in the Old and New Testaments.

73. Schonfield, *The Passover Plot*, pp. 165–6.

74. Ibid., p. 166.

75. *See*, for instance, Peter Hebblethwaite, *The New Inquisition? Schillebeeckx and Küng* (London: Fount Paperbacks, 1980).

76. Gerd Lüdemann, *The Great Deception: And What Jesus Really Said and Did* (Amherst, NY: Prometheus Books, 1999).

77. *See*, for instance, Julius Wellhausen, *Prolegomena to the Heritage of Ancient Israel* (New York: Meridian, 1967); Emil Schürer, *The History of the Jewish People in the Age of Jesus Christ (175 BC–AD 135)*, 3 vols (Edinburgh: T. and T. Clark, 1973–1987) and *The Literature of the Jewish People in the Time of Jesus* (New York: Schocken Books, 1972); also Ernst Troeltsch, *Religion in History* (Edinburgh: T. and T. Clark, 1991).

78. Lüdemann, *The Great Deception,* p. xii (in Preface to the US edition).

79. Ibid. He provides a list of his earlier works dealing with the various topics mentioned in the quotation: *The Resurrection of Jesus: History, Experience, Theology* (London: SCM, 2000); *Heretics: The Other Side of Early Christianity* (London: SCM, 1996); *The Unholy in Holy Scripture: The Dark Side of the Bible* (London: SCM, 1997); *Virgin Birth: The Real Story of Mary and Her Son Jesus* (London: SCM, 1998).

80. *See* Lüdemann, *The Great Deception,* 'A Letter to Jesus', p. 1.

 81. Ibid., pp. 25-64.
 82. Ibid., p. 58.
 83. Ibid.
 84. Ibid., p. 59.
 85. Ibid., p. 110.
 86. Fricke, *The Court Martial of Jesus*.
 87. Ibid., p. 3.
 88. Ibid., p. 4.
 89. Ibid.
 90. Ibid.
 91. Ibid., p. 5.
 92. Ibid.
 93. Ibid.
 94. Recently, there has been a vigorous debate in Israel over the claim by some Israeli archae-
     ologists that there is little or no evidence to substantiate much of the earlier books in the
     Bible. A newspaper article by Ze'ev Herzog, a leading Israeli archaeologist, led to a
     prolonged and animated debate in the media and in academic circles; for an analysis of
     this issue, see his article, 'Deconstructing the Walls of Jericho: Biblical Myth and
     Archaeological Reality', *Prometheus – Firing the Mind* 4 (2000). *See also* reference to his
     work, and a general discussion of the ongoing debate in Israel, in Amy Dockser Marcus,
     Rewriting the Bible: How Archaeology is Reshaping History (Boston: Little, Brown,
     2000); and for his research, see Herzog, *Archaeology of the City: Urban Planning in
     Ancient Israel and its Social Implications* (Tel Aviv: Yass Archaeology Press, 1997 –
     Monograph Series of Institute of Archaeology, Tel Aviv University, No. 13).
 95. Ahad Ha-am, *Selected Essays* (Philadelphia: The Jewish Publication Society, 1912),
     'Moses', p. 306. He writes: 'I care and whether this man Moses really existed; whether
     his life and activity fully correspond to our traditional account of him ... We have another
     Moses ... whose image has been enshrined in the hearts of the Jewish people for genera-
     tions, and whose influence on our national life has never ceased from ancient times till
     the present day ... His character is ... not liable to be altered by any archaeological
     discovery.'
 96. Fricke, *The Court Martial of Jesus*, p. 58.
 97. Ibid.
 98. Ibid.
 99. Ibid., chapter 9.
100. Ibid., p. 109.
101. Ibid., p. 111.
102. Ibid., p. 149
103. Ibid., p. 109
104. Ibid., p. 175.
105. Ibid.
106. Ibid., p. 222.

COMPLEX CHARACTERS

4
Messiah

Throughout their history, Jews have known false Messiahs. One of the earliest was almost exactly 100 years after the crucifixion of Jesus when, in a desperate, yet futile (perhaps foolish) gamble, the Jews frontally challenged the might of the Roman Empire. The rebellion was led by Simon Bar-Kochba, whose name is derived from the word 'star' (*cochav*); yet it has been claimed that his name was really Bar-Kozbah, a name that embodies the idea of falsity (*kozav*).[1]

More recently, a few years before the end of the Second Christian Millenium, the followers of the Hasidic Rabbi, the Lubavitcher Rebbe from Brooklyn, were dropping blatant hints that the advent of the Messiah was at hand; and there were suppositions that the official announcement as to his renowned status would be made on the occasion of his forthcoming ninetieth birthday. A few weeks before the date, he suffered a paralytic stroke and died several months later after a lengthy period of hospitalization, unconscious and kept alive only by sophisticated medical technology (part of the time being apparently clinically dead). Some of his followers were reported to have accepted his death not just with equanimity but even joy, breaking out into song and dance, and confidently declaring (apparently unaware of its historical and theological incongruity for a Jew) that he would return in three days' time.[2]

Inbetween these two false Messiahs have been other colorful, yet tragic, figures who made similar claims as to their messianic status: the most noted being Jacob Frank, a mystic who glorified deviant actions,[3] and more particularly, Shabtai Zvi, whose many followers throughout the Middle East had to cope with the shock of his last-minute conversion to Islam shortly before their hopes of the full messianic age, with a return to the Holy Land, were to be fulfilled.[4]

These messianic figures all claimed divine inspiration, but none of them claimed divinity as the Son of God. This is a concept totally foreign to Judaism, as many scholars who have studied the topic have clearly explained.[5]

In this context, it may well be argued that any such claim by Jesus to be the Son of God may well have led to a vicious response by the Jewish religious authorities. This is certainly true, but it begs the question as to whether Jesus did indeed clearly and openly make this claim, or only claimed to be a Messiah (as understood in Jewish tradition). Or was the issue of his divinity raised only after his death, indeed, only some four or five decades after his death, in a unique historical context?

At the time of the Crucifixion, the followers of Jesus were totally devastated. The Crucifixion was, at the time, a disastrous event; it symbolized the failure of a potentially interesting incipient movement within Judaism (like other religions, Judaism has been characterized throughout by its ability to develop new approaches to existing religious situations).[6] Indeed, it was only the creative powers of rabbinical author- ities that saved Judaism when, almost 40 years after the crucifixion of Jesus, in the year 70 CE, the Temple in Jerusalem was destroyed. Rabbi Yochanan Ben-Zachai then made his way southwest to the town of Yavne, and there re-created Judaism around the idea of synagogue life in lieu of the temple.[7] Later, the Talmud was to develop as an outgrowth of the Old Testament, allowing for further developments in interpretation of the laws and the commandments that had been laid down – perhaps even in some respects partly along the lines that Jesus had envisaged.[8]

But this juxtaposition of two tragedies – the crucifixion of Jesus and the destruction of the Temple – created a unique situation for the followers of Jesus. There was for them now a possible, divine, causative connection between the two incidents: the rejection of their teacher, with his critique of the happenings in the temple, had led to the divine punishment of the destruction of the Temple.

It was at this time, probably shortly afterwards, that the Gospels were written. It is certain that the latter three were written subsequent to the destruction. The only Gospel about which there is some doubt as to whether it was published before or after the cataclysmic event is the Gospel by Mark. It was probably written some time in the 70s CE, but it was possibly written just shortly before.[9] As regards the two most critical aspects of Jesus' divinity, this Gospel is one of the two Gospels that totally ignores the virgin birth while, as for the Resurrection, it deals with this momentous phenomenon in an almost offhand manner. First, Mark has three women come to the sepulchre where Jesus had been buried, only to discover that the stone at the entrance had been rolled away. In the sepulchre itself sat a man who was not known to them, and whose identity is left unclear. He is the one who apprises them of the amazing fact that the body of Jesus is no longer there since, in his words, as quoted by Mark, 'he is risen; he is not here'.[10] He then informs them that Jesus has gone to the Galilee, and that all of his disciples should be informed of this. To this he adds, 'there shall ye see him, as he said unto you'.[11]

The reaction of the women is one of amazement and fear. However, Jesus shortly afterwards appears to one of the three women, Mary Magdalene. In this first reference to her, Mark mentions that she was the one 'out of whom he [Jesus] had cast seven devils'.[12] She then informs others, and so the information spreads until it is briefly mentioned that Jesus has appeared to other people, including the 11 disciples (Judas no longer being in the reckoning). They are then urged to go out and preach the gospel: 'He that believeth and is baptized shall be saved; but he that believeth not shall be damned.'[13] And thus, with one more general sentence, the Gospel of Mark comes to an end.

There is no description of what transpired in this miraculous meeting between their recently-crucified leader and his remaining disciples; no mention of the joy, the awe, the gratitude they must surely have felt; no indication of whether Jesus then resumed his ministry. Casually, non-committally, Jesus is reunited in the Galilee with his disciples. Some of the other Gospels are slightly more detailed, especially that of Matthew. His Gospel is actually the first book of the New Testament, though written later than that of Mark. A possible reason for this is that he provides more information, some of it crucial for the unique message of Christianity, particularly in regard to the virgin birth. (My own surmise is that Mark did not recount this story because he had possibly written before the destruction of the Temple or immediately after, before the full implications and possible interpretations had emerged, and before the critical connection between the crucifixion of Jesus, as the Son of God, and the destruction of the Temple as a punishment to the Jews, had been established.)

Matthew reports that those responsible for his death (Pilate and the priests) were apprehensive that the body of Jesus might well disappear from the tomb: not because of his actual resurrection, but because he had been heard to say, 'After three days I will rise again.'[14] Because of this, they were apparently, according to Matthew, fearful that the body might actually be stolen, so that his disciples would be able to state that he had indeed been resurrected. They determined to forestall this possibility. Thus, according to Matthew, an order is given 'that the sepulchre be made secure until the third day, lest his disciples come by night, and steal him away, and say unto the people "He is risen from the dead"'. These orders are carried out; the sepulchre is made secure 'sealing the stone, and setting a watch'.[15]

Yet they seem to have reacted too late, for in the next sentence in Matthew, the women are described as coming to the tomb, with a similar outcome to that in Mark's account: that is, the body has disappeared (though there is cryptic mention also of an earthquake and the appearance of an angel).[16] What happened? Did the guards fall asleep; were they bribed, were they part of a conspiracy? Many alternatives exist, but Matthew opts for a deliberately concocted explanation of a conspiracy between the delinquent guards and the scheming priests in which bribery is used: not by the disciples to allow them to take the body, but by the priests in order to cover up the miraculous disappearance. He writes:

> Now when they were going, behold, some of the watch came into the city, and shewed unto the chief priests all the things that were done. And when they were assembled with the elders, and had taken counsel, they gave large money unto the soldiers, saying, 'Say ye, His disciples came by night, and stole him away while we slept. And if this comes to the governor's ears, we will persuade him, and secure you.' So they took the money, and did as they were taught.[17]

Then, immediately, comes the *coup de grâce:* 'And this saying is commonly reported among the Jews until this day'[18] – the implication being that given the fact of the disappearance of the body, the Jews have perforce provided a simple, yet false, explanation for it. Interestingly enough, in a Hebrew translation brought out by the Society for Distributing Hebrew Scriptures, the term used is not 'saying' but 'rumor'.[19]

In Luke, the earlier accounts are expanded even more. First, he reports that the body's disappearance is checked and confirmed by Peter. Then there is a description of a meeting between Jesus and the 11 disciples where they eat together, and then Jesus says to them, 'Thus it is written, and thus it behoved Christ to suffer, and to rise from the dead the third day.'[20] It is then, and only in this Gospel, that an attempt is made to describe the full ending of the earthly life of Jesus. Luke writes, 'And it came to pass, while he blessed them, he was parted from them, and carried up into heaven.'[21]

Writing much later, John, in what is generally known as the Fourth Gospel, is more explicit and detailed; here, Mary Magdalene, this time alone, specifically sees Jesus near the sepulchre. At the sepulchre this time are two angels, 'the one at the head, and the other at the feet, where the body of Jesus had lain'.[22] As in Mark, she is the one who informs the disciples; and then confirmation is provided when:

> The same day at evening, being the first day of the week, when the doors were shut where the disciples were assembled for fear of the Jews, came Jesus and stood in the midst, and said unto them, 'Peace be unto you.' And when he had so said, he shewed unto them his

hands and his side. Then were the disciples glad, when they saw the Lord.[23]

Here, at least, John attempts to convey some of the emotions that the disciples must surely have felt: a factor ignored by Mark.

At this stage, the doubts that might well have arisen at this remarkable development are expressed through the person of Thomas, who, according to John, was not present at this meeting and, on being told of it, refused to believe it without concrete proof. Eight days later, the doubts are resolved: Thomas is enabled to see and touch the corporeal body of Jesus. This is the opportunity for a major theological pronouncement by Jesus (found only in the Gospel of John), 'Thomas, because thou hast seen me, thou hast believed: blessed are they that have not seen, and yet have believed.'[24] A statement that has obvious implications for all succeeding generations.

The import of this aspect of the story of Jesus is that, in order for the divinity of Jesus to be proved, the Crucifixion is totally irrelevant (incidentally, apparently none of the disciples were present at Golgotha, having fled at his arrest).[25] What is crucial is the virgin birth and the post-crucifixion Resurrection. As for the former, it is partly based on an incorrect translation from the Hebrew of the Old Testament. A Christian scholar who is most forthright in this matter is Gerard S. Sloyan, who notes that the 'Septuagint Greek Bible has chosen to render a word in Isaiah as "virgin" instead of "young woman"'.[26] Furthermore, two of the four Gospels do not even mention the unique nature of his birth, while the remaining two differ as to how the information was provided (by a dream of Joseph's in Matthew, or in Luke through information supplied by an angel directly to Mary of impregnation through the Holy Spirit[27]). All four of the Gospels refer to the Resurrection, but only laconically and briefly in the light of its momentous meaning, with only Luke closing the narrative by describing a second demise and Jesus' disappearance directly into heaven.

The very brevity of these accounts raises doubts as to their accuracy. This is not a peripheral issue, it is of the essence. The Crucifixion is not crucial for proof of divinity, but it is mentioned in detail (if ambiguous detail at times) because it did take place. It was not, in any case, an unusual event; but a resurrection was certainly almost unique, although not entirely so, since Jesus himself was reported to have raised Lazarus, and a teenage girl, from the dead.[28] Furthermore, unlike the issue of the virgin birth, which can only be based on pure belief since there are no means of empirical proof, the Resurrection must have concrete evidence, such as the body's disappearance and Jesus' interaction with others.

Reading these texts as a non-believer, the possibility clearly emerges – given the fact of the humiliating crucifixion of the beloved leader – that the virgin birth and the Resurrection are addenda. They enabled his movement to revive, to be born again, to be resurrected. The timing was crucial. The message was given during a disastrous tragedy for the Jews: the destruction, for the second time, of their Temple; the very Temple for which Jesus had been accused by false witnesses of predicting destruction and then reconstruction in three days.[29]

The Old Testament is full of such repetitive interconnections.[30] The Evangelists now draw on this tradition to present a version of reality that, if believed, can lead to the revival of their incipient, but damaged, movement. To an extent, they succeeded. The bulk of the Jews remained loyal to mainstream leadership and adapted the injured body politic and body religious to the new reality, by creative change, replacing the Temple with the Synagogue, the Temple service with prayers, the priests with rabbis, and adding later talmudic exegeses to the original sacred book, the Bible. However, the minority, in their despair and anguish, turned to the message provided by Jesus: which, on the one hand, warned of impending doom, and on the other hand spoke a message of the Kingdom of God – with the addition, subsequent to Jesus' death, of his virgin birth and miraculous resurrection. This minority forms the kernel from which an internal Jewish movement becomes universal, not through the Gospels alone but through the inspired work of Saul, the former arch-foe of Jesus and his followers, later named Paul and the bearer of the message of Jesus to the Gentiles, which then spread throughout the Roman Empire.[31]

This missionary zeal focused on the religious aspect of a belief in God, and in the Trinity, but had to be wary not to revive the political implications of a challenge to the secular authority. It is at this stage that, in both subtle and blatant ways, the emphasis for the responsibility for the death of Jesus was increasingly attributed, not just in the Gospels but in later books of the New Testament, to the Jews.

Nevertheless, the problem still remained of the humiliation of the Crucifixion: not for its cruel finality but for its ubiquitousness, particularly in its use against petty criminals and political rebels. The *Akedah* provided the solution. The demand made on Abraham (as interpreted by religious leaders) to sacrifice his son as a sign of belief was now transposed to God's willingness to sacrifice His son, His only begotten son, as a sign of His love for humanity, as a sign of His willingness to redeem it. In Abraham's case, the sacrifice was averted at the last moment and Isaac was saved;[32] in the latter case, Jesus was sacrificed momentarily, but saved through the Resurrection. This was not only proof of God's love, but also a sign of eternal life.

Isaac therefore provides the prototype within the Jewish tradition; but, as already noted, just as the demand for his sacrifice was by no means a novelty for that era or for an area in which filicide was widely practiced, so the idea of the birth of a son through divine intervention and the idea of a resurrected, young, dying God, was fairly widespread at the time throughout this region.

The idea of the Son of God being sacrificed probably had its basis in the mirror image of the father of the Jewish people being prepared to sacrifice his son, but it soon took on added meaning and impact through syncretism, made possible by the widespread idea of human–divine interconnections and widespread filicidal practices (not just the actual sacrifice of children to the gods as a form of pagan worship, but stories of the gods themselves sacrificing their sons). The competing religions of the time, popular and powerful, provide ample examples.[33]

But this approach presents a certain dilemma. On the one hand, it presents an attractive syncretism. It is often pointed out that Paul, going beyond Jesus, introduced changes that would make the religion compatible to outsiders, by downplaying and even abandoning the strict observance of Old Testament rules: for instance, the need for male circumcision in order to enter into a covenant with God.[34] However, less noticed is the overlap between aspects of the new faith and the prevalent beliefs in divine–human unions and of young gods dying, some of whom were also resurrected. This very similarity created a dilemma: it was a threat, not just to the political, secular authority (which many commentators have suggested), but also to the religious culture, not of the Jews, but of the Romans.

In this sense, it may well have been easier for the Roman political authorities to come to terms with the Jewish religion (with its amorphous, unseen God in sole monotheistic splendor in the heavens above) than with a physical God, who came into the world, performed miracles, and then, after the penalty of death had been imposed upon Him, rose again and, by His resurrection, outwitted his enemies – obviously with the possibility of a second advent.

This is a key factor explaining why the Christians were often persecuted by the Romans more severely than the Jews (apart from their open rebellion, leading to the destruction of the Temple and of much of Jerusalem in the year 70 CE, and then their further decimation and exile in the year 132 CE, after the failure of Bar-Kochba's revolt).[35] A son of God, in the person of Jesus, with a universal message to all, as presented by Paul, was more threatening than a distant God, with his insistence on the observance of a myriad of commandments by a select group of 'chosen people'. This led to a further crucial aspect in Christian theology and in Jewish–Christian relations: the need to present the bench-mark act of the Crucifixion as being the responsibility of the Jews, and not the Romans, in order to ward off Roman enmity. This was a desperate theological development that had, however, little practical success, as the persecution of the Christians continued for three centuries, until the history of the world was fundamentally and irretrievably transformed by Constantine's declaration of Christianity as the official religion of the empire.[36] But the theology failed only in the political area; as the Roman rulers were not concerned with who bore responsibility for Jesus' death, it succeeded in the religious area, since those entering the Christian fold focused responsibility for the death of Jesus on the Jews, thus leading to hostility and hatred.

It is in this light – of the destruction of the Temple 40 years after the Crucifixion, of the nadir of Jewish life at that time, of the dates when the Gospels were written – that these books must be read and interpreted. Reading between the lines is essential, as is a closer analysis of textual usage.

Thus, for instance, most of the Gospels refer to those outside of the group of Jesus' followers as Jews, even though Jesus himself clearly lived and died as a Jew, as is true of his disciples. The incipient Christian Movement might have been emerging when the Gospels were being written, but this distinction being made between Jesus and his followers and the Jews is, I would submit, extremely revealing, since it reflects conditions that prevailed at the time of writing, not during Jesus' lifetime, allowing us to understand its anachronistic nature.

More significant are the references made to Jesus specifically as the Son of God, or as the Son of Man, or the Son of David, or references to God as a Father. This last reference presents no problems as, both in Judaism and Christianity, much formal prayer involves supplication by believers to God as a Father: for instance, 'The Lord's Prayer' in Christianity, with its opening words of 'Our Father', or Jewish references to *Av Ha-Rachamin* (Father of Mercy), and similar usages. There is nothing unusual in casual references to God in paternal terms.

Of more interest is the importance attached to the repetitive references to the Son of Man. This may stem from the Aramaic or the Greek, with special connotations. However, in Hebrew, both at that time and in modern parlance, the Son of Man is no more than a person: *Ben Adam*. The word *Adam* itself may be used on its own to express the word 'person', but a slightly more common use is '*Ben Adam*', the word '*Ben*' meaning son (as in Ben-Gurion, or in the English use of the suffix 'son' at the end of a family name – Robinson, Ferguson, Harrison). It is also often customary for prominent people to refer to themselves in the third person, so that all the theological discourses as to the use in the New Testament of the phrase the 'Son of Man' may likely have no real relevance, since the term is merely a common vernacular in Hebrew or other Semitic languages that posed problems only in later translations, especially in English.

In C.H. Dodd's book on the *Interpretation of the Fourth Gospel*, he devotes a whole chapter to this nomenclature. Admittedly, he opens with a reference to the Greek term;[37] however, he does note that in the Old Testament, the Greek term 'frequently renders the Hebrew Ben-Adam in the sense of "human being"'. He then adds that, 'There is little evidence to show that in pre-Christian Judaism the term "Son of Man" was used as a Messianic title.'[38] However, he claims that, whatever the earlier situation may have been, for John, 'Son of Man is the Son of God; He descended from heaven and ascends to heaven again. He is in intimate union with God, "dwelling in him".'[39] Based on Hellenistic concepts, Dodd argues that:

> For John the true life for men is attained only by those in whom Christ dwells, and who dwell in Him ... as Son of Man He is in some sort the inclusive representative of ideal or redeemed humanity. He descends into the world and dies in order that He may draw all men to Him. He ascends to God in order that where He is they may be also.[40]

Even the use of capitals to refer to the Son of God is, to a certain extent, problematic, as the Hebrew language, and other Semitic languages, have no capital letters.

Dodd claims that, 'This corporate significance of the term is not alien from the Jewish and Old Testament tradition lying behind the Gospels.'[41] His authority for this is sparse – Daniel (a problematic book in many respects, with mystical overtones, written in Aramaic and barely incorporated into the Bible); one reference in the Psalms; and, most particularly, the story of 'Jacob's Ladder' from Genesis. However, since the term 'Son of Man' does not appear in this story, he is forced to resort to a convoluted argumentation. He opens with a reference to the first use of 'Son of Man' in the Gospel of John, 'Verily, verily, I say unto you, Hereafter ye shall see heaven open, and the angels of God ascending and descending upon the Son of Man.'[42] This picture of angels going up and down obviously conjures up the well-known image of the angels ascending and descending the ladder in Jacob's dream. However, by a deft grammatical manipulation, Dodd points out that going up and down the ladder could also have referred to going up and down Jacob's body, since the genitive in Hebrew, '*Bo*', could grammatically refer to either Jacob or the ladder. This is certainly so grammatically, but even so, there is still no mention of the Son of Man. Here, Dodd takes theological disputation to its extreme; he writes that:

> It seems clear that John knew and accepted the interpretation which understood Gen. 28:12 to say that angels of God ascended and descended upon Jacob, or Israel [which is when Jacob's name was changed to Israel – L.S.], and that for 'Israel' he substituted 'Son of Man'. As Burney puts it, 'Jacob, as the ancestor of the nation of Israel,' summarizes in his person the ideal Israel *in posse,* just as our Lord, at the other end of the line, summarizes it *in esse* as the Son of Man (*Aramaic Origin*, p. 115). For John, of course, 'Israel' is not the Jewish nation, but the new humanity, reborn in Christ, the community of those who are 'of the truth', and of whom Christ is King. In a deeper sense He is not only their King, He is their inclusive representative; they are in Him and He in them.[43]

Thus, a simple phrase, in daily use in Israel today – and quite likely so in Palestine 20 centuries ago – *Ben Adam*, Son of Man, meaning a person, takes on mystical proportions in exegetical interpretation, which also involves a certain amount of manipulation of words – instead of going up and down the ladder (the generally accepted version), the angels go up and down Jacob; Jacob now takes on, for this purpose, his new name, Israel, and 'Israel' refers to all the Jews. Therefore, by the universal message of Jesus, the going up and down of the angels now refers to all of humanity – QED the use of the term 'Son of Man' (*Ben Adam*) takes on divine implications as applied to a messianic figure; and all of this is presumed to be in John's mind at the time of writing. This is not a peripheral matter; it enables Dodd to conclude:

> It is clear that this conception raises a new problem. It challenges the mind to discover a doctrine of personality, which will make conceivable this combination of the universal and the particular in a single person. A naive individualism regarding man, or a naive anthropomorphism regarding God, makes nonsense of the Johannine Christology. Ancient thought, when it left the ground of such naive conceptions, lost hold upon the concrete reality of the person … A Christian philosophy starting from the Johannine doctrine of Jesus as Son of Man should be able to escape the *impasse* into which all ancient thought fell, and to give an account of personality in God and in ourselves.[44]

One might well claim that this grammatical cum theological excursus is much ado about nothing. Yet the use of 'Son of Man' (*Ben Adam*) clearly poses problems for Christian theology without such an interpretation, for under normal circumstances, the Son of Man cannot be the Son of God. Hence the need to provide a sophisticated interpretation of the meaning behind the term, thereby making it possible to synchronize the use of the 'Son of Man' and the 'Son of God' in the alternative references to Jesus. And, indeed, the chapter following on from the one entitled 'Messiah' is entitled 'Son of God'.

The succeeding chapter opens with a revealing and significant admission. Dodd writes that:

> The idea of a being affiliated to a deity, in one sense or another, was extremely widespread in the ancient world ... there were demigods and heroes sprung from the unions of gods with mortals, and royal clans like the Heraclidae traced their descent from such beings.[45]

Furthermore:

> In Egypt, and among various oriental peoples, the reigning King was divine, and was described as the son of the god worshipped as the special patron of the royal house, whether this was understood to mean that his descent could be traced to the god, or that his actual birth was miraculous, or that he was in some sense an 'epiphany' of the god himself.

In sum, 'the idea of divine or deified men was familiar'.[46]

Thus, just as I posed the question as to how the *Akedah* represented the special nature of a divine test of faith for Abraham, when all around, similar demands were being made by countless pagan gods, so the question arises as to the uniqueness of a special relationship between a particular human being and a universal God, given the prevalence (as even acknowledged by Dodd) of similar relationships among the pagans in their beliefs. Here, Dodd is actually surprisingly rather circumspect, and indeed quite flexible, in his liberal interpretation (paradoxically in contrast to his complicated explanation of 'Son of Man'). He writes that, 'The question whether in pre-Christian Judaism the title "Son of God" was used of the Messiah is not entirely settled. The evidence is not satisfactory.'[47] He notes the problematics that arise from the fact that the term was used to refer:

... both to the nation as a whole (Exod. 4:22; Hos. 11:1) and to its anointed King (II Sam. 7:14, Ps 2:7) might easily have led to its application to an ideal figure who was conceived as the perfect representative of the Davidic monarchy, and as embodying in Himself the ideal relation of Israel to God and to the world.[48]

Furthermore, Dodd states that, 'The first clear and explicit allusion to "My son the Messiah" in Jewish literature appears in IV Ezra, which is about contemporary with the Fourth Gospel.'[49] Dodd then admits that:

This brief survey of the background will have shown that the expression 'Son of God' might suggest to various classes of readers in the public to which the Fourth Gospel might appeal, a wide variety of ideas. It might suggest a man of god-like character or power, a prophet or initiate, the Messiah of the Jews, or a supernatural being mediating the knowledge of the Supreme God.[50]

My own presumption would be that some of the alternative possibilities suggested by Dodd in this quote are far closer to the reality of the time, as well as to the traditions of Judaism, than the connection to an actual son, born of a virgin mother through the intervention of the Holy Spirit. The latter are certainly non-Jewish concepts, and would have been foreign to Jews of that period.

Nevertheless, Dodd presents an interesting analysis to indicate the inner meaning attached to the phrase, and then ends the chapter with the statement that:

The love of God in Christ creates and conditions an active ministry of word and deed ... which ... ends in a victory of life over death through death. The love of God, thus released in history, brings men into the same unity of which the relation of Father and Son is the eternal archetype.[51]

But, in the final analysis, it is not the terms 'Son of Man' or 'Son of God' that are historically crucial, it is the concept of the Messiah, the Anointed One. What is meant by this Old Testament term 'Mashiach'? In a modern concordance of the whole Bible (Old Testament and New Testament),[52] there are only two references to the word Messiah, both taken from the Book of Daniel. All the other references to the Hebrew word 'Mashiach' are translated as 'the Anointed'. On its own, this word – neither the Hebrew 'Mashiach' nor the English 'Anointed' – has no clear-cut connections to the divinity of a particular individual. It is true that, over the years, as already noted, Jews had appeared who had claimed to be the Messiah; but they never claimed to be the Son of God and in many instances, they may well have been motivated as much by the impact and influence of Christianity as by the original Jewish writings. (Parenthetically, it might be noted that the latest attempt to put forward a Messiah – the Lubavitcher Rebbe from the Chabad movement[53] – stemmed from a movement whose headquarters was in the Christian world, in New York City, towards the end of the second millenium, at a time when a certain amount of anticipatory excitement was starting to build up in books and magazine articles, prior to the turn of the millenium.[54])

Dodd argues that, of all the Gospels, it is the Fourth that deals most thoroughly with the idea of the Messiah: to a large extent, this is related to the idea not of Sonship of God, but of kingship on earth. This is the title with which Jesus was mocked at the Crucifixion – and this is, according to Dodd, how Matthew and Mark deal with the episode. But he notes, 'it is accepted by John as a legitimate title of Christ'.[55] For much of the rest of the chapter, Dodd is involved in a discussion of the connection between the Messiah and the Lamb of God,[56] and surprisingly makes almost no mention of the New Testament reference to a Son of God born of a virgin mother. In general, this is a disappointing analysis, since it avoids the key issues in the person of Jesus: the nature of his birth and his resurrection.

It is these factors that are crucial to the idea of the Messiah, yet among the 12 leading ideas to which Dodd devotes special chapters, there is no mention of these terms; in the chapter on 'Eternal Life', Dodd discusses the 'Raising of Lazarus',[57] but not the Resurrection of Jesus. I do not wish to impute ideas to an obviously learned scholar, but one senses that perhaps Dodd has doubts as to these two key Christian beliefs; that perhaps, writing in 1968, he was a hesitant forerunner of the spate of books written in recent years by Christian theologians, such as Crossan and the other members of the Jesus Seminar.[58]

In fact, the only time in the chapter on 'Eternal Life' that Dodd even uses the word 'resurrection' is in a general context, when he writes:

> The evangelist agrees with popular Christianity that the believer will enter into eternal life at the general resurrection, but for him this is a truth of less importance than the fact that the believer already enjoys eternal life, and the former is a consequence of the latter.[59]

So, devoid of the specific references to a virgin birth and a personal resurrection, Dodd's understanding of John deals mainly, in a most impressive, scholarly manner, with the general and abstract (and sometimes abstruse) ideas in the Fourth Gospel. In fact, he places more emphasis, in some respects, on external influences (such as Greek and Oriental religions) than on the text itself.

In the Old Testament, there are many uses of the root word for Messiah (*Mashiach*), but almost always in the context of anointing someone with oil, often in a sacred context, as when Aharon and his sons are anointed with oil in preparation for the sacred duty to be imposed on them of being priests.[60] The one exception in which a specific reference is made to the Messiah is in Daniel, a mystic writer, living in exile in Persia, who makes one reference to an anointed one, the Messiah (*Mashiach*). He writes:

> Know therefore and discern, that from the going forth of the word to restore and to build Jerusalem unto one anointed [*Mashiach*], a prince [*Nagid*], shall be seven weeks ... And after the threescore and two weeks shall an anointed one [*Mashiach*] be cut off, and be no more.[61]

So here the reference to a Messiah is in the context of being a prince, and then in the context of a personal tragedy (being cut off).

Since it is so important for there to be a direct connection between New Testament descriptions of specific events that happened and Old Testament prophecies as to future events, this is flimsy evidence to work on. The regular attempts to use references in the Prophets as to a child being born to a virgin is certainly no stronger, especially since the translation is blatantly wrong. The word for virgin is *betulah*, but the prophetic text refers to *almah*, a maiden, or young woman.[62] There is no basis in the wording of the Old Testament for a belief in a virgin birth.

I do not wish to delve any further into New Testament theology; my only aim is to set the record straight in terms of alleged Jewish responsibility for denying the arrival of the Messiah as the Son of God. Christian theology and Christian history may well be disappointed at its inability to convince Jews – 2,000 years ago, and ever since, until this day – that Jesus was divine. He may indeed be so, and there are certainly enough people who, both in the past and today, believe so, and who belong also to a dominant civilization centered around Christianity. However, aside from the question of who actually killed Jesus and why, there is the theological issue for Christianity of Jewish obtuseness and obstinacy in rejecting a son of their people who was also the Son of God;

and, by so doing, betraying the trust that God had placed in them by choosing them in the first place.

Categorically, it may be said that there is no divine messianic figure in Jewish sacred writings, no future Son of God, no redeemer who, whether prospectively or retrospectively, is required to sacrifice his life in order for his heavenly Father to grant forgiveness to humanity for its sins. The Christian message may or may not be a good or inspiring message: some Jews, even today, accept it, either by converting or by joining groups such as 'Jews for Jesus'; but Jews who reject the message are not betraying their heritage. Their heritage is of a belief in one God (with no Trinity), and of a vague messianic vision of an eschatological world which is a vast improvement on the one in which they live. Their heritage is of a tribal loyalty to the patriarchal (and matriarchal) generations; to Moses, as a Lawgiver of the Ten Commandments; and to the prophets, with their courageous and critical messages against corruption of kings and priests. Jesus was indeed in this tradition. His Sermon on the Mount (provided only by Matthew) is magnificent in its eloquence, sensitivity and humanity; it is one of the great orations of history.[63] It obviously stirred those who heard it, as it can stir those who read it today. These are the words of an inspired – and inspiring – human being. But there is no connection with such inspiration and physical divinity. This is, and always has been, the issue at the center of the tragic conflict between the two religions, Judaism and Christianity.

From the Jewish perspective, the issue is not of the divinity of Jesus, but of the Christian attribution to him of such a status. The full answer to this issue is not to be found in the biblical texts alone, but the historical context in which they were written; and beyond the biblical text and the historical context is an underlying culture, a culture that is congenial to the idea of a sacrificed son. I have tried to suggest how Abraham, trying to break away from the prevailing norms, might have struggled on his own with this concept; and I have added that, from this perspective, there is a thread linking the *Akedah* to the Crucifixion. There is much additional evidence as to the power of this idea – in mythology certainly (as already mentioned), but also in drama, fiction, as well as in real life and in other religious frameworks. An understanding of the impact of this background may well clarify the theological underpinnings of Christianity, inasmuch as it deals with a divine son who is sacrificed because of God's love of humanity and in order to redeem it from its sins.

NOTES

1. For a good, succinct discussion, *see* Stephen G. Wilson, *Related Strangers: Jews and Christians, 70–170 CE* (Minneapolis, MO: Fortress Press, 1995), chapter 1, 'The Political and Social Context', especially the sub-section, 'The Jewish Revolts and their Consequence', pp. 2–11; *see also* Gedaliah Alon, *The Jews in Their Land in the Talmudic Age* (Cambridge, MA: Harvard University Press, 1989), pp. 622–32. He writes, 'What ... was the nature of that messianic belief that so many of his contemporaries, Sages included, fastened on to Bar Kochba? It must have been an expression of hope and faith that great things were about to happen?' (p. 622).
2. This information is based on media reports. Exactly what transpired during these few months has not been fully divulged. For a critical analysis of the Lubavisher movement by an Orthodox rabbi, *see* David Berger, *The Rebbe, the Messiah and the Scandal of Orthodox Indifference* (London: The Littman Library, 2001).
3. *See*, for instance, Abba Hillen Silver in his book, *Messianic Speculation in Israel: From the First Through the Seventeenth Centuries* (Boston, MA: Beacon Press, 1959; first published in 1927). He writes of:

    > The Messianic adventures of Jacob Frank and his followers. They were tainted with grossness and moral corruption ... One of their doctrines was that the way to purge one's soul from sin was through physical debaucher ... They even charged their fellow Jews with the dread blood accusation ... The Frankists finally went over to Christianity *en masse.* (p. xv)

4. Gershom Scholem, *Sabbatai Sevi: The Mystical Messiah* (Princeton, NJ: Princeton University Press, 1973).
5. For a leading Jewish scholar on the topic, see Joseph Klausner, *The Messianic Idea in Israel: From its Beginning to the Completion of the Mishnah* (New York: Macmillan, 1955). *See also* the statement by Herbert Bindley, a Christian scholar, who in his book, *Religious Thought in Palestine in the Time of Christ* (London: Metheun, 1931), devoted a chapter to the concept of the 'Messiah'; he writes:

    > The word Messiah since early Christian days has acquired a personal and concrete connotation which did not originally belong to it. To us it denotes our Lord Jesus Christ, and it has no other signification. It was not so with the Jews. With them the word Messiah, or Anointed ... was not a distinctively characteristic title of the promised and expected Saviour. (p. 74)

    He goes on to explain that 'any instrument used by God, and especially the King of Judah or Israel, might be called God's Anointed One or "Christ"'.
6. For an interesting discussion on marginal movements in Judaism, see Shaya J.D. Cohen, *The Beginnings of Jewishness: Boundaries, Varieties, Uncertainties* (Berkeley, CA: University of California Press, 1999).
7. For a discussion of the work carried out at Yavne in the specific context of Jewish-Christian relations, *see* Wilson, *Related Strangers*, pp. 176–83, in the sub-section entitled, 'The Yavneh Sages'.
8. For a positive assessment of Jesus' qualities by a Jewish scholar, *see* Geza Vermes, *Jesus the Jew: A Historian's Reading of the Gospels* (Philadelphia, PA: Fortress Press, 1973). He concludes his interesting analysis by stating that Jesus is 'an unsurpassed master of the art of laying bare the inmost core of spiritual truth', and that, though his message on behalf of the poor and weak, was similar to those in the prophets, he 'went further by his willingness to take his stand among the pariahs of his world'. (p. 224) *See also* David Flusser, who writes:

    > The present volume not only reflects the truism that Jesus was a Jew and wanted to remain within the Jewish faith but argues that, without the long preparatory work of contemporaneous Jewish faith, the teaching of Jesus would be unthinkable.

    David Flusser (in collaboration with R. Steven Notley), *Jesus* (Jerusalem: The Magnes Press/Hebrew University, 1997), p. 13.

See also Susannah Heschel, *Abraham Geiger and the Jewish Jesus* (Chicago, IL: The University of Chicago Press, 1998). In discussing the works of Geiger, a founder of Reform Judaism in the nineteenth century, she writes: 'His argument that Jesus was a Pharisee who sought nothing more than the liberalization of Jewish religious practice became modern Judaism's favorite tale of Christian origins'. (p. 6)

9. There is no absolute certainty as to the dates of publication. *See*, for example, the dates suggested in Dwight N. Peterson, *The Origins of Mark: The Markan Community in Current Debate* (Leiden: Brill, 2000). *See* pp. 15–19, where he refers to the debate among scholars as to whether the Gospel of Mark was written pre-70 or post-70.
10. Mark, 16:6.
11. Ibid., 16:7.
12. Ibid., 16:9.
13. Ibid., 16:16.
14. Matthew, 27:63.
15. Ibid., 27:64–6.
16. Ibid., 28:2.
17. Ibid., 28:11–15.
18. Ibid. Even so, it is not clear what significance can be attached to the disappearance of the body, in and of itself, without the actual appearance of Jesus in real life – it is not his dead body that is relevant to prove resurrection, but his living presence.
19. *The New Covenant in Hebrew and English* (Edgware: The Society for Distributing Hebrew Scriptures, n.d.), translated from the Greek into Hebrew by Professor Franz Dalitsch.
20. Luke, 24:46.
21. Ibid., 24:51.
22. John, 20:12.
23. Ibid., 20:19–20.
24. Ibid., 20:29.
25. *See*, for example, Matthew, 20:56, 'Then all the disciples forsook him, and fled.'
26. Gerard S. Sloyan, *Jesus in Focus: A Life in its Setting* (Mystic, CN: Twenty-Third Publications, 1983), p. 127. He explains that:

> The Greek translation of Isaiah … calls the woman a virgin. The Hebrew had merely called her a young woman. It all fits in perfectly with the virgin symbolism of the fruitful people Israel. That is probably what influenced the translator of the Septuagint Greek Bible to render 'young women' by 'virgin' in the first place … The virgin symbol has influenced the Christian church ever since. (p. 127)

27. Matthew, 1:2, 'For that which is conceived in her is of the Holy Ghost'; Luke, 1:35, 'And the angel answered and said unto her, "The Holy Ghost shall come upon thee".'. It should, however, be noted that John, writing much later (and apparently reluctant to choose between the two contrasting versions as to how the divinity of Jesus was made known) makes only passing reference to 'the only begotten son' (1:18).

Sloyan discusses frankly the problematics of the descriptions of a virgin birth by Matthew and Luke in *Jesus in Focus*. He writes that:

> Matthew and Luke call on the biblical tradition that knew Israel as the Lord's bride, hence virginal by definition, and make Jesus' mother a virgin at the conception of the child. The symbolism is understandable in light of the conviction that Jesus is the fulfillment of Jewish hopes of all the ages.

But, then, all the chaste were virginal at the conception of their first child. Luke hints at more, while Matthew is explicit. The impregnation of this woman, the latter says, is not the doing of Joseph with whom Mary is arranged to be married. This just man, a dreamer like the patriarch whose name he bears, is told in a dream that Mary has conceived and that it is the doing of God's holy spirit. (p. 127)

Stressing the influence that this inaccurate translation had on Matthew, Sloyan asserts that, 'The virgin symbol has influenced the Christian church ever since.' But the question then becomes as to the intent of Matthew and Luke for:

> It is hard to be certain that [they] meant to describe Mary as physically virginal in her conception of Jesus. They probably did. But they were more intent on describing her as virginal in another way.
>
> 'Virginal in another way' makes moderns guffaw. Even the third- and fourth-century church of Greeks and Romans had trouble with it. Their virginity was the physical kind ... the symbolic Semitic symbols escaped them. As a result of the two different outlooks of the Jewish-oriented evangelists and the literalist Greeks and Romans, some students of the Gospels hold that while early Luke and Matthew are symbolical, they are not historical. That ... is what really matters. They point out that the brothers and sisters of Jesus in the Gospels are so evidently his siblings that Mary's ever-virginal status cannot be a fact. Others hold that while Luke and Matthew may be symbolical, they are historical. This ... is what really matters. They hold that 'brothers' and 'sisters' describe nonsiblings in an extended family. (pp. 128–9)

This discussion, it should be noted, appears in a chapter dealing not with the crucial factor of a virgin birth, but with Christian attitudes to the renunciation of sex. What makes the issue of the virgin birth, and Jesus' consequent divinity, even more problematical is that Luke's account of the birth of Jesus is preceded by a similar description of a birth to a married couple, Elizabeth and Zacharias, who had been childless, and were beyond child-bearing age. The descriptions are admittedly not identical, but contain strong similarities, certainly more than the vague statements in the Old Testament that claim to foretell of the virginal birth of Jesus. Thus, Luke writes of 'a certain priest named Zacharias ... and his wife was of the daughters of Aaron, and her name was Elizabeth' (Luke 1:5). The passage then describes (Luke 1:11–15) how:

> ... there appeared unto him an angel of the Lord standing on the right side of the altar of incense. And when Zacharias saw him, he was troubled, and fear fell upon him. But the angel said unto him, 'Fear not, Zacharias; for thy prayer is heard; and thy wife Elizabeth shall bear thee a son, and thou shalt call his name John ... And he shall be great in the sight of the Lord ... and he shall be filled with the Holy Ghost, even from his mother's womb.

After Elizabeth conceived, the description moves on to the sixth month of her pregnancy, when:

> The angel Gabriel was sent from God unto a city of Galilee, named Nazareth, to a virgin espoused to a man whose name was Joseph, of the house of David; and the virgin's name was Mary. And the angel came in unto her, and said, 'Hail, thou that art highly favored, the Lord is with thee; blessed art thou among women' (Luke 1:26–8);

Mary's reaction is now similar to that of Zacharias, as in the dialogue with the angel:

> And when she saw him, she was troubled at his saying ... And the angel said unto her, 'Fear not, Mary; for thou hast found favor with God. And, behold, thou shalt conceive in thy womb, and bring forth a son, and shalt call his name Jesus.' (Luke 1:29–31)

Like Zacharias, who 'said unto the angel, whereby shall I know this? for I am an old man, and my wife well stricken in years' (Luke 1:18), Mary reacts with a query:

> Then said Mary unto the angel, 'How shall this be, seeing I know not a man.' And the angel answered and said unto her, 'The Holy Ghost shall come upon thee, and the power of the Highest shall overshadow thee; therefore also that holy thing which shall be born of thee shall be called the Son of God. (Luke 1:34–5)

The connection between the two narratives is then clarified when Luke (1:36) quotes the angel as referring to Mary's cousin Elizabeth, and her capacity to conceive despite her old age, because, in both instances, 'with God nothing shall be impossible' (Luke 1:37).

28. Luke, 16:20–4; *see also* John, 11 and 12.

29. Mark, 14:58, 'We heard him say, "I will destroy this temple that is made with hands, and within three days I will build another made without hands".'

30. For discussion of these aspects in the Old Testament, see Meir Sternberg, *The Poetics of Biblical Narrative: Ideological Literature and the Drama of Reading* (Bloomington, IN: Indiana University Press, 1987), chapter 11, 'The Structure of Repetition: Strategies of Informational Redundancy', p. 365.

31. *See* Joseph Klausner, *From Jesus to Paul* (New York: Macmillan, 1944).

32. As noted in chapter 2 above (*Akedah*), later legends claim that Isaac was actually killed.

33. *See*, for instance, the comment by Mark Juergensmeyer, when discussing issues of sacrifice and violence in connection with fundamentalist religion. He writes:

> Sometimes it was God him- or herself who was offered up, or a divinely inspired person such as Jesus … It was not just their sacrifice that made them divine; rather their almost unhuman holiness was what made them candidates for slaughter.

Terror in the Mind of God: The Global Rise of Religious Violence (Berkeley, CA: University of California Press, 2001), p. 170.

34. See Klausner, *From Jesus to Paul*, pp. 504–5.

35. The revolt started in 132 CE, and was finally stamped out in 135 CE.

36. *See* chapter 7, 'Constantine'.

37. C.H. Dodd, *The Interpretation of the Fourth Gospel* (Cambridge: Cambridge University Press, 1968).

38. Ibid., p. 241; *see also* discussions of the term 'Son of Man' in Vermes, *Jesus the Jew*, chapter 7, 'Jesus the *Son of Man*', p. 160; and Flusser, *Jesus*, chapter 9, 'The Son of Man', p. 124. My approach to this term is similar to theirs (based on Hebrew linguistics), but I have added extra philological facts.

39. Dodd, *Interpretation of the Fourth Gospel*, p. 244.

40. Ibid.

41. Ibid.

42. John, 1:51.

43. Dodd, *Interpretation of the Fourth Gospel*, pp. 245–6.

44. Ibid., p. 249.

45. Ibid., p. 250.

46. Ibid.

47. Ibid., p. 253.

48. Ibid.

49. Ibid.

50. Ibid.

51. Ibid., p. 262.

52. James Strong, *The Exhaustive Concordance of the Bible* (New York: Abingden Press, 1965).

53. *See* note 2.

54. Conversely, the approach of the millenium had an impact in Israel. Mark Juergensmeyer (*Terror in the Mind of God*) writes of Christian groups who had come to Jerusalem in 1999:

> … to prepare for the coming of the millenium … with the expectation that the end of the millenium would be the occasion for the apocalyptic confrontation predicted in the book of Revelation – Armageddon – after which Christ would return to earth. (p. 138)

55. Dodd, *Interpretation of the Fourth Gospel*, p. 229.

56. *See* discussion of this aspect in chapter 8, 'Easter'.

57. Dodd, *Interpretation of the Fourth Gospel*, pp. 147–8.

58. The first publications by members of the Jesus Seminar were in the 1980s. *See*, for instance, John Dominic Crossan, *The Cross that Spoke: The Origins of the Passion Narrative* (San Francisco, CA: Harper and Row, 1988).

59. Dodd, *Interpretation of the Fourth Gospel*, p. 148.

60. Exodus, 30:30.

61. Daniel, 9:26.
62. Isaiah, 7:14.
63. Matthew, 5:1–29.

5

Rustum

Religions deal with both eternal and mundane themes; with issues that confront and concern average persons in their regular daily lives and in their larger cosmic understanding. The solutions that they provide are sometimes conservatively oriented, offering a comforting continuation of accepted ideas or entrenched customary practices, and sometimes radically innovative, presenting challenges to existing modes of thought and current patterns of behavior. They also oscillate between periods of creativity, with prominent characters acting as catalytic agents of change, and periods of conformity, in which bureaucratic frameworks give rise to clerical officialdom intent on consolidating its power over the populace. Religions have their charismatic founders and their later loyal disciples; they have their maverick prophets and they have their appointed priests.

The messages that religions bear sometimes have unique and novel aspects, and sometimes are additions and adumbrations to prevailing situations. Sometimes they expand through cataclysmic change, and sometimes through synthesis and syncretism; sometimes through exclusive adoption, and sometimes through co-optative adaptation.

The idea of monotheism, as perceived by Abraham and expounded by Moses – the idea of One Divine Being, creating a universe, centered on Planet Earth, focused on human beings in constant communion with Him – is considered generally to be a breakthrough in conceptualization. This is the special contribution of the Jewish people to world civilization; but linked to this universalistic theme of what was always considered the Fatherhood of God and its resultant Brotherhood of Man (all in the male gender), was an exclusivity which acknowledged a tribal primacy to the Chosen People.

It was into this culture that Jesus was born. Within this tradition, tension had often existed between the official keepers of the faith (the priests – an inherited office through the line of Aharon) and the prophets, and both the priesthood and the people were castigated for their aberrant ways. It is one of the features of Judaism that it is the work of the latter, at the margins of the society, that was recorded, preserved, and finally sanctified.[1] In terms of inspiring messages, the priesthood became peripheral, involved only in the minutiae of religious ritual, most of it within the precincts of the temple.

When the age of the prophets – an impressive list of almost two dozen challenging thinkers – came to an end, their heritage was still sustained by isolated individuals. One contemporary of John the Baptist and of Jesus Christ was Hillel, a liberal interpreter of the law[2] and, to this day, a recognized authority when choosing the progressive and humanistic alternative when considering the different options for either religious or secular decision-making. Thus, politicians, officials, judges and other decision-makers in Israel will often invoke the name of Hillel in order to justify a tolerant or flexible interpretation of a law, a rule, or a prevailing norm.

All three – Hillel, John and Jesus – were, in one way or another, at odds with the religious and political establishment. It has been claimed that there is a great deal of similarity in the sayings and teachings of all three men. In historical terms, Hillel occupies an honored place in Jewish history as a symbol of liberal and progressive interpretation, especially at the present time among those who seek to transform Judaism in a modern direction. John is remembered mainly as the forerunner of Christianity, and Jesus has, of course, retrospectively become the founder of the religion which is at the heart of the dominant civilization in the world.

Judaism itself has never been considered a missionary religion, even though there have been periods in which it has absorbed outsiders.[3] One of the most noted women in the Bible, Ruth, was a Moabite, who voluntarily linked her personal fate to the Jewish people after her Israelite husband died. She is a progenitor of King David, himself considered in Jewish tradition a progenitor of a future *Mashiach*, and also, in Christian theology, of Joseph, the husband of Mary, the mother of Jesus.[4] Furthermore, a little-noticed factor is that, at the time of the Exodus, the Israelites left Egypt in the company of a motley band of camp followers, whose identity is not classified, about whom there is almost no research, but who may well have been, like them, slaves, or in some parallel servile situation, and who took advantage of the prevailing turmoil in Egypt to make their escape.[5] Their presence amongst the Israelites is mentioned both before and after the events at Mount Sinai, so it is very possible that, besides the 'tribal' or ethnic Israelites, there were others who accepted the Torah given to Moses and were then absorbed into the community.[6]

The Old Testament also displays a great deal of vacillation in dealing with relations to outsiders. On the one hand, there is clear instruction about the need to be considerate to the aliens living in the midst of the Israelites; on the other hand, certain specified peoples – the Amelikes, the Moabites, the Hittites and others – are attacked and devastated. However, since Ruth was a Moabite and King David married the widow of a Hittite, it is possible that these strictures as to certain peoples were not universally observed. Furthermore, Abraham, Joseph, Moses and King Solomon, amongst others, all had marriages or less formal liaisons with non-Israelites.[7]

These clarifications are necessary in order to understand the differences in historical terms between Judaism and Christianity: the former lacking missionary zeal, remaining for the most part within its original tribal format (with undoubted additions as noted); the latter breaking out of its Palestinian environment to become a world religion, an integral part of the dominant western civilization.

The key question that has to be addressed for understanding the relationship between Judaism and Christianity is: what was the unique aspect of Christianity that enabled it to reach out and attain the mass following that Judaism never achieved (but also never sought)? After all, in terms of the basic message, they have common roots: in the concept of one God, in the Ten Commandments, in the key stories of the Garden of Eden, the Flood, the Exodus and the Holy Land.

Amongst Jewish thinkers, it is generally considered that Jesus himself concentrated his efforts solely on his Jewish brethren; his disciples were all Jewish, as were those to whom he preached and ministered.[8] It was Paul who, on undergoing a major transformation after the death of Jesus – from foe to follower, from skeptic to believer – changed the nature of the movement by both preaching to the Gentiles in the area, and by making the religion more palatable by abolishing most of its stringent legal commandments.[9] This, of course, was done in the name of Jesus.

Success was not immediate. It was the official intervention on Christianity's behalf by Constantine the emperor that ensured its ultimate triumph (as will be discussed in chapter 7). Nevertheless, during its three centuries of repression by the Romans, it grew and attracted many people who were willing to suffer the consequences of their membership in the Church.

Undoubtedly, the positive messages contained in the Bible (both Old and New Testaments), the recounting of the miracles performed by Jesus, and the charismatic personality presented through his work and life, all contributed to Christianity's attraction. Some of this was innovative but much of the message was not crucially different from its original source in the Old Testament, which in itself was also an integral part of this new religion.[10] (Parenthetically, it was theoretically possible for

Christianity to eschew the Old Testament when it reached out to convert the Gentiles and start afresh, but it apparently needed the descriptions of One Divine Being, as described there, to provide the framework for an only-begotten son, as also to link in to some of the stories, especially the *Akedah*).

The key differences between Judaism and Christianity arose from the controversial matters of the virgin birth and the Resurrection, as well as the actual details of the undoubted empirical fact of the Crucifixion. I use the word controversial because these were then, just as they are today, the key factors differentiating the two religions. The issue now is to examine the nature of these two factors. To what extent were the ideas of a virgin birth, leading to a divine sonship and a resurrection following the Crucifixion, major factors in the success of Christianity? Leading off from this, and in terms of the background just outlined, the question is whether the success was related to the utterly innovative nature of these two factors, or whether it was the consequence of their syncretic possibilities, that is, their similarity to current ideas? In this chapter, I shall argue that it was syncretism that provided the possibility of the easy acceptance of Christianity and guaranteed its early successes. Later, of course, it was official recognition that provided its ultimate triumph, through the edict of Constantine, which made Christianity the official religion of the Roman Empire.

Simply put, the idea of a divine son, and the idea of an early death and a later resurrection, were not novel ideas.[11] Furthermore, the idea of a father sacrificing his son, or killing him in other circumstances, was also a prevalent idea. This aspect will also be examined in this chapter, partly through the concept of the Rustum Complex, based on a story, Persian in origin but also part of English literature, in which a father, Rustum, inadvertently kills his son, Sohrab. This speaks, as will be argued, to a deep and meaningful factor in society.[12] It is, I believe, of major relevance for understanding, on the one hand, the message of Christianity, and on the other hand, its missionary success.

In religious terms, as Christian theology developed, the ideas of virgin birth and resurrection took on special meaning because of the intervening variable of God's willingness to sacrifice his own son. If there was no virgin birth, the very idea of sacrificing one's progeny does not arise; and if there was no resurrection, the divinity itself might possibly be doubted, especially given the plaintive cry of Jesus on the Cross to God, 'Why have You abandoned me?' As already mentioned, the Crucifixion itself is no more than a cruel act, and not even, at that period, unusual; its theological meaning stems from the willingness of God to sacrifice his son for the benefit of humanity. The Crucifixion is an empirical fact with no intrinsic importance attached to it; its significance arises from the meaning subsequently attributed to it.

Thus, there are three interlinking factors: a birth, a death, and a resurrection of a divine son. All three aspects will be examined, partly in terms of religious beliefs, partly in terms of ancient mythical narratives, and partly in terms of modern social science perspectives. This examination must move beyond theology to take account of sociological factors and, in particular, the aspect of the sacrifice of a son, as most sociological analysis does not, after all, deal with concepts of virgin births and resurrection – although it does deal with the sacrifice or the killing of a son, not just in fulfillment of a religious demand, but in ordinary social interaction. The Bible itself contains a classic example in the story of Jephta, who sacrificed his daughter (name unknown),[13] not in response to a divine command but in fulfillment of the vow that he had made that if he were to be successful in battle he would sacrifice the first creature to exit his house on his return, which happened to be his daughter. Of course, he could not have known definitely that this would be the outcome, but the sheer recklessness of the vow, given the high possibility of a family member being the potential victim, is an indication of the underlying reality. Greek mythology has a similar tale in the exploits of Agamemnon, with his victory also being marked by the sacrifice of his child.

In effect, the three aspects of virgin birth, sacrificed son and miraculous resurrection have to be examined at two different levels: on the one hand, the dual aspects of a virgin birth and a resurrection, which occur both in pagan religions and mythology but are not necessarily linked to a sacrificial act for the purpose of assuring redemption; on the other hand, the killing of a son, which is also not always linked to an act of redemption.

Indeed, the most unique aspect of Christianity might specifically be the idea of a divine being who sacrifices his son out of a love of humanity in order to redeem it; and it is perhaps precisely this additional factor that gave Christianity its special attraction. The killing of a son as an empirical act was, in any case, prevalent, but it was the reasoning behind this particular death, the subtle message and the powerful symbol (of the Cross), that provided the positive and divine dimension. Instead of the sacrifice of a young son or daughter taking place in order to placate a demanding god, the motive is inverted: it is not the god who is the recipient of a human token, but humanity which, because of the sacrifice, is to be the beneficiary of God's benevolence. And this particular God does not share His status with a pantheon of similar beings, but stands alone and supreme. Within the religious ritual, this sacrifice is re-enacted through the ceremony of communion, in the belief that those who partake of the wine and the wafer are not taking part in a symbolic act but are actually in contact with the blood and the body of the sacrificed son.[14] Today, this is still found in Catholic ritual.

My argument is a simple one, if admittedly rather blunt and brash. Given prevalent norms involving the sacrifice of a son, either for religious or non-religious reasons, and given the fairly widespread existence of ideas about virgin births and post-mortem resurrections, Christianity offered an explanation and a justification which, till then, had been lacking . The sacrifice is not of one's own progeny but is effected by the Divine Being Himself as a means of assuring redemption for those who believe in Him and in His son's birth, death and resurrection. *The uniqueness of Christianity lay not in the facts that were presented, but in the explanation that was provided.*

The Bible itself, as already noted, contains examples of child sacrifice among the population then living in Canaan. Perhaps this was a key reason for the stringent attitude adopted by the Bible toward some of these people (while emphasizing the need to be considerate to the alien as an individual). One of the Gospels (that of Matthew) even provides a link to a cruel edict passed by the Jewish King Herod the Great, who is a problematic figure in Jewish history for several reasons: that is, his cruelty, his collaboration with the Romans, and his disputed status.[15] This edict, according to Matthew, called for the massacre of all babies born in Bethlehem at the time of Jesus' birth.[16] The Evangelist then has Joseph and Mary taking Jesus to Egypt in order to safeguard him, and returning only when word is sent that the tyrant is dead and the danger has passed.

As for the virgin birth, many examples exist of stories of unions between divine and human beings; in fact, Genesis possibly contains an example. After describing the development of the generations from Adam and Eve through to the three sons of Noah, and before describing the wickedness that led to the flood, the Bible contains a passing comment whose full meaning is difficult to fathom:

> And it came to pass, when men began to multiply on the face of the earth, and daughters were born unto them, that the sons of God saw the daughters of men that they were fair; and they took them wives, whomsoever they chose. And the Lord said: 'My spirit shall not abide in man for ever, for that he also is flesh; therefore, shall his days be a 120 years.' The *Nephilim* were in the earth in those days, and also after that, when the sons of God came in unto the daughters of men, and they bore children to them; the same were the mighty men that were of old, the men of renown.[17]

This passage poses a real problem for both Judaism and Christianity, since it suggests that there were divine–human relationships at an early stage of human history. For Christianity, this implies prior connections before the virgin birth of Jesus; for Judaism, it totally contradicts its strict monotheistic belief, and its denial of the very possibility of a virgin birth arising out of a union with the Holy Spirit, which lies at the center of its rival religion.

To appreciate the nature of the dilemma for Judaism, one must study the attempts in modern times to explain (or perhaps explain away) this problematic text, which reveal the depth of the difficulty posed. A major publication of Orthodox Jewry, the Soncino *Chumash* (that is, the Five Books of Moses), which was first published in 1947 and is widely used throughout the English-speaking world, provides the following dubious explanations for parts of the text.[18] For instance:

1. "*the Sons of God*": that is, the sons of princes and judges, "*Elohim*" [that is, God] always implying rulership …'
2. "*that they were fair*": By a play on words, Rabbi Judah taught that when the maidens were adorned for the marriage ceremony, the chieftain used to have intercourse with them first (an allusion to the practice of "*ius primae noctis*") [the right to sex on the first night[19]].'
3. "*and they took*": By force [their wives], *whomsoever they chose*: even those married to others.'
4. "*Nephilim*": They were so named because they "fell" [Hebrew for fall is from the root, actually similar in sound to the English, "naphal"] and caused the world to fall'. Another explanation for the *Nephilim* (considered to be large) was that '… the heart of whoever saw them fell in wonder at their enormous stature'; 'and also after that' [possibly after the flood] '… the words imply that either the wives of Noah's sons were descended from them, so that the children they bore after the Flood were giants' – alternatively it is possible to interpret 'the whole passage on the supposition that Adam and Eve are designated *the sons* (children) *of God* (verse 2) as well as Seth and Enosh [Seth was born after the death of Abel, and Enosh was his son]. Their children are referred to as "*the Nephilim*" who, though no longer bearing the visible impress of God's creation, nevertheless stood out from their fellow-men. "*Nephilim*" then signifies the "inferior ones", and they were so called because they were inferior to their parents' – 'yet a further possibility is that the "*Nephilim*" were angels who fell from heaven, the place of their sanctity'.
5. "*came in*": And begot giants like themselves.'

It should be stressed that this book, first published in 1947, was edited by a leading rabbinical authority who explained (in the Foreword) that 'an ambitious plan was adopted which has never been attempted before, viz. to present a digest of the commentaries of the most famous Jewish expositors'.[20] A similar book had been published by the Chief Rabbi of England, Rabbi Hertz, sometime before (in 1936) by the same Press; this also provided a succinct (and similar) summary of earlier authoritative commentaries.[21] These two books in tandem indicate how, in the modern world, earlier commentaries are presented for easy mental consumption. Older ideas are presented not as anachronistic leftovers, but as important and relevant. Rabbi Hertz writes:

> *Sons of God*: ... Among several ancient peoples there was a belief that there once existed a race of men of gigantic strength and stature who were the *offspring of human mothers and celestial fathers* [my emphasis], and we are supposed to have an echo of that Legend in this Biblical passage. Philo, Josephus and the author of the Book of Jubiless were misled into this interpretation by the analogy of these heathen fables. There is, however, no trace in Genesis of 'fallen angels' or rebellious angels; and the idea of inter-marriage of angels and human beings is altogether foreign to Hebrew thought. The mythological explanation of this passage was in all ages repelled by a large body of Jewish and non-Jewish commentators, though it has been revived by many moderns. Others render *beney Elohim,* by 'sons of the great' (in poetic Hebrew, *elohim* often means mighty ... ([i.e. not God, which would be its normal meaning]. This verse would thus state that the sons of the nobles took them wives of the daughters of the people, who were powerless to resist [Question: who were these nobles and from whence did they come?] ... 'Sons of God' may, however, also mean those who serve God and obey Him ... It is quite in accord with Biblical usage that those who adhered to the true worship of God – the children of Seth – were called 'Sons of God'; and that, in contrast to these, the daughters of the line of Cain should be spoken of as 'daughters of men'.[22]

This is a convoluted explanation and, I presume, not too convincing for the average reader. Thus, the Bible hints at celestial–human inter-marriage, or sexual interaction. To this day, biblical interpretations have no easy explanations for this reference. Even modern authoritative Jewish summaries provide rationalizations rather than rational explana-tions. Often, the basic text gave rise not just to intellectual explanations, but also to legends that enabled the believer to avoid confronting the holy text and to take refuge in the fertile imagination of legend. Louis Ginzberg, in probably the most authoritative compendium of such legends,[23] explains the awkward story of the *Nephilim* in terms of the temptation by Cain's female descendants (Cain, the fratricidal killer of Abel) of the angels. He writes that the women's

> ... beauty and sensual charms tempted the angels from the path of virtue. The angels, on the other hand, no sooner had they rebelled against God and descended to earth than they lost their transcendental qualities, and were invested with sublunary bodies, so that a union with the daughters of men became possible. The offspring of these alliances between the angels and the Cainite women were the giants, known for their strength and sinfulness.[24]

Ginzberg himself explains in a general context in his introductory remarks that, surprisingly, among the legends are 'palpable reminiscences or relics of pagan mythology'. He explains that:

> Reported in the name of renowned scholars flourishing in the third century, they clash patently not only with legacy of the biblical faith, but with the austere monotheism which these founders of rabbinic Judaism consistently maintained and invariably sought to implant and enforce in their people.

He then claims that it was not these noted scholars who created the stories but that they were merely repeating stories which were 'harking back to the earliest tales of their remote ancestors or *heathen neighbors*' [my emphasis].[25]

The importance of this passage, however, is not to reveal Jewish confusion or embarrassment but to point out that within the Old Testament is the hint of a prior instance of celestial–human progeny. From a Christian perspective, however, it is still possible to claim a unique status for Jesus, not through angels but through the Holy Spirit via a virgin birth. But, for the moment, I wish only to point out the awareness within the overall culture (of 2,000 years ago) of the possibility of celestial males and human females enjoying intimate associations.

At that time, however, the religion, or the mythology, of the dominant cultures of the time (Greek and then subsequently Roman) was far more prevalent, and there were many overlaps between them: for instance, between the Greek Zeus and the Roman Jupiter. Much of this semi-religious mythology also found an outlet in the developing religions that rivaled early Christianity: Gnosticism and the Mystery religions.[26] Greek mythology (and Roman mythology, which supplanted it, or perhaps rewrote it using different names) was based on a pantheon of gods who possessed human qualities and were differentiated according to social class and division of labor.[27] Inevitably, confusion often arose as to differentiation between the divine and the human, with hints, or even direct description, of divine–human interconnections. Kirk, in his book on Greek myths, provides several pertinent examples, and shows there was often much ambivalence associated with the issue of divine–human sexual relations. He writes:

> The gods do not normally tolerate the later adulteration of their seed within a mortal woman; if they do, there are twins, of which the elder is the semi-divine offspring (as Heracles was), the younger the mortal one ... Apollo's son Arclepius grew up to be a great healer, and was worshipped both as god and hero; but he went too far...and tried to raise a man from the dead – an impious act that earned a thunderbolt from Zeus.[28]

In discussing some of Apollo's actions, Kirk writes that, 'He had a habit of loving, but failing to win, mortal women...he was more successful with Hyakinthos ... but actually the beautiful boy must have been...a pre-Hellenic god whom Apollo merely absorbed into his own worship'.[29]

In general terms, Kirk writes that, 'The blood or seed of gods, if it falls on the ground, is nearly always fertile.' Furthermore, he discusses the 'Cretan dying-and-reborn god'.[30] Then, focusing in one chapter on one interesting character, Heracles,[31] Kirk writes that he:

> ... is not only the most important of the heroes, he is also the most difficult to reconstruct. In some ways he was a source of mystery to the Greeks themselves, particularly because of his ambivalent status as both hero and god; he alone started as a hero and was raised up to be a god on Olympus ... Despite Hera's persistent hatred of him, in the end he was taken from his funeral pyre ... and made immortal.[32]

Kirk points out that when sacrifices were offered up, different rituals would be followed for human heroes and for gods. In the case of Heracles, he '... uniquely received both types of sacrifice and worship'.[33] According to mythology, Heracles was born as a twin: his mother gave birth to one son born of sexual relations with Zeus, who had succeeded in pre-empting her husband, who, later that same night, returned from battle and also impregnated her. Heracles was the son of Zeus. In discussing his mortal aspects, Kirk notes that, 'Another unusual thing about him as a hero was that he had no grave ... A grave would have caused a scandal, because the point about him was precisely that his body was burned and subsumed into heaven.'[34] In discussing his status as a 'hero-god', Kirk writes that:

> The idea of making Heracles into a god seems not to be very old, no earlier than the seventh century BC ... the Homeric poems twice specifically assert that he was mortal, but in one case he is also said to be a god.[35]

Kirk also describes how those who provided the narrative of his life and death tried 'to reconcile the view that Heracles *died* and went down to Hades like anyone else with the contradictory idea ... that he went to Olympus, married Hebe and lived for ever'.[36] Kirk notes that 'the problem of Heracles' divinity exercised the ancient world as well as the modern'.[37] Linking Heracles to other similar figures, he continues:

> Most of the heroes rather expectedly die remarkable deaths, usually violent ones, and continue to operate from beneath the earth as protective spirits or daemons ... Cults of healing tended to gain heroic connections for the same sort of reason, and also because the heroes turned into chthonic powers with the gift of life as well as death.[38]

Much ambiguity persists because, as Kirk comments, 'Making a man into a god was a difficult business, as the Romans found when they tried to deify their emperors.'[39]

There is one particular aspect of Heracles' life that must be specially noted, namely that he killed his own children. This is generally considered to be an aberrant act, one that points to a degree of madness in his character. Kirk makes several passing references to this fact. On one occasion, he asks quizzically, 'why should Heracles so unpredictably kill his children, or his music-teacher Linus in a fit of uncontrollable rage?'[40] Later, Kirk discusses this action in broader terms of his power, which might occasionally become destructive. Thus he writes that:

> He does, after all, bring death in manifold forms to others. In that he is not unique, but the killing of his own children through inexplicable madness shows that his quality of excess spills over into lethal forms as well as into vitality and life. He is superhuman,

but still, until the gods decide otherwise, all too mortal. And then his own death by burning, followed by resurrection and glory, must have some bearing on the situation.[41]

So, here we have a figure – part human, part divine, a central character in Greek mythology and in Greek religion – with a problematic birth (a divine son with a human twin brother), a dual character during his life, who commits infanticide against his own children, who has a death with no recognized tomb, and who later enjoys resurrection and glory.

The key point that requires further examination is the specific fact that Kirk refers to only peripherally: that is, the killing of his own children. Kirk suggests that this is a violent act that flows from madness. I shall argue that this is not necessarily so; it is obviously a deplorable violent act, but it cannot be brushed aside as something totally irrational, as it is far too prevalent for such a conclusion to be drawn. Indeed, despite its prevalence, similar acts are far too often ignored, or dealt with superficially. After all, a major story in the Old Testament is Abraham's exposure to a test which involved committing a similar act (this shortly after sending another son into an unknown fate in the desert), while the New Testament attributes a similar act to a divine being in terms of the fate of his son – an act which, in Christian tradition, is, of course, interpreted as aimed at offering redemption to humanity.

There is a far greater awareness in the modern world of the phenomenon of infanticide or filicide, as there is of the general problem of violence within the family, but much of the evidence, as well as the theoretical perspective linked to it, is the product of only the last few decades. Indeed, when Kirk published his book in the early 1970s, there were only the first initial hints of a disturbing phenomenon of major proportions. The first investigations were being carried out into what had, until then, been an almost taboo topic, with researchers such as David Gil and Richard Gelles attempting to provide both empirical facts and a theoretical perspective.[42] Parallel to these activities, there were preliminary attempts to measure and cope with the similar problem of wife abuse.[43]

I stress the novelty of this academic work because, until the late 1960s and early 1970s, there was little prospect of accurately measuring and perceptively evaluating any negative phenomenon linked to the intimate framework of the family. Kirk himself, had he been writing some years later, may have shown a little more sensitivity to Heracles' killing of his own children instead of casually attributing it to a moment of madness. The late 1960s and early 1970s were also important because of the many manifestations of generational conflict; in the United States, much of this focused on opposition by the young to the war in Vietnam, as well as general tensions on university campuses.[44]

Responding to criminological evidence as to violence in the family, and to the vicious responses to student protests in a number of countries in Europe as well as in the United States, I embarked on a research project into a phenomenon that I designated as 'Adult hostility to the young', dealing with this phenomenon both in the family and in society at large.[45] The empirical facts presented involved not just family violence and youth protests, but also examples taken from biblical stories (including the *Akedah* and the Crucifixion), mythology, literature and academic analysis.[46]

Part of the analysis involved a direct confrontation with a dominant concept in western society, that is, the Oedipus Complex,[47] which is based on Greek myth, and drama by Sophocles, and concerns a patricidal act by Oedipus against his father, Laius. This theory suggested that – for deep, inbred reasons (a yearning for incest) – sons were liable to develop hostile feelings against their fathers, the sexual rival for the love of the mother/wife. Many scholars, including psychologists, had pointed out many of the fallacies of this theory,[48] and several had even suggested an alternative concept, the Laius Complex,[49] referring to the harm that Laius attempted to inflict on his son, Oedipus – starting with his abandonment in a forest shortly after birth – because of an oracle that Laius would be harmed by his son in the future.

My own suggestion at this time was to offer an alternative concept that would reflect generational tensions but would not be related to the prominent Oedipal theme. Persian mythology has a story of a dominant character, a popular warrior, who inadvertently kills his own son in a one-on-one clash set up by two opposing armies. The story was introduced into western culture by Matthew Arnold, who wrote an epic poem based on it.[50] On this basis, I suggested the possibility of a Rustum Complex – Rustum being the father who killed his son,[51] and I argued that much of social life could be better understood through the use of this theoretical perspective rather than the well-known, but controversial, Oedipus Complex. I believe that it is of great relevance for the interpretation of literature, mythology, art – and the Bible.

The story of the generational conflict between Rustum, the father, and Sohrab, the son, is of major relevance as it is part of both oriental culture (as a Persian myth) and occidental culture (as an epic poem by a well-known British poet, Matthew Arnold), and it is also, in many respects, a mirror image of the Oedipus–Laius struggle. Rustum and Sohrab meet in a one-on-one struggle as representatives of two opposing armies, without being aware of their family connection. Oedipus also did not know that the person who challenged him at the crossroads was his paternal father, since the latter had abandoned him shortly after birth and he had been brought up by foster parents who had discovered and saved him. Rustum and Sohrab also did not recognize each other, as Rustum, a renowned warrior, 'abandoned' his son at birth; on being informed by his wife (or mistress – there are different versions) that a daughter had been born to them, Rustum never bothered to return home from his military exploits. This false information had been supplied because the mother wished to avoid her son following in his father's footsteps as a military man. However, her plans went awry: when Sohrab reached physical maturity, he also entered upon a military career. Sohrab knows that he has an illustrious father and possesses an amulet left behind by Rustum to be given as a memento to the child that is born.[52]

Unknown to each other, Sohrab and Rustum are in opposite camps. When the idea is suggested that, instead of a wholesale carnage, a prominent fighter from each side should be designated to fight each other in direct combat, the choice falls on the renowned warrior, Rustum, from the one camp, and the young warrior, Sohrab, from the other. After several bouts, Rustum gains the upper hand and fatally wounds Sohrab. As his life ebbs away, he calls out that he shall be avenged by his father, Rustum. The latter, on hearing his name pronounced, states that Rustum has no son – but Sohrab pulls out the amulet to prove his identity. Rustum is overwhelmed by the tragedy that has befallen him.[53]

In an attempt to provide some balance to the dominant theoretical perspective of the Oedipus Complex, I suggested that the concept of a Rustum Complex would provide a useful theoretical framework for understanding many hidden aspects of generational conflict. The initial empirical basis for this idea were the twin factors, as already mentioned, of the growing evidence as to widespread child abuse and the vicious and violent reactions to youth protest in many parts of the western world, highlighted at the peak of the protests against the war in Vietnam by the Kent State University killings, when four students were shot to death by members of the National Guard in Ohio during the demonstrations on campus.[54]

The idea of a Rustum Complex seemed to provide a balance to the pervasive power of the Oedipus Complex and offer a theoretical framework for divulging hitherto hidden aspects of generational relations, not only from empirical data from the social sciences, but when interpreting symbolic messages in various subjects in the humanities. Inevitably, the latter include biblical references, with obvious implications for the *Akedah* and the Crucifixion.[55]

In my initial foray into this area of research, it was clear that other researchers were divulging facts of social life that had been mainly unknown until then (particularly in terms of the nether side of family life), while theorists were struggling to make sense of generational conflict and, as noted, several writers had independently suggested the concept of a Laius Complex, based on the earlier failings of the father in abandoning his infant son.[56] From a theoretical perspective, it seemed advisable to break away from the confines of the Greek myth and to seek a totally new framework for expressing the phenomena associated with the opposite of filial hostility.

It is this framework that, I believe, has great utilitarian capacity to facilitate deeper understanding of the meaning of the two major biblical stories dealing with generational contact: of a father (the forerunner of the Jewish people) willing to sacrifice his son in response to a divine command, but then, at the last moment, withdrawing the threatening hand; and of a divine being who allowed his son to be crucified ('*Eli, lama azavtani?*', 'My God, why has Thou forsaken me?') for the positive purpose of assuring redemption for humanity.

The burning question arises, not so much as to the authenticity of these two stories, but as to the credibility of the interpretations given by authoritative sources. Was Abraham really supinely meek in immediately acquiescing to God's demand (especially when contrasted to his obverse behavior over the fate of the wicked people of Sodom and Gomorrah)? Did a benevolent God really wish for his only son to be humiliated, tortured and executed, in order to identify with human suffering as part of a beneficent act of redemption?

My biases on these two questions are clear. First, as a Jew, I do not accept traditional rabbinical interpretation of Abraham's conduct. In a secular age, with the accumulation of knowledge as to human behavior, I claim that Abraham (within the framework of the biblical story, and retaining maximum fidelity to the text) was intent on sorting out his own ambivalent feelings, within the framework of a deep love toward his son, Isaac: a need made essential by his prior abandonment of his other loved son, Ishmael. Second, as a Jew, I do not accept the Christian description of the life and death of Jesus Christ – not the virgin birth, not the resurrection, and not the retrospective explanation given for his crucifixion. In doing so, I am, of course, responding as generations of Jews have done for the past 2,000 years. This is a basic human right in modern terms of the freedom of religion. However, in presenting my ideas, within the framework of an academic analysis, in moving beyond faith and theology, and in presenting historical and sociological issues, and in posing personal, generational questions, I am fully aware of the potential offense that might be occasioned to those for whom the Christian interpretation is the only truth, and for whom Jesus is indeed the Son, the Messiah, the Savior.

However, Jewish history is replete with the suffering inflicted on those who refused to abide by the prevailing norms in European society. This denial led to their persecution, to expulsions, pogroms, the tragedy of the Inquisition, and the ultimate destruction of most of European Jewry during the Holocaust. This is evil committed in the name of a loving God. This is, to a large extent, the other side of the universality of Christianity – that it too often insists on exclusivity, not for a chosen people, but of exclusion for those who choose not to join the universal religion – and, for many years, the Jews were the epitome of a minority group in a sea of Christian majority.

Much of Christian behavior is a denial of the beauty in Jesus' acts and sayings. Is there perhaps something hidden in Christian theology that facilitates this discrepancy? Is there not, perhaps, an inconsistency in the willingness of a divine being to sacrifice his son – even if on behalf of humanity, even if because of humanity's sins? Is there perhaps something intrinsic in familial concepts that lies at the basis of anti-Semitic ideas and practices – for instance, the failure of the 'children' of Israel to recognize the Messiah, to recognize, as the Chosen People, the arrival on earth of God's son?

These are broad, abstract ideas. But, more specifically, and perhaps far more pertinently, what is the meaning for the ultimate success of Christianity – within the Roman Empire – of the fact that Constantine, the emperor who declared Christianity to be the official religion (ending the persecutions and guaranteeing access to power), had his own son put to death when he was about the age of Jesus at the time of the latter's crucifixion. These are known, incontrovertible, historical facts, but they have never, to the best of my knowledge, been subject to probing interpretation – particularly the question of the real motivations behind Constantine's radical action.

My own reflections on these subjects over the years have been made easier given the sincere attempts recently by many Christian theologians to reassess their sacred writings.[57] It is certainly easier for them, in the modern world, to raise such issues without endangering their lives or their livelihoods, as was the case in earlier periods, such as during the Inquisition. Even so, those committed to their religious belief, yet intent on an open discourse in theological matters, might still have to endure stern reactions, such as excommunication.

At the same time, it is necessary to be both wary and humble as to the full willingness of a secular and a scientific world to openly and objectively analyze data and assess their interpretations. Science is not just open to new ideas, but often intent on preserving existing ones. No less than religion, as pointed out at the beginning of this chapter, science has its periods of progress and its periods of consolidation. This is true even of the physical sciences, where, as John Horton points out, the guardians of existing knowledge are often as 'tradition' oriented as the traditional societies[58] – that is, concerned about maintaining existing knowledge. Breaking existing paradigms is part of the problem of modern-day science.[59] Even more so is this true of the social sciences: Karl Mannheim long ago warned of the biases that often affect the purity of social science.[60] This is particularly true when dealing with sensitive matters, such as, for instance, family relations and religious beliefs. When these two factors are combined, it becomes even more complicated.

In this context, my argument is that, as adults, it is not easy to accept the basic idea of the Rustum Complex, which attributes the fault for tensions between the generations, in large measure, to adults, or for that matter, to related ideas, such as a potential Laius Complex. It is far easier to accept the idea of an Oedipus Complex, with its explanation as to why inherent factors in the developmental process of a child might lead to hostility toward the parent.

Thus, while it is only in the modern world that certain awkward questions may be raised about dominant theologies (for instance, the problematics of an idea of a God wishing to sacrifice his only begotten son as a savior for humanity), similar inhibitions arise from the very source that enabled the questions to be asked – from academic research, from the sometimes constrictive parameters of dominant social science theories. One such theory is the Oedipus Complex. Its present influence is so overwhelming, despite the critiques that have been made of many of Freud's ideas, that it prevents the development of insights that are necessary to probe certain aspects of theology, particularly when dealing with the key stories that have familial overtones (beyond the religious belief itself) – the *Akedah* and the Crucifixion.

In order to realize how difficult and complex it is to deal with these stories and their interpretations, it is advisable to examine the impact of the Oedipus Complex on modern society and on modern lives – that is, not the complex itself, but the very idea of the complex and the impact it might have on people's perceptions of social reality, of academic ideas, of mythology and literature, of biblical narratives and theological claims.

An analysis of the Oedipus theme is also important for an understanding of the relations between Judaism and Christianity, as a number of writers have used an Oedipal perspective to analyze the relations between the 'father-religion' or 'mother-religion' of Judaism and the 'son-religion' or 'daughter-religion' of Christianity. Freud himself had, on several occasions, made references to religion and the Bible;[61] no less important is the work of those, working within a Freudian perspective, who are striving to understand expressions of anti-Semitism. These broader themes will be discussed at a later stage, but in the next chapter, an attempt will be made to understand the oedipal theme – in its historical context, in comparative terms with other generational stories, and in its impact, sometimes direct, sometimes subtle, on the discourses of the modern world.

NOTES

1. *See*, for instance, Abraham J. Heschel, *The Prophets* (Philadelphia, PA: The Jewish Publication Society, 1962).
2. *See*, for instance, James Charlesworth and Loren Johns (eds), *Hillel and Jesus: Comparative Studies of Two Major Religious Leaders* (Minneapolis, MI: Fortress Press, 1997).
3. *See*, for instance, J.R. Rosenbloom, *Conversion to Judaism from the Biblical Period to the Present* (Cincinnati, OH: Hebrew Union College Press, 1978).
4. This fact is presented in the opening chapters of the Gospel of Matthew, which opens with the sentence: 'The book of the Generation of Jesus Christ, the son of David, the son of Abraham', and then states, 'So all the generations from Abraham to David are 14 generations; and from David until the carrying away into Babylon are 14 generations; and from the carrying away into Babylon unto Christ are 14 generations' (1:17).
5. *See*, for instance, Exodus 12:38, 'And a mixed multitude went up also with them.'
6. It is of some interest to note that Ben-Gurion, during his premiership, became involved in a theological dispute as to how accurate the Bible was in providing a number of 600,000 who left Egypt. He argued that the number was far too large for the time (a period of 400 years) in which the Israelites had stayed in Egypt, but it is possible that such a large number could be the result of the assimilation of outsiders. For a controversial discussion of a similar absorption of non-Jewish population, *see* Paul Wexler, *The Non-Jewish Origins of the Sephardic Jews* (Albany, NY: State University of New York Press, 1996); and Arthur Koestler, *The Thirteenth Tribe* (New York: Random House, 1976).
7. Abraham and Joseph with Egyptian women (Hagar and Osnat), Moses with Tzipporah (a Midianite), and King Solomon, amongst others, with an Egyptian woman for whom he built a house parallel with the building of the Temple.
8. For interesting analyses, *see* Geza Vermes, *Jesus the Jew: A Historian's Reading of the Gospels* (New York: Macmillan, 1973); Harvey Falk, *Jesus the Pharisee: A New Look at the Jewishness of Jesus* (New York: Paulist Press, 1985); and Susannah Heschel, *Abraham Geiger and the Jewish Jesus* (Chicago, IL: The University of Chicago Press, 1998).
9. *See*, for instance, Joseph Klausner, *From Jesus to Paul* (New York: Macmillan, 1944), translated from the Hebrew by William Stinespring.
10. There are slight differences between the Old Testament, as determined by Christianity, and the *Tanach* (the Jewish Bible). Some books accepted in the Christian canon are only apocryphal books in the Jewish definition.
11. *See*, for instance, Jon Levenson, *The Death and Resurrection of the Beloved Son: The Transformation of Child Sacrifice in Judaism and Christianity* (New Haven, CT: Yale University Press, 1993). *See also* my discussion of this book in chapter 2.
12. *See* Leon Sheleff, *Generations Apart: Adult Hostility to Youth* (New York: McGraw-Hill, 1981).
13. Judges, 11:29–40; *see also* discussion in Phyllis Treble, *Texts of Terror: Literary-Feminist Readings of Biblical Narratives* (Philadelphia, PA: Fortress Press, 1984), chapter 4, 'The

Daughter of Jephthah: An Inhuman Sacrifice', p. 93.
14. *See* discussion in chapter 8, 'Easter'.
15. On the negative attitude to Herod, *see* discussion by Gedalyahu Alon, *Jews, Judaism and the Classical World* (Jerusalem: Magnes Press, 1977), pp. 18–47: 'The Attitude of the Pharisees to Roman Rule and the House of Herod', especially at pp. 38–41.
16. *See* Matthew, 2:13–16:

> The angel of the Lord appeareth to Joseph in a dream, saying, 'Arise, and take the young child and his mother, and flee into Egypt, and be then there until I bring thee word: for Herod will seek the young child to destroy him.' When he arose he took the young child and his mother by night, and departed into Egypt. And was there until the death of Herod: that it might be fulfilled which was spoken of the Lord by the prophet, saying, 'Out of Egypt have I called my son.' Then Herod, when he saw that he was mocked of the wise men, was exceeding wroth, and sent forth, and slew all the children that were in Bethlehem, and in all the coasts thereof, from two years old and under.

17. Genesis, 6:1–4.
18. Rev. Dr A. Cohen (ed.), *The Soncino Chumash: The Five Books of Moses with Haphtaroth* [Hebrew text and English translation with an Exposition Based on the Classical Jewish Commentaries] (London: The Soncino Press, 1947).
19. For examples of sexual relations between fathers-in-law and daughters-in-law in different parts of Eastern and Central Europe in former times, *see* Samuel Kacherov, 'Indigenous and Foreign Influences on the Early Russian Heritage', *Slavic Review*, 31 (1972), p. 265; and Bela Gunda, 'Sex and Semiotics', *Journal of American Folklore*, 86 (1973), p. 147.
20. Cohen, *Soncino Chumash*, p. ix.
21. Rabbi Dr J.H. Hertz (ed.), *The Pentateuch and Haftorahs: Hebrew Text, English Translation and Commentary* (London: Soncino Press, 1936).
22. Ibid., pp. 18–19.
23. Louis Ginzberg, *Legends of the Bible* (Philadelphia, PA: The Jewish Publication Society of America, 1968) [abridged edition of original seven-volume work] . The book is publicized, on the cover, as, 'Variations of Stories in the Scriptures as Told and Retold in the Ancient East from the Days of Abraham in Synagogues and Churches and the Homes of a Hundred Generations of Men.'
24. Ibid., pp. 69–70.
25. Ibid., p. xxxiv.
26. *See*, for instance, Wilson, *Related Strangers: Jews and Christians 70–170* CE (Minneapolis: Fortress Press, 1995), chapter 7, 'Gnostics and Marcionites', p. 195; *see also* Elaine Pagels, *The Gnostic Gospels* (London: Weidenfeld and Nicolson, 1979), especially chapter 1, 'The Controversy over Christ's Resurrection: Historical Event or Symbol?', p. 3. Pagels writes that: 'The gnostics stood close to the Greek philosophic tradition (and, for that matter, to Hindu and Buddhist tradition) that regards the human spirit as residing "in" a body.' She points out that:

> The orthodox teaching on resurrection...legitimized a hierarchy of persons through whose authority all others must approach God. Gnostic teaching...was potentially subversive of this order; it claimed to offer to every initiate direct access to God of which the priests and bishops themselves might be ignorant. (p. 27)

It should be noticed that the gnostic writings, especially those discovered in Upper Egypt in 1945 at Nag Hammadi, raise further serious questions for traditional Christianity – and these are well brought out in Pagel's book, as she discusses issues such as: 'The Politics of Modernism' (pp. 28–47), 'God the Father/God the Mother' (pp. 48–69); and 'The Passion of Christ and the Persecution of Christians' (pp. 70–101). However, she makes only brief, passing reference to the issue of Jesus as the Son of God.
27. *See* discussion in the next chapter, 'Oedipus'.
28. G.S. Kirk, *The Nature of Greek Myths* (Harmondsworth: Penguin Books, 1974), p. 127.
29. Ibid., p. 128.

30. Ibid., p. 116.
31. Ibid., chapter 8, 'The Mythical Life of Heracles'.
32. Ibid., p. 176.
33. Ibid.
34. Ibid., p. 177.
35. Ibid.
36. Ibid., p. 178.
37. Ibid., p. 179.
38. Ibid., pp. 202–3.
39. Ibid., p. 203.
40. Ibid., p. 201.
41. Ibid., p. 210.
42. David Gil, *Violence Against Children: Physical Child Abuse in the United States* (Cambridge, MA: Harvard University Press, 1970); and Richard Gelles, *Intimate Violence in Families* (Thousand Oaks, CA: Sage Publications, 1997).
43. For a critical analysis of the legal aspects, *see* Cynthia Gillespie, *Justifiable Homicide: Battered Women, Self-Defense and the Law* (Columbus, OH: The Ohio State University Press, 1987).
44. *See*, for instance, Kenneth Keniston, *Young Radicals* (New York: Harcourt Brace, 1968).
45. *See* Sheleff, *Generations Apart*; and *also* Leon Sheleff, 'Behind the Oedipus Complex: A Perspective on the Myth and Reality of Generational Conflict', *Theory and Society*, 3 (1978), p. 1.
46. Sheleff, *Generations Apart*, chapter 2, 'The Myths of Generational Conflict'.
47. Sheleff, *Generations Apart*, part 1, 'Oedipus at the Crossroads', and part 2, 'The Uses of the Oedipus Complex'.
48. *See*, for instance, Seymour Fisher and Roger Greenberg, *The Scientific Credibility of Freud's Theories and Therapy* (New York: Basic Books, 1977).
49. *See* especially, Ian Suttie, *The Origins of Love and Hate* (London: Kegan Paul, Trench, Trubner, 1935); Erich Wellisch, *Isaac and Oedipus: A Study in Biblical Psychology of the Sacrifice of Isaac – the Akedah* (London: Routledge and Kegan Paul, 1954); and Thomas Vernon, 'The Laius Complex', *The Humanist*, 32 (1972), p. 44.
50. *See* Kenneth Allot (ed.), *The Poems of Matthew Arnold* (London: Longmans, 1965), pp. 302–30.
51. Sheleff, *Generations Apart*, part 3, 'The Rustum Complex'.
52. *See* reference in John D. Yohannan, *A Treasury of Asian Literature* (New York: Mentor, 1956).
53. The original story is from the *Shahnamah* by Firdausi who lived from 932 to 1020 CE. The figure of Rustum is well-known in Persian mythology, and the story itself obviously made a strong impression on Matthew Arnold.
54. For an account of the event, see James Michener, *Kent State: What Happened and Why*, 2nd edn (New York: Fawcett Books, 1982).
55. *See*, for instance, Philip Rieff, *Freud: The Mind of the Moralist* (London: University Paperbacks, 1965), p. 165, where he discusses both the *Akedah* and the Crucifixion in the context of a critique of Freud in these particular aspects.
56. *See* note 49; for general review of these ideas, see Note, 'More on the Laius Complex', *Journal of Individual Psychology*, 29 (1973), p. 88.
57. *See*, especially, the ongoing work of the Jesus Seminar.
58. John Horton, 'African Traditional Thought and Western Science', *Africa*, 37 (1967), p. 50 (Part 1) and p. 155 (Part 2).
59. *See*, for instance, Thomas Kuhn, *The Structure of Scientific Revolutions* (Chicago, IL: University of Chicago Press, 1962).
60. Karl Mannheim, *Ideology and Utopia: An Introduction to the Sociology of Knowledge* (New York: Harcourt, Brace, and World, 1936).
61. *See* discussion in chapter 11, 'Freud'.

6
Oedipus

During the period of anticipation leading up to the celebration of the millenium, many newspaper editors and television and radio producers presented lists of those who were considered to have been the most prominent personalities of the past century. Sigmund Freud figured in most lists, and there can be little doubt that many of his ideas have had a major impact on the manner in which people perceive of themselves and understand their relations with others.[1]

One of the most significant of these ideas is the concept of the Oedipus Complex. Yet the strange fact is that this complex, conceived and presented by Freud, was never ever set out by him in one authoritative statement.[2] Slowly, over the years, Freud wove references to this ancient Greek myth into much of his writings:[3] from references to the original myth itself, or to Sophocles' play, through the twin ideas of incestuous inclinations and parricidal tendencies, to explanations of patients' dreams and wish-fantasies. Thus, a concept recognized as a major contribution by Freud was never systematically set out by him. Yet, from being initially a marginal factor, even in Freud's work, Oedipal ideas have become a significant part of western culture. Various phenomena, from juvenile delinquency to student unrest,[4] have been attributed to the impact of Oedipal feelings, the explanation often being that patricidal impulses from an early age were never satisfactorily resolved and in later life find an outlet in violent or deviant behavior. Furthermore, there are endless interpretations of novels, poems, plays, movies and biographies based on the Oedipus Complex,[5] sometimes even in circumstances totally unjustified, where the popularity of the concept overwhelms the facts.

The story of a son, Oedipus, killing his father, Laius, during an altercation between the two of them after a chance meeting at a crossroads, when their identities were unknown to each other, is presumed by Freud to speak to some factor hidden deeply in the psyche of every human being. In this respect, the patricidal aspect of the story in the myth of Oedipus is the symbolic opposite of the two biblical stories at the center of generational contact – the *Akedah* and the Crucifixion.

My argument is that both the *Akedah* and the Crucifixion not merely deal with divine interactions and interventions, but are part of ongoing human drama dealing indeed with deep, personal emotions. I have argued that Abraham had valiantly attempted to cope with the ambivalence inherent in parental concerns, and have suggested that the Crucifixion is, in many respects, a continuation of this theme – with a different outcome, and therefore also with a different interpretation.

Given the traditional power of the Church in controlling the nature of commentaries on biblical themes, I have claimed that it is only within modern, secular society that issues such as these can be discussed and that attempts of this nature to fathom a hidden or subtle message, or form such critical non-conformist analyses, have become possible. The very number of Christian theologians engaged in this debate, from the Protestants in the Jesus Seminar in California[6] to the individual Catholic thinkers who are risking papal condemnation or even excommunication,[7] is indicative of the intellectual fermentation that characterizes biblical study in the modern, secular and scientific age.

Yet – and this is the dilemma posed in this chapter – a dominant non-religious personality has suggested that the major theme of familial relations is filial patricidal tendencies. If this is correct, then the theological implications of the *Akedah* and the Crucifixion lead to different conclusions than those which stem from the basis of a Laius Complex or a Rustum Complex.[8] In my book, *Generations Apart*,[9] I suggested that the oedipal perspective, as laid out by Freud, was based on incorrect assumptions. It even ignored the basic fact that, throughout the story, the impetus for generational conflict emerged from the parental side – Laius, with the connivance of his wife, Jocasta, attempted to be rid of their new-born infant by abandoning him in a forest in order to avoid the prediction of an oracle that spoke of the fatal danger posed by the son. Oedipus, on being apprised in young adulthood of the same oracle, but not knowing that the people who had found him and saved him and then brought him up as their son were not his real parents, left home in a vain attempt to thwart the oracle, only to encounter his real father, Laius, at the crossroads near Thebes. The initial violence of this encounter stems from Laius' provocation. With these additions, the nature of generational contact, and conflict, becomes much more complex than is contained in a simplified account of inherent incestuous feelings for a mother leading to patricidal tendencies toward the father. It ignores the flow of hostile actions from the parental generation. Hence, the suggestion of a Laius Complex, and the alternative suggestion of a Rustum Complex.

But, since Freud himself took the basis of his concept from Greek mythology, and since the stories linked to Greek mythology were widely prevalent in the areas where Christianity initially spread, including Greece itself (where, also, many Jews lived), and since there is a syncretic overlap between Greek and Roman mythology, it behoves us to examine the essence of this mythology. Such an examination will show not only the defects in Freud's reasoning *vis-à-vis* the story itself (and, indeed, the problematics of much of his own empirical data, taken from his case studies,[10] as I have outlined in my earlier book), but also the fact that the Oedipal story, with its climax of the killing of the father, is an exception to other stories which are no less central to Greek mythology. In fact, these stories are far more significant, and far more numerous, and their *coup de grâce* is an act of filicide akin to the underlying themes of the *Akedah* and the Crucifixion. The idea of the syncretic nature of the biblical narrative must be given due consideration: the line from the *Akedah* to the Crucifixion passes through the catalytic influence of Greek mythology, providing both general understanding of the theme in universal terms and a glimpse of the cultural factors existing in the Roman Empire at the time, including in Greece and the surrounding areas such as Syria, and in Rome itself, where Paul preached in his first attempts to bring the message of the Bible to the Gentiles.[11] The question is, was there a familiarity, was there a similarity, to some of the biblical narratives, with the addition of a comforting theological explanation for the sacrifice of a son, that was lacking in the mythological accounts of such acts?

The essential facts of Greek mythology are clearly and unequivocally stated by Richard Buxton who, in a chapter entitled 'Family',[12] explains that, 'there is no reason to think that the Greeks *themselves* [emphasis in original] gave special status to the Oedipus story as a model for parent/child relationships. On the contrary, in mythology...we find a wide range of contrasting paradigms'.[13] Buxton then provides a list of parental figures who, in one way or another, caused harm to their offspring: Meobe, Medea, Agamemnon, Hella, Daedalus, Ouranus, Kronos and Zeus. In addition, Buxton includes Oedipus himself in the latter category, for Oedipus, as a father, is aware of fraternal strife between his two sons, but instead of seeking to pacify them, calls down a curse upon them that one of them would, in the course of their struggle, kill the other one, which is exactly what later transpired.[14] This part of the drama, this aspect of the full Oedipal family tragedy, is totally ignored by Freud and almost all the various commentators who rely on the Oedipus Complex for their theoretical analysis. Buxton himself does not go into the details but merely mentions his name in setting out his list of characters whose actions were harmful to their children.

This list contains parents who, for various reasons, killed their children: for instance, Medea, who put two of them to death for selfish reasons;[15] Agamemnon, whose story is so similar to the biblical account of Jephtha's tragedy, namely he sacrifices his daughter after giving a rash promise of sacrifice if successful in battle;[16] Kronus, the first major figure in Greek mythology, the father of Zeus, who devoured his children immediately after birth, of whom only Zeus survived due to the wily action of his mother who, aware of Kronus' habitual infanticidal practices, managed to outwit him; and Zeus himself, who, in a different manner, carried on the family tradition.[17] Buxton then states simply, yet categorically, 'Amid all this diversity, the Oedipus story, far from being typical, *seems actually to be unique* [my emphasis] in linking the theme of parricide with that of incest with the mother.'[18] To which he adds that:

> There is not entirely negligible difference between a son desiring to eliminate his father, and a father feeling threatened – for example, as a result of a prophecy – by the prospect of being ousted (in the case of a king, being overthrown by a son). Greek mythology is very much richer in the latter motif than the former.[19]

Here it should be mentioned that the oracle surely meant, and should so have been interpreted, that the son, in the normal course of events, would supercede the parent and succeed to the throne. This is the way of nature, and the oracle spoke, perhaps, of no more than this, even if in a more dramatic fashion by referring to a killing. In modern terms, an American poet, Donald Hall, has expressed similar feelings in writing of, 'My son, my executioner',[20] in a sense indicating that the change of generations is an inevitable reminder of mortality, while also guaranteeing some modicum of 'immortality' through the very existence of offspring.

This was the subtle message of the oracle that Laius failed to perceive, and – far more important – that those working within an oedipal framework continue to ignore. The oracle aspect of the story comes full circle when Oedipus himself, apprised of an unsolved riddle set at the oracle, solves it – 'What walks on four in the morning, two at noon and three at night?': a person moving relentlessly through the stages of life, with the third stage (the need for a walking stick) hinting also at future demise.[21]

Even more relevant for our theme are Buxton's comments on divine–human interactions. Referring first to 'the complex relationships between the Olympians and their various heroic offspring',[22] Buxton goes on to describe how:

Another relevant group of roles involves the gods. One of the basic types of genealogy for Greek heroes was birth from a liaison between a god and a nymph or mortal women. In these instances the relationship between father and son interacted with that between god and mortal.[23]

Amongst the most important of these cases, leading to further complications, were those in which a mortal woman gave birth to twins, one of whom was born of a divine king, and one of whom was born of an ordinary mortal. In the previous chapter, the key example of Heracles (Hercules in Roman mythology) was provided, but there are other examples.

Buxton describes the inevitable problematics that arise from such a dual parentage and notes that:

> Some of the most moving episodes in Greek mythology derive from an exploration of the latter imbalance, as with the tears of blood shed by the Iliadic Zeus over his son Sarpendon. A particular set of problems was highlighted by cases of double parentage, notably Heracles (son of Zeus and Aphitryon) and Theseus (son of Aigeus and Poseidon). With the intellectual and moral daring characteristic of tragedy, it was possible for the suffering hero of Euripedes' *Heracles* to express a preference for his mortal over his divine father ... Of all the heroes, few are at a greater distance from their father than those who are the offspring of gods.[24]

Thus, it appears that the idea of a birth arising out of divine–human contact had existed as part of the general culture in the Roman Empire before Christianity presented a similar phenomenon of a virgin birth.

In the case of Greek and Roman mythology, because of the existence of a pantheon of gods, almost all of whom possessed human qualities, it was possible to present a direct sexual contact out of which an infant would be born. In contrast, the monotheistic nature of the new religion, the unique presence of only one Divine Being, obligated a different approach: a Holy Spirit, who would allow for pregnancy without direct contact.[25] But the basic principle is similar. This comparison between mythical figures, who no longer have any religious connotations in the modern world, might seem unnecessarily provocative and even demeaning to an existing religion in the twenty-first century. However, this is not a probing into Christianity's present status, but the nature of the culture into which Jesus was born, in which Paul set out on his mission of conversion of the pagans, and in which the immediate disciples of Jesus and the writers of the Gospels all lived. My argument is that it was not necessarily the unique aspects of Christianity (the monotheistic belief, for instance) that enabled it to make inroads into the culture of heathens in the areas surrounding Palestine, but the fact that it had a shared basis with non-Israelites.

Put in other terms, the capacity of Christianity to convince Jews to accept Jesus as a savior was linked to a belief deeply embedded in Judaism of a special personality – an Anointed One, a Messiah (from the original Hebrew) – who would bring succor and hope in times of national disaster and human distress. In this respect, the destruction of the Temple 40 years after the Crucifixion was, as noted, a crucial stage in reviving the fortunes of Jesus' message, the movement associated with it, and the status of Messiah attached to Jesus.

The Temple's destruction was, however, irrelevant for non-Israelites, but the missionary zeal of Paul, and others, was to a large extent facilitated by the fact that a key aspect of Christian theology, the virgin birth, shared certain parallels with aspects of Greek and Roman mythology (that is, mythology as understood in retrospect, but at the time a religion with its temples, rituals and belief-systems). Put simply, the idea of a divine–human relationship, foreign to post-Abrahamic Judaism,[26] was an acceptable and recognized idea in Greek and Roman culture. What Christianity also offered, giving it an added attraction, was the monotheistic idea of an omnipotent and benevolent God, in contrast to a pantheon of gods who possessed human-like characteristics, each being responsible for different aspects of social life. Indeed, it is quite likely that Greek and Roman religions had exhausted their attractive and creative potentialities and, at the advent of Christianity, were losing their capacity to provide satisfactory answers to eternal questions. This left fertile ground for missionary activity, made easier by the divine–human link and a monotheistic God (a new idea) who had an only begotten son (an idea that had been prevalent in the religious culture).

This concept of direct divine–human interconnection was expressed in other ways: first, the Roman emperors themselves often sought/assumed divine status (a trend started by Augustus); and second, some of the major gods were themselves believed to have originally been ordinary mortals.

A leading Jewish scholar, Joseph Klausner, explains some of the background to the social and cultural situation extant at the time of Christianity's inception. After describing the manner in which 'the Graeco–Roman religion became ritualistic and mechanical',[27] offering satisfaction to the masses but lacking a similar capacity to satisfy the more educated people, he writes that:

From the fifth century BCE in Greece and from the second century BCE in Rome, the educated people, who were gradually increasing in number, began to ask questions and raise difficulties about the nature of the gods and the destiny of man, and about rewards and punishments in life and after death. These questions and difficulties undermined the pagan religion. And in this educated group, which grew larger and larger, Christianity in the beginning of its growth was able to find its first admirers.[28]

Even in terms of the essential nature of the dominant deities, Klausner describes a book, written by Ephemeris in the third century before the common era, and entitled *Sacred History,* in which the writer:

> Sets forth in the form of a travelogue, the 'Acts' of the gods Uranus, Cronus, and Zeus, as he had found these acts recorded on a column of gold in a temple of Zeus on one of the isles of the Indian Ocean. These 'Acts' seek to show that all three of these gods were at first only historic men, who after death attained the rank of gods because they had benefited humanity, although they had died like all men.[29]

Increasing dissatisfaction was expressed by many in the educated classes, particularly as to the recording of immoral aspects in the lives of the gods. Thus, even before the appearance of Christianity, there had been a move toward other religious beliefs, particularly the mystery religions, which offered a prospect, lacking in the Graeco–Roman religions, of a clear differentiation between the body and the soul, with a corresponding possibility of spiritual life continuing after corporeal death. Klausner explains that:

> The mysteries of Eleusis, which were founded upon *the death and resurrection of a god* [emphasis in original], offered hope to man that he also would not die with the death of the body, and that if he could be 'sanctified' in these mysteries, he would rise again and live a blessed life after death.[30]

Furthermore, the very expansion of the Greek and Roman Empires into Asia had exposed their cultures to oriental religious influences, which contained even more examples of special births, deaths and resurrection.

This latter aspect is of particular import, and must now be examined. To the idea of divine–human connections already embodied in the religion and mythology of the Greek and Roman culture, the Orient added the idea of a resurrected deity.

Klausner describes the situation that had developed in the Roman Empire. He writes:

> The Oriental gods most familiar in Greece and Rome were dying and rising gods. Such was the Egyptian Osiris, such was Adonis in Phoenicia, such was Attis in Phrygia. Likewise, the Babylonian Baal-Bet-Marduk died and rose again; he was arrested, he was sentenced, he was chastised, and together with a malefactor he was sent away to death, while another malefactor was freed. A woman cleansed away the blood from the heart of the god, which, it would appear, was pierced by a spear or a javelin. Afterwards he was found in a 'mountain', that is, in the underworld, where he was being watched over. A goddess had made a nest for him. Finally Bel-Marduk came back alive and well from the mountain (the 'underworld').[31]

Klausner explains that in polytheistic frameworks, the possibilities are always available for a move from the divine to the human. Thus:

> The god Apollo, son of Zeus, became a man (servant of Admetus) in order to expiate a murder which he had committed. After he had served for some time, he went up to Olympus, and thereafter remained by the side of the glorious throne of Zeus. By contrast, Heracles, the man, son of the god Zeus and the princess Alemene ... became a god by virtue of his great and good deeds.[32]

There is even, according to Klausner, a story which states that Plato may well have had a divine father, in the person of Apollo.[33] In his chapter entitled 'Religious Syncretism',[34] Klausner notes similarities between aspects of the fundamentals of Christianity and prevailing ideas in Graeco–Roman culture and history, including the key idea of resurrection. He states clearly that the events associated with Jesus' life are factually correct, and that even the interpretations are probably independent of external influences; for instance, that 'belief in the resurrection of the dead was ... widespread in the period of the Second Temple'.[35] Thus he concludes that: 'The fate of Jesus is not just a reflexion of the fate of the gods Osiris, Attis, Adonis, Mithras, and other such divinities.'[36] However, he immediately clarifies that:

> There can be no doubt that, had it not been for the general influence – however obscure and remote – of those pagan stories, a *Jewish Messiah* would never have become the *Christian Son of God,*

who ... rose to life again in the vision of his followers and became
not only Christ-Messiah, but also the only son of God the Father, a
son who was begotten of the Holy Spirit, and rose to life again
from the darkness of his tomb.[37] [emphasis in original]

A further aspect that must be noted is the desire of the more powerful
emperors to be given the status of a god; however dubious some of the
evidence on this score is, Klausner claims that:

The large number of inscriptions in which the Caesars are called
'God,' 'son of God,' and 'Savior,' the statues and monuments which
were erected in their honor, the libations which were poured out
before their statues, and the incense which was burned to them –
all these proved that in Rome as in ... Egypt, it was customary to
deify the man who became emperor.[38]

Klausner's book, which attempts to understand Paul's role in the
success of Christianity, sums up the syncretic aspect of Christianity, and
the mutual influences through cultural contact with the various
religions:

Here we have the solution to the great and relatively swift success
of Paul. He *consciously* opposed paganism and brought over the
pagans to Judaism in the new Christian form which he had created;
but he was *unconsciously* influenced by paganism and took over
from it most of its sacred practices (sacraments) insofar as he could
find for them a precedent in Judaism; or, he unintentionally
colored Jewish customs with a pagan-mystery color. He also took
over from the pagan mystery religions and from pagan philosophi-
cal-religious thought a part of their terminology.[39]

The parallels between the story of Jesus, as described in the New
Testament, with narratives recounted in the surrounding cultures,
suggests a reasonable conclusion: the New Testament account of Jesus'
birth, life, death and resurrection is by no means a unique story (except
for the monotheistic aspect). But the very fact of this similarity poses an
inevitable contrary question. What caused Christianity's success in the
long run, while all the religions (and mythologies) then prevalent (such
as the mystery religions) disappeared, remaining only as a historical
memory, and with ongoing impact only in terms of myths and legends?
Was there something special in Jesus' acts and sayings that ensured the
spread of his message? Was there something special in his suffering on

the Cross that attracted sympathy and identification? Was there some degree of authenticity in the reports of his resurrection that contained a persuasiveness lacking in the similar stories from the Orient?

Furthermore, on the balance of the evidence presented, much of it widely known – at least to those with some modicum of knowledge of Greek mythology – the inevitable question arises as to why there is not a wider recognition of the *lack* of uniqueness in the narrative about Jesus. For, in contrast to the mythologies of the Graeco–Roman religions, or the stories of the mystery religions, uniqueness is essential to the very validity of the claims made for Jesus, specifically because of the monotheistic basis: the one God has only one begotten son. The authenticity of the stories in Greek or Roman mythologies are not undermined by similar stories, whether within the same mythology, or learned from other cultures. But the authenticity of the story of Jesus, the very belief in his divinity, is predicated on its uniqueness.

The mere fact of similar stories in nearby cultures does not, of course, automatically negate belief in Jesus as the Son of God. There is, admittedly, the possibility that the other stories were indeed no more than stories, whereas the account of Jesus' life, with its various vicissitudes, was thought to be based on proven, empirical fact. The others, mostly from an earlier time, contained no more than the fruit of somebody's imagination, later recorded by outstanding poets such as Homer.

For Jesus, on the other hand, there is definite evidence – unlike them, it is known that he lived, his crucifixion was witnessed, he was believed to have been in physical contact with his disciples after being resurrected. Some claim that this is supported by his presumed image on the Shroud of Turin, although these claims have always been controversial and have been undermined in recent years, even by official church pronouncements.[40]

Again, assuming that the kind of issues being raised here and the kind of questions being asked were beyond the pale of possibility during the years of Church supremacy, when its secular power had been consolidated and the full force of the Inquisition could be activated against heretics challenging doctrinal truths, what is to prevent these questions being raised now, as indeed I am raising them? This is to raise questions beyond those dealt with in the Higher Criticism of the modern world, for the claim being made here is based not merely on religious disputation, but on sociological and psychological reasoning.

Freud argued that the Oedipus story had an attraction for people in different societies and periods because they could so easily identify with the basic theme of incestuous, and related patricidal, tendencies, since these were universal processes which all people experienced. This was, he argued, the reason for the popularity of the story as expressing a universal truth. But, as we have seen in this chapter, the Oedipal theme is a marginal theme in contrast to the far more dominant theme of filicidal tendencies – in Greek and Roman mythology, in oriental cultures (including experiences undergone by such religious figures as Krishna[41] in India, or the life story of Buddha[42]), and in the Bible itself.

Why, at least in the modern age, is the story of the *Akedah* not interpreted in terms of potential paternal hostility? Why is there no awareness of a truth embedded in this story, warning of possible hostile feelings of the parental generation to the younger generation? Why, on the other hand, is there such easy and wide acceptance of the Oedipal theme? If it is truly a marginal theme in Greek mythology, why is the Oedipus Complex so popular in modern Western society, not only for medical purposes (for instance, as the basis for methods of treatment), but also as a constant framework for the analysis of literature in its various forms, and the analysis of social phenomena (student protest being defined as no more than an expression of unresolved Oedipal problems), and of historical processes (where leading figures in politics, philosophy, the military, etc. are subject to biographical analyses based on the impact of the Oedipus Complex on their actions and beliefs)?[43]

Why is the blame for generational conflict so facilely attached to the younger generation? Freud claimed that the popularity of the Oedipus story lay in its capacity to speak to feelings inherent in all. Yet, what of the capacity of the *Akedah* and its central role in Judaism? And, in purely psychological terms *à la* Freud, what of the central role of the Crucifixion in Christianity? Are these stories also not speaking to some widespread sentiment: of parental power *vis-à-vis* the filial generation?

I wish to argue that there are two parallel processes at work. On the one hand, a patricidal theme – in the *Akedah*, in the Crucifixion, and in much of Graeco–Roman mythology, as also in other oriental cultures from that period – is prevalent and popular, because it speaks to latent feelings, hidden feelings. The *Akedah* was intended to reveal them in a subtle manner; perhaps too subtle, because it has been, as I have argued in an earlier chapter, misrepresented.[44] On this basis, there is an added justification for the Crucifixion since, unlike other similar stories – the *Akedah*, Cronus and Zeus, Mithra, Dionysius, etc. – the official interpretation is that the harm done to the son, the cruelty inflicted on him, has (at least in retrospect) divine sanction, since this was God's way of identifying with human suffering. By offering His son in order to redeem humanity, God commits a one-time act with colossal and universal implications for humanity.

On the other hand, there is an alternative process at work. The very critique that is needed of the *Akedah* and the Crucifixion is not forthcoming, as the opposite theme, that of the Oedipus Complex, has become dominant in modern society, including academic research.

Beyond any niceties associated with critiques of theological themes, the Oedipus Complex prevents any major thrust of research into the inner meaning behind the *Akedah* and the Crucifixion. The attempts by several theorists to suggest an alternative theme, such as a 'Laius Complex', even if only for the purpose of achieving some minimum balance in dealing with generational contacts and generational conflicts, has failed.[45] There has been almost no follow-up to any of these attempts.

A similar fate has befallen my own efforts to suggest a 'Rustum Complex' as a preferred alternative. I have to concede that little use has, to the best of my knowledge, been made of this concept, despite the fact that I have tried to show how it could be used to understand not just conflict in sociological terms (the main thrust of the book), but also to re-assess inner meanings of literature, biography, and the Bible itself.[46] For instance, Shakespeare's *Hamlet*[47] (not as Oedipal, but parental hostility, as Shakespeare had a son, Hamnet – whom he barely knew as he lived apart from his family – and who died at the age of 11, just before Shakespeare wrote his greatest play with a similar name),[47] Dosto'evski's work, for example, *The Brothers Karamazov*, which, I argued, discussed parental hostility),[48] and Kafka (and his well-known tensions with his father, and the manner in which this affected his major work in *The Trial, The Castle, Metamorphosis*),[49] are merely outstanding examples of the desire of so many critics and researchers to enlarge upon Oedipal themes and their inability to discern the exact opposite. However, I argue that the real message contained in fiction actually lies in the Rustum Complex and is often linked to the personal background of the author.

This is pre-eminently the case of Matthew Arnold and the message he was trying to convey in his classic epic poem, *Sohrab and Rustum* (incidentally originally entitled *The Death of Sohrab*). There is almost no doubt that, in writing this poem, indeed in being excited and entranced on encountering the original Persian myth, Arnold was relating to the plight of Sohrab from a very personal perspective – as the sensitive son of the authoritarian Thomas Arnold, the renowned principal of Rugby School (immortalized in the novel *Tom Brown's Schooldays*).[50] Arnold was known for his strict discipline and authoritarian control and, according to most of his biographers, for his dominance over his children, and his displeasure for many of Matthew's aims and endeavors, particularly his poetic inclinations.

It seems clear that in writing this poem, which reaches a tragic climax in a filicidal act, Arnold was attempting to express his own identification as a member of the younger generation facing the power and insensitivity of the parental generation. Yet, most of the biographers of Arnold either ignore this aspect (this 'cry in the wilderness'), or actually utilize the Oedipus Complex to interpret the story.

An example of partial recognition of what Arnold was almost certainly trying to express is the reference by Lionel Trilling to the poem:

> It is almost impossible not to find throughout *Sohrab and Rustum* at least a shadowy personal significance. The strong son is slain by the mightier father, and in the end Sohrab draws his father's spear from his own side to let out his life and end the anguish. We watch Arnold in his later youth and we must wonder if he is not, in a psychical sense, doing the same thing.[51]

More practically and precisely, William Madden writes that:

> In *Sohrab and Rustum* the threatening forces which Arnold is indirectly resisting ... find successful embodiment in the figure of Rustum; like all viable poetic personae, the figures of both Sohrab and Rustum had their roots beyond the reaches of the poet's discursive awareness in his most deeply felt experience ... We can only speculate in such matters, but it seems probable that the tragedy in which an unrecognized son is unwittingly killed by a famous father found a responsive chord in the lonely poet-son of the famous 'Arnold of Rugby'.[52]

He concludes that, 'It is not too much to say that in the poem Arnold portrays his father as unwittingly instrumental in his own "death" as a poet.'[53]

On the other hand, in contrast to these sympathetic approaches are other interpretations that draw on the Oedipal perspective. For instance, Dwight Culler, in his analysis of Arnold's poetry,[54] totally ignores the filicidal aspect and focuses on the incestuous aspect in Oedipus (which appears nowhere in the Sohrab–Rustum story); he states categorically that, 'Sohrab and Rustum is often interpreted as an expression of the Oedipus conflict.'[55] Thus, the fact of a son's killing is inverted. In his analysis, Culler also focuses on the sexual aspect of the Oedipus story, and since there is no sexual aspect in the Rustum story, plays with the idea of the brandished weapon being a phallic symbol. Thus, he writes:

> The redoubtable masculinity of Rustum, as witnessed by the vast
> club he wields, the tower and pillar by which he is symbolized,
> together with the presumed effeminacy of the son, make it a
> conflict between the masculine and feminine principles, and in the
> end, when the virility of the son has been established by planting a
> far-seen pillar over his grave, replacing the fallen pillar of his father,
> he is clearly the sexual victor. At the level of the Super-Ego he has
> been conquered, and, of course, it is his joy to be so conquered.[56]

Bruce Mazlish, in a dual biography of the Mill family – James, the
father and John Stuart, the son – which is based on an Oedipal
framework, refers to Arnold's poem in a similar vein to Culler, and
suggests that the 'son offers grateful submission to the now tender
father'.[57] In a general discussion of Asian literature, John Yohannan
ignores the plea for understanding Arnold's plight that the poem
suggests, and argues that 'the myth has recoiled upon Matthew Arnold,
who has been charged with projecting his own suppressed desire to do
battle with a stronger father, the renowned Thomas Arnold of Rugby'.[58]

William Buckler also suggests that the poem is a desperate attempt by
the son to gain recognition and praise from his omnipotent father.[59] He
uses a biblical framework to deny that 'Sohrab and Rustum represents a
veiled parable by which a variation on the Judeo-Christian myth of God
the Father and God the Son is examined and critiqued',[60] although he
does see 'an oblique analogue of that myth'.[61] (It is not clear what myth
Buckler is referring to, especially in terms of a concept of God the Son,
which is attributed to a Judeo-Christian myth – one doubts whether
Judaism has any myth that allows for a concept of God the Son. In any
event, Buckler refers to 'Sohrab's slightly distorted Christ imagery.')[62] In
terms of Sohrab's fate, he suggests that:

> 'Elementary feelings' like those at the foundation of the story of
> Sohrab and Rustum perhaps led, at some primitive stage in man's
> imaginative thought, to speculations that eventually emerged as the
> sophisticated and humanly satisfying myth of a son who allayed his
> father's wrath by dying of a totally self-immolating love of him and
> thereby reconciled the father's omnipotent imperviousness to the
> catastrophic errors to which even the best of them are prone.[63]

What Buckler seems to be suggesting is that while there was parental
error, it was neutralized by a filial sacrifice born of love!

David Riede, in a book entitled *Matthew Arnold and the Betrayal of Language*,[64] also ignores the message of a patricidal act, and presents the poem as 'The struggles of humanity under the authoritative decree of fate', which he sees as being 'The voice of God that makes the world comprehensible'.[65] Yet he feels that the poem does not resolve the issue of fate. According to him:

> Sohrab protests too much, and his assertion about fate's decree is only a conjecture *ex post facto* exploration that reflects a desire for order rather than a conviction of it ... When Sohrab concludes, 'But it was writ in Heaven that this should be,' one is tempted to respond that it was not writ in Heaven by Fate, but was writ in Persia by Firdawsi [the writer of the original story].[66]

The story, surely, is not of unavoidable fate being acted out in some typical Greek drama, but a heartfelt cry of a young sensitive poet, trying to come to terms with the harm done to him by his famous father, the stern headmaster of Rugby School.

How deeply the son was affected by the home in which he grew up may be noted in an extract of a story that appears on the opening page of another biography (by Park Honan), where the seven-year-old Matthew writes to 'Dear Papa' as follows:

> Now it came to pass that when they were come to about the middle of the wood that LOVE saw a monstrous cave, and all that he could see of it was blood ... two great giants their names were Hurt and Cruel.[67]

From this quote, and other similar ones, one senses the difficulty that a younger generation has in expressing its innermost feelings towards the parental generation – or at least in being understood. Part of this reason, as noted, is a direct consequence of the impact of the Oedipus Complex in modern society. But even aside from that, the deeper appreciation of the perspective of a younger generation is not easily acquired. Those who read poetry, fiction, historical accounts and biblical stories are adults (and often parents) with the biases and related perspectives that are associated with that status.[68]

In the *Akedah*, a son is almost killed – and Abraham is highly commended for his willingness to prove his belief in, and love for, God, by preparing to sacrifice his son. Rabbis prefer this interpretation (as do Christian scholars) over the possibility of according to Abraham not blind faith, but perceptive probing into the deepest recesses of his heart and soul. In the Crucifixion, Christian theology claims that a benevolent divine being is actually willing to offer his son as a sacrifice on behalf of humanity.

My argument is basically that while the Oedipus story is attractive because it assigns blame to the younger generation (and provides an explanation for it by referring to incestuous feelings at a young age), the *Akedah* and the Crucifixion appeal because they have an indirect justification for patricidal tendencies – in the *Akedah*, at God's command, and in the Crucifixion, with God's acquiescence.

The theme of the Crucifixion is a central aspect of Christianity, even though, as pointed out, the theme of the dying god who is reborn is not unique. Yet, for all its initial success, for all the achievements linked to the missionary activity of Paul, the fact is that the success of Christianity as a widespread universal religion was not attained by the success of proselytizing, but by imperial edict. It was not the zealous efforts of Paul, or the determination of his successors to persist despite ruthless persecution conducted by the Roman State, that laid the basis for Christianity's triumph, but the decision of Empĕror Constantine to declare Christianity the official religion of the empire.

Constantine was not the first emperor to adopt Christianity on a personal basis, but he was the first to impose it on all of his subjects. He is a key figure in the history of Christianity.[69] Unfortunately, his personal history also includes his order to have his son, Crispus, put to death in his early thirties. Shortly before this, Christianity had been declared as the official religion. This troublesome fact of the death of Crispus has been largely ignored in the history of the dominant religion in the world; the implications of this fact will be addressed in the next chapter.

NOTES

1. *See* Sigmund Freud, *The Standard Edition of the Complete Psychological Works*, 24 volumes (London: Hogarth Press, 1953–1966).
2. The first indication of a use of the story of Oedipus is in Sigmund Freud, *The Interpretation of Dreams* (London: Hogarth Press, 1900).
3. The first use of the term Oedipus Complex was in a minor article that appeared in 1910; *see* Sigmund Freud, 'A Special Type of Choice of Object Made by Men', in *The Standard Edition of the Complete Psychological Works*, Vol. 11. The first fuller explanation of the term appeared seven years later in Freud, *Introductory Letters on Psycho-Analysis* (London: Hogarth Press, 1917).
4. On juvenile delinquency, *see* Kate Friedlander, *The Psychoanalytical Approach to Juvenile Delinquency* (London: Routledge and Kegan Paul, 1951); *see also* Franz Alexander and Hugo Staub, *The Criminal, the Judge and the Public: A Psychological Analysis* (Glencoe, IL: The Free Press, 1956). On the student revolt, *see* Lewis S. Feuer, *The Conflict of Generations: The Character and Significance of Student Movements* (New York: Basic Books, 1969); and Morton Levitt and Ben Rubenstein, 'The Student Revolt: *Totem and Taboo* Revisited', *Psychiatry*, 34 (1971), p. 160.

5. *See* M. Kallich, A. MacLeish and G. Schoenbaum (eds), *Oedipus: Myth and Drama* (New York: Odyssey Press, 1968).

6. *See*, for instance, the recent work of the person who helped found the group, Robert W. Funk (with the Jesus Seminar), *The Acts of Jesus: The Search for the Authentic Deeds of Jesus* (San Francisco, CA: Harper, 1998).

7. *See*, for instance, Peter Hebblethwaite, *The New Inquisition: Schillebeeckx and Küng* (London: Collins-Fount Paperbacks, 1980). *See also* the relevant books that challenged the official Catholic approach: Edward Schillebeeckx, *Jesus: An Experiment in Christology* (London: Collins, 1979); and Hans Küng, *Infallible? An Enquiry* (London: Collins, 1971).

8. *See* discussion in previous chapters of the Laius Complex and the Rustum Complex.

9. Leon Sheleff, *Generations Apart: Adult Hostility to Youth* (New York: McGraw-Hill, 1981).

10. For detailed discussion, *see* ibid., chapter 3, 'Beyond Incest and Parricide'. For other critiques of some of Freud's classic case studies, *see* Steven Marcus, 'Freud and Dora', *Partisan Review*, 61 (1974), pp. 12–23 and 89–108; Morton Schatzman, *Soul Murder: Persecution in the Family* (New York: Signet, 1974); and Schatzman, 'Paranoia or Persecution: The Case of Schreber', *Family Process*, 10 (1971), p. 171.

11. For an interesting recent analysis of Paul, *see* Daniel Boyarin, *A Radical Jew: Paul and the Politics of Identity* (Berkeley, CA: University of California Press, 1994).

12. Richard Buxton, *Imagining Greece: The Contexts of Mythology* (Cambridge: Cambridge University Press, 1994), chapter 7, 'Family'.

13. Ibid., p. 131.

14. The story of Oedipus' conflict with his two sons appears in the second play of Sophocles' Oedipal trilogy, *Oedipus at Colonnus*; *see* Robert Fitzgerald (trans.) *The Oedipus Cycle* (New York: Harvest Book, 1949), scene 6.

15. *See* comparison of the stories of Medea and Oedipus in A.J. Levin, 'The Oedipus Myth in History and Psychiatry', *Psychiatry*, 2 (1948), p. 287.

16. Ibid. The story of Jephthah appears in Judges, 11:29–40. *See* discussion of Jephthah's sacrifice of his daughter in Virginia Stern Owens, *Daughters of Eve: Women of the Bible Speak to Women of Today* (Colorado Springs, CO: Navpress, 1995). She writes:

> Interestingly, in his previous negotiations with the Ammonites Jephthah had mentioned the god Chemosh, to whom children were routinely sacrificed ... Jephthah's religious understanding of his own deity is too limited and his recognition of Chemosh too substantial ... Did he ignorantly fall back on a practice meant to honor Chemosh ...
>
> In an attempt to find something edifying about the story, commentators have often praised Jephthah's daughter for her obedience, for submitting to her father's misdirected piety. But the whole business was a sordid blot on Israel's history, in contrast to the story of Abraham and Isaac on Mount Moriah. (pp. 108–9)

17. *See* Kirk, *The Nature of Greek Myths* (Harmondsworth: Penguin Books, 1974), pp. 113–18.

18. Buxton, *Imagining Greece*, p. 131.

19. Ibid.

20. Donald Hall, 'My Son, My Executioner', in *The Alligator Bride* (New York: Harper and Row, 1969), p. 12.

21. *See* Edith Hamilton, *Mythology* (New York: Mentor, 1971), p. 257.

22. Buxton, *Imagining Greece*, p. 132.

23. Ibid., p. 133

24. Ibid., p. 140.

25. As described in Luke, 1:35, 'The Holy Ghost shall come upon thee, and the power of the Highest shall overshadow thee; therefore also that holy thing which shall be born of thee shall be called the Son of God.' In Matthew 1:20 the description is based on a dream by Joseph in which an angel says to him, 'Joseph, thou son of David, fear not to take unto thee Mary thy wife; for that which is conceived in her is of the Holy Ghost.'

26. However, there are hints of such a relationship in the story of Samson's birth. Over several paragraphs, the Bible describes 'a certain man of Zorah ... whose name was Manoah; and his wife was barren and bore not', and two visits of an angel to them, who brought assurance that she would conceive and bear a son. After the first visit, when this assurance is given, Manoah entreats God:

> 'O Lord, I pray Thee, Let the man of God whom Thou didst send come again unto us, and teach us what we shall do unto the child that shall be born.' And God hearkened to the voice of Manoah; and the angel of God came again unto the woman as she sat in the field; but Manoah her husband was not with her. (Judges, 13:8–9)

27. Klausner, *From Jesus to Paul* (New York: MacGraw-Hill, 1944), p. 96.
28. Ibid.
29. Ibid.
30. Ibid., pp. 97–8.
31. Ibid., p. 103.
32. Ibid., p. 106.
33. Ibid.
34. Ibid., chapter 3, p. 95.
35. Ibid., p. 107.
36. Ibid.
37. Ibid., pp. 107–8.
38. Ibid., pp. 111–12.
39. Ibid., p. 118.
40. For contrasting recent views on this controversial topic, *see* Ian Wilson, *The Blood and the Shroud* (London: Weidenfeld and Nicolson, 1998); W.C. McCrone, *Judgment Day for the Turin Shroud* (Chicago, IL: Microscope Publications, 1996); and Lynn Picknett and Clive Prince, *Turin Shroud: In Whose Image – How Leonardo da Vinci Fooled History* (London: Corgi Books, 2000).
41. Krishna's life was threatened, on his birth, by his uncle (the King), and he was hidden by his parents. George Foot Moore explains that 'his uncle had been informed by an oracle that the eighth son of this pair would kill him, and to avert this fate put his nephews out of the world as fast as they came into it', *History of Religions* (New York: Scribner's Sons, 1922), p. 330.
42. It is of interest to note that Buddha, immediately after his Enlightenment, left his home, his wife and son, never to return – raising serious questions as to the price that children have to pay for the spiritual needs of their parents. George Moore, *History of Religion*, writes:

> Immediately after the birth of this son, at the age of 29 Siddharta abandoned his home, wife, and child, and wandered forth, like thousands of others in his day, in search of salvation. Legend has surrounded the great renunciation with a halo of poetry ... the last look at his sleeping wife and child. (p. 282)

43. On biographies, *see*, for instance, Richard Solomon, *Mao's Revolution and the Chinese Political Culture* (Berkeley, CA: University of California Press, 1971).
44. *See* Chapter 2, '*Akedah*', with the critical analysis of the emphasis placed on Abraham's faith and not potential parental harm.
45. *See* discussion in previous chapter. The works in which the term 'Laius Complex' is used include Ian D. Suttie, *The Origins of Love and Hate* (London: Kegan Paul, Trench, Trubner, 1935); George Devereux, 'Why Oedipus Killed Laius?', *International Journal of Psychoanalysis*, 34 (1953), p. 1; Erich Wellisch, *Isaac and Oedipus: A Study in Biblical Psychology of the Sacrifice of Isaac – the Akedah* (London: Routledge and Kegan Paul, 1954); Thomas S. Vernon, 'The Laius Complex', *The Humanist*, 32 (1972), p. 27. *See* discussion in Note, 'More on the Laius Complex,' *Journal of Individual Psychology*, 29 (1973), p. 88. All of these suggestions were made independently of each other, and none of the later writers seem to be aware of the earlier works.
46. *See*, especially, Sheleff, *Generations Apart*, chapter 2, 'The Myths of Generational Conflict', and chapter 4, 'Fictional Worlds of Childhood'.

47. Ibid., pp. 106–8. For a typical Freudian analysis, see Ernest Jones, *Hamlet and Oedipus* (Garden City, NY. Doublday Anchor, 1954).

48. Sheleff, *Generations Apart*, pp. 99–106. *See also* Sigmund Freud, 'Dostoevsky and Parricide' (1928) in vol. 21 of *Standard Edition of Complete Psychological Works* (London: Hogarth Press, 1953–1966).

49. Ibid., pp. 111–15. *See also* Michael Carronges, *Kafka Versus Kafka* (The University of Alabama Press, 1968); and Frederick J. Hoffman, 'Escape from Father in Angel Flores' (eds), *The Kafka Problem* (New York: New Directions, 1946).

50. Thomas Hughes, *Tom Brown's Schooldays* (1857); *see* discussion in John R. de Symons Honey, *Tom Brown's Universe: The Development of the Victorian Public School* (London: Millington, 1977), chapter 1, 'The Conception of the School in Arnold and in the First New Victorian Public Schools'.

51. Lionel Trilling, *Matthew Arnold* (New York: Meridian Books, 1955), p. 124.

52. William A. Madden, *Matthew Arnold: A Study of the Aesthetic Temperament in Victorian England* (Bloomington, IN: Indiana University Press, 1967), p. 27.

53. Ibid., p. 32.

54. A Dwight Culler, *Imaginative Reason: The Poetry of Matthew Arnold* (New Haven, CT: Yale University Press, 1966).

55. Ibid., p. 229.

56. Ibid.

57. Bruce Mazlish, *James and John Stuart Mill: Father and Son in the Nineteenth Century* (New York: Basic Books, 1975), p. 33.

58. John Yohannan, *A Treasury of Asian Literature* (New York: Mentor, 1956), p. 108.

59. William E. Buckler, *On the Poetry of Matthew Arnold: Essays in Critical Reconstruction* (New York: New York University Press, 1982).

60. Ibid., p. 153.

61. Ibid.

62. Ibid., p. 154.

63. Ibid., pp. 153–4.

64. David G. Riede, *Matthew Arnold and the Betrayal of Language* (Charlottesville, VI: University Press of Virginia, 1988).

65. Ibid., p. 106.

66. Ibid.

67. Park Honan, *Matthew Arnold: A Life* (London: Weidenfeld and Nicolson, 1981), p. 1.

68. *See* Sheleff, *Generations Apart*, chapter 1, 'Who Speaks for the Young?'.

69. A recent book, written by a Christian, and documenting historical examples of official anti-Semitism by the Church, uses the name of Constantine in its title: *see* James Carroll, *Constantine's Sword: The Church and the Jews, A History* (New York: Houghton Mifflin, 2001).

7

Constantine

In his broad and comprehensive study of the impact of Christianity on the Graeco–Roman world, *Christianity and Classical Culture,* Charles Cochrane concludes his chapter on Constantine with the intriguing statement that, 'He is perhaps unique as the one human being to have enjoyed the distinction of being deified as a pagan god, while, at the same time, he was popularly venerated as a Christian saint.'[1]

Whatever success Christianity might have had as a persecuted religion attempting to prosclytize by the power of its ethical message, the charisma of its founder, the persuasion of its theological doctrines, and its promise of future rewards in the Hereafter, a basic historical fact is that its ultimate success was assured the moment Constantine the Great declared it to be the State Religion. From this moment onwards, the full authority of the State was placed at the disposal of the Church – from a struggling movement, competing with rival religions, some pagan, some mystery, some similar, it became a dominant force that grew and thrived, despite the future disasters that befell the very empire under whose protective aegis it had been placed.

Christianity was made the State Religion by the Council of Nicaea[2] almost exactly three hundred years after Jesus began his ministry. A year later, in 326, Constantine had his son, Crispus, put to death on what many considered to be a trumped up accusation of treasonable activity against the empire.

Cochrane describes briefly what happened, putting it within the historical/mythical context of Rome's foundation (where, in its early days, another leader, Brutus, had also killed his son)[3] and the religious context of the Old Testament (the *Akedah*). He writes:

> Absence of any real evidence connected with the trial and execution of the young prince, coupled with vague hints thrown out by the ecclesiastical historians of a sordid palace intrigue in which the Empress Fausta (Crispus' stepmother) was cast for the role of Potiphar's wife, lends support to the suggestion that the true motive of the murder was political. For such an act the Roman

annals afforded a precedent in the myth of Brutus, who had slain his offspring for the good of the republic; but it is probable that Constantine, whose point of view was becoming more and more Hebraic, conceived of himself rather as an Abraham, prepared to sacrifice his first-born to the glory of God.[4]

Cochrane is probably correct that no intrigue with tempting sexual overtones was involved (such as the biblical incident between Potiphar's wife and Joseph),[5] but he may not be quite so accurate in attributing the imposition of an ultimate penalty on his son to the other factors mentioned.

Far more likely is a personal factor – the emperor's envy of the very success of Crispus as a loyal lieutenant in Constantine's struggle against his rival, Licinius. Cochrane notes the son's military prowess in a short comment, 'The easy defeat of Licinius was followed, within two years, by the destruction of Crispus, the man who, in forcing the Dardanelles, had made that defeat possible.'[6] However, a far more authoritative statement as to Crispus' capacity and loyalty may be gleaned from a contemporary account, one of the first comprehensive histories of the Church, written by Bishop Eusebius.[7] In the final page of this work, he writes, under the sub-title of 'Conclusion':

> Thus was Licinius cast down prostrate. But Constantine the most mighty Victor, resplendent with every virtue that godliness bestows, together with his son Crispus, an Emperor most dear to God in all respects like unto his father, recovered the East that belonged to them, and formed the Roman Empire as in the days of old, into a single united whole.[8]

In the appendix to Eusebius' work, prepared for a modern audience by the editors, the following comment appears: '*Crispus:* The eldest son of Constantine, who had been made Caesar in 317. He was in command of the navy, and won a notable victory over Amandus, Licinius' admiral, in the Hellespont.'[9] Eusebius' concluding comments, at the end of his book, exclaim proudly, 'Thus verily, when all tyranny had been purged away, the kingdom that belonged to them was preserved steadfast and undisputed for Constantine and his sons alone.'[10] These words were written probably about a year before Crispus was executed, since Licinius was defeated in September 324, while Crispus was killed in 326.[11]

Eusebius' description of the unison between Constantine and Crispus, between father and son, can be considered a reliable reflection of reality, for he knew Constantine personally and apparently had a close friendship with him. What happened then, in the short time to disrupt this positive familial relationship, to undermine the sanguine hopes for the future empire under Constantine and his sons? A very real possibility is that Constantine was motivated by fears of the popularity of his son, especially given his military successes. Cochrane's suggestion is that the *Akedah* served as a model because of his increasing Hebraic nature: like Abraham, he was prepared to sacrifice his son. However, an alternative explanation seems far more likely. Not the *Akedah*, but the Crucifixion.

Constantine – in Cochrane's own definition, part 'pagan god', part 'Christian saint'[12] – was no less likely to be swayed by the message embodied in the Crucifixion, of a benevolent God willing to sacrifice his son on behalf of humanity, especially given his own status within paganism, as a god. The juxtaposition between the official declaration of Christianity as a state religion in 325 (a year after the defeat of Licinius) and the execution of Crispus in 326, a year later, must surely allow for a serious assessment of this contention. As is known, Constantine had made a personal decision to convert to Christianity about a decade before, but basically continued to live, as did many of his contemporaries, in two religious worlds; in fact, he was only baptized shortly before his death in 337.

In family terms, far more is known of his mother, Helena. It was she who made a pilgrimage to the Holy Land, and it has been claimed that on her visit to Jerusalem, she found part of the Cross on which Jesus had been crucified and brought it back to Rome.[13] In any event, as Cochrane notes:

> On the occasion of Constantine's twentieth anniversary the magnificent Church of the Holy Sepulchre was dedicated at Jerusalem with elaborate pomp and ceremony; at the same time Jews who tried to rebuild the Temple had their ears cut off and were flogged to death by the public executioner.[14]

Within the framework of this book, which attempts to understand the familial background to relations between Judaism and Christianity, the execution of the son of the Emperor, who declared Christianity the State Religion, obviously requires further, deeper analysis. Cochrane's surmise as to the influence of the *Akedah* on this action is also revealing, for a number of reasons.

First, it obviously totally ignores the fact that Isaac was, in the end, not killed. Second, it fails even to provide the slightest hint that an emperor, emerging from a pagan religion that afforded many emperors divine status (with temples in their honor), might very conceivably relate to the central theme of the monotheistic religion that he had just adopted in terms of the sacrifice that the God in whom he now believed had made of his son on behalf of humanity.

I acknowledge that the essential point that I am making is not easily amenable to definitive proof, especially given the centuries that have elapsed since then. But the theoretical possibility exists. Let me repeat the basic facts. An all-powerful emperor, considered by his pagan citizens to have some degree of divinity, decides to become a Christian on the basis of a personal decision. Some ten years later, he ends almost 300 years of persecution of that religion by formally declaring it to be the State Religion: an action that he takes a year after the significant defeat of his rival (himself a committed pagan) – a victory gained with the substantial support of his eldest son, whom he then puts to death a year later. This is what would be considered, in legal parlance, circumstantial evidence, but of a particularly strong nature. There are, of course, far-reaching implications for the thesis; namely that the success of Christianity was ensured by the official decision of a politically powerful figure who re-enacted a central theme of the religion – the sacrifice of the son of a divine being.

In order to appreciate the personal impact of Christianity on the political and military happenings of that time, it is instructive to note the manner in which Eusebius, Church historian and Constantine's friend, described what he defines (in a sub-title) as 'The Madness of Licinius'. He opens this section by stating that:

> Such then were the gifts that the divine and heavenly grace of our Saviour bestowed upon us by his appearing, and such was the abundance of good things that the peace which came to us procured for all mankind.[15]

He then goes on to describe the ingratitude of Licinius toward Constantine, who had made him joint-emperor and arranged for him to marry his sister. Licinius was, according to Eusebius, '... daily contriving all kinds of devices against his superior, and inventing all manner of plans to reward his benefactor with evil'.[16] However, these plans proved futile, as:

> God proved to be Constantine's Friend and Protector and Guardian, who brought to light the plots that were devised secretly and in darkness, and confounded them ... our Emperor, most dear to God, escaped the plots of this ill-famed master of intrigue.[17]

Eusebius then places the conflict in basically religious terms: of the pagan, Licinius, against the Christian, Constantine; the former 'was already hastening to battle also against the God of the universe, whom, as he knew, Constantine worshipped'.[18] Finally Licinius, 'turned aside from the path of sound reason, and becoming altogether mad, decided to make war on God Himself, as the Protector of Constantine'.[19]

Eusebius describes the actions that Licinius took against churches and bishops, and his initial successes in the war that he had initiated. Indeed, he claims that Licinius:

> ...had power to accomplish his purpose, and there was nothing to hinder him carrying it into effect, had not God, the Champion of the souls that are His own ... caused to shine forth ... out of deep darkness and most murky night, a great luminary and saviour of them all, leading thither *with a lofty arm his servant* Constantine.[20]

(The words in italics, as in the original, have footnote references to two verses in Exodus from which these phrases are taken.)[21] The final development is then described by Eusebius:

> Wherefore, mingling a hatred of evil with a love of goodness, the defender of the good went forth, with that most humane Emperor, his son Crispus, stretching out the right hand of salvation to all who were perishing. Then, inasmuch as they had God the universal King and Son of God, the Saviour of all, as their Guide and Ally, the father and son both together divided their battle array against the haters of God on all sides and easily won the victory; for everything in the encounter was made smooth for them by God according to His purpose.[22]

A year later, shortly after the book itself was published, with its idyllic account of family bonding, Crispus was dead. To what extent was the symbol of the Cross, with the message contained in the act of crucifixion, appealing to a pagan turned Christian, to a worldly emperor who bore a semblance of divinity from his pagan past?

Some idea of the degree of syncretism that was involved in this religious transformation may be gleaned from a decisive action taken by Constantine in a rather marginal sphere, but whose consequences are still with us today. Several years prior to the official declaration of Christianity as the State Religion, Constantine enacted a law that is seen by Cochrane as having direct effect on subsequent developments. Early in his reign, an edict was passed, known as the Edict of Milan, which basically allowed greater religious freedom for everybody, including Christians – in some respects similar to the guarantees of freedom of religion recognized in modern constitutions. As described by Cochrane, 'Toleration, or rather complete religious neutrality, was embraced, not merely as a political expedient, but as a fundamental principle of public law ... Thus envisaged, the Edict of Milan constitutes a milestone in the history of human relationships.'[23]

Nevertheless, in 321, Constantine enacted a Lord's Day Act, marking the very day that commemorated the resurrection of Jesus as a holiday (holy day). After noting this fact, Cochrane states that:

> It became apparent that the emperor was becoming deeply involved in a line of policy which was in flagrant contradiction to the spirit of official neutrality embodied in the Edict of Milan. This policy was presently to give rise to a second great crisis of his career, the break with Licinius and the subsequent destruction of Crispus, his eldest son. For, despite the evidence (contained on coins and inscriptions) of a desire to reassure his pagan subjects, despite his retention of pagan titles and of the traditional hocus-pocus of public divination, it was increasingly evident that the divorce between religion and politics contemplated in the Edict could hardly be maintained. In other words, Constantine's personal religion was rapidly becoming the religion of state.[24]

Throughout his life, Constantine was apparently unable to fully resolve the conflicting pressures emanating from the paganism he had grown up with and from which he derived so much honor from his subjects, because of its divine expressions, and the Christianity that he had discovered and accepted in a manner reminiscent of Paul's conversion (seeing a cross in the sky on the eve of a battle that he won decisively the next day).[25]

This continuing ambivalence is reflected in the enactment of the Lord's Day Act. In modern European languages, some use the term the Lord's Day (for example, Domingo, in Spanish); while others, as in English, use the term Sunday (a reference to the Sun god). This day of rest, now standardized throughout the western world, and even beyond that, is no longer based on the culmination of six days of work (as set out in Genesis), but precedence is given to the day on which Jesus rose from the dead – hence 'the Lord's day'. Yet languages, such as English, that refer to this day of rest as Sunday, reflect the ambiguity that existed way back in Roman times.

The complications involved in the nomenclature, and the religious background to this determination, are laid out in a book dealing specifically with the overlap of 'Greek Myths and Christian Mystery'.[26] The author, Hugo Rahner, a Catholic priest (whose book contains, on the title page, the imprimatur of the Church that it is 'free from doctrinal or moral error'), discusses the manner in which Christianity changed the day of rest from the Jewish Sabbath to the day on which the Resurrection took place, necessitating also a change in its name. As he notes:

> This change really marks the point at which the young Church severed itself from its native Jewish soil ... The day following the sabbath had been turned into the Lord's day, and on that day the primitive community celebrates the 'Lord's supper'

the intention being, 'to give cultic expression'[27] to 'the belief in the Resurrection and the acceptance of the Eucharist as a feast commemorating to the end of time the death and glorification of the Lord'.[28]

However, Rahner explains that in the century before Jesus, a custom had arisen of naming the days of the week after the seven planets:

> A custom that may have originated in Chaldean and Egyptian astrology ... Under the dictates of this custom the first day after the Jewish sabbath was made into ... day of the sun, and it may well be here that we should see the first encounter between Christianity and a form of the Hellenistic sun-cult. The members of the early Church must have observed that Christ had risen from the dead on the day sacred to Helios, the second day of the planetary week which began with Saturn. Their great day, therefore, the day on which they solemnized the mysteries of the resurrection and the *eurichrista*, was not the sabbath of the Jews nor the day of Saturn which began the pagan week, but the day of Helios.[29]

From this basis, Rahner goes on to describe the close association between the idea of the ascension of Jesus from the grave and the idea of the rising sun. 'Thus,' he explains, 'the Christians had begun to think of Christ rising under the figure of the rising sun and of his death under that of a sunset – to be followed of course by the sunrise of his glory.'[30] Rahner notes the great significance attached to the determination of both the day to be declared the weekly day of rest and the name to be given to it. According to him:

> Sunday is at one and the same time regarded from two points of view, that of the first of the six biblical days of creation and that of its Greek significance as the day of Helios, and in both aspects is

already perceived something of the character that it was ultimately to possess for the Christian. It is both 'Sun' day and creation day because it is the day of Christ's resurrection.[31]

Furthermore, he quotes Pliny as commenting that:

> On that day the Christians turned in prayer to the rising sun as a symbol of Christ arising from the dead ... so unusual was the Christian worship on the day of Helios to the pagan way of thinking that they regarded the Christians as a species of sun-worshippers.[32]

(Rahner denies this aspect and has his own interpretation of the connection with the various cults as related to sun-worship.[33])

If pagan outsiders were drawing these kind of conclusions as to the nature of Christian worship and belief, it was rather inevitable that the Church leaders themselves would be concerned at the manner in which their presumably monotheistic doctrine was being misinterpreted by their pagan neighbors. The question becomes who was at fault?: the pagans for superimposing their ideas on the Christians, or the latter for being affected by the former? In modern times, most European languages still retain some relics of the original intertwining of a biblical seven-day week with the terminology of pagan myths – for example, all the days of the week in the English language have pagan roots.

Rahner discusses this dilemma, of the mystery in the connection between a day marked as being that of the sun (or sun god) also being the very day on which Jesus arose. He writes that:

> It is true that Christians never quite lost the feeling that it would be more truly Christian to speak of 'the Lord's day' ... yet so attached had the faithful grown to the idea of a mysterious secret connexion between the Lord's day and the sun that they were less inclined to depart from what was becoming accepted practice in the case of Sunday than in that of any other day of the week. Further, there is evidence to show that the Romans themselves had begun to count Sunday and not Saturday as the first day of the week, and this seems to have happened, not as a result of Christian influence, but of the growing spread of sun-worship in the late Roman empire.[34]

This excursus into the background of the naming and meaning of Sunday leads to the following extremely relevant statement by Rahner that:

This would seem to explain why Constantine himself when giving orders for the celebration of the Lord's day among the people and in the army, expressly refers to it as 'Sunday' in his edicts. Eusebius lays some stress on this: 'He instructed his whole army,' he writes, 'to celebrate with zeal the day of the redeemer which was also named after the light and the sun.' It is clear from all this that the after-effects of certain pagan conceptions had lingered on, conceptions according to which Sunday was regarded as a day of light and good fortune.[35]

The outcome of all of this is that a recurring event, aimed not at commemorating God's creation (as the original idea of the Sabbath, one day in seven) but at commemorating the resurrection of God's son, retains in many languages its pagan antecedent. Rahner concludes that, 'In most countries Sunday has triumphed over its rival'; in fact, he affirms that 'the name of Sunday is the most lasting legacy which astrology left us centuries ago and which lives on even after astrology's demise'.[36] However, despite making this concession, which has obvious far-reaching implications for the purity of religious symbols or the syncretic influence of pagan ideas, Rahner takes consolation from the fact that:

> On the whole it is not such a bad legacy, since for millions of people – though they may not be quite aware of the fact – the day of the Lord is illuminated by a sense of the beneficent physical brightness of the day of the sun.[37]

Not content with this partial apologia for what is really an embarrassing relic of pagan influence in a basic aspect of Christian theology, Rahner then ends on a very personal basis by lamely suggesting that, '… this is only so, because the early Church gave new content to this day of Helios by filling it with her own mystery of the resurrection'.[38] In the Hebrew language, the reference to the days of the week is based simply on their numerical order: the first day, the second day, *yom rishon, yom sheini,* etc.; or sometimes they are referred to in their alphabetical order of *yom aleph, yom beth,* etc. The single exception is the seventh day, which is always referred to as Shabat – the Sabbath – and which starts at sundown on Friday evening to fit with the biblical description of 'it was evening, it was morning'.[39]

However, the importance of this excursus into a seemingly marginal issue – but one which is obviously linked to deep symbolic messages – of the cyclical pattern of the passing of the days is not the personal thoughts of Rahner, or the meaning in the modern world of the word Sunday, or my skeptical response to it, but the personal considerations of Constantine, and the clear ambivalence that is manifested in his behavior. On the one hand, he violates the role of neutrality offered by the Edict of Milan to lay down legislation enforcing 'celebration of the Lord's day', but then, on the other hand, 'expressly refers to it as "Sunday"'.[40] Through the prism of this ambiguity, it is possible to understand the quandaries that constantly beset him, as he slowly divested himself of his pagan beliefs and increasingly adopted those of the religion to which he had been converted, though apparently not fully so, as he had not undergone baptism. In any event, he apparently constantly vacillated between the attractions of both. Pagan religion certainly offered clear inducements – for example, in the deification of an earthly ruler, in the temples dedicated to his honor, in the religious ceremonies lauding his achievements.

Had Constantine decided to call Sunday 'the Lord's Day', the possibility would have existed of making a major clean break from paganism, just as the change of the day of rest from the last day of the week – the Jewish Sabbath – to the first day of the week (the resurrection of Jesus) was, as noted, a significant break from the Jewish religion. Yet it did not happen: for despite Constantine's tremendous practical contribution to Christianity's success, and despite the fact that much of the conflict with Licinius revolved around the latter's paganism, it seems clear that he never fully resolved the opposing tendencies. This may be true of many people moving from one religion to another, and in some cultures it is allowed: Japan, for instance, is a notable example, where belief in both Shintoism and Buddhism is considered an acceptable situation; and in the rest of the modern world, with a greater degree of intermarriage, many couples are trying their own solutions to bi-religious families – for instance, Jewish and Christian couples celebrating Christmas and Chanukah, Easter and Passover, despite the obvious incongruities given the clashing perspectives ensconced in these festivals.[41]

However, Constantine was not a mere individual. Politically, he was an omnipotent emperor; religiously, he was, as noted at the beginning of this chapter, both a 'pagan god' and a 'Christian saint'. There can be little doubt that these dual influences affected his policy-making in the secular world. The question inevitably arises as to whether it had an impact on his decision to justify the execution of his son? Did a powerful emperor, with the status of a pagan god, use the message conveyed by the Crucifixion to perform an act not unknown in the general culture of that time, and apply to it, within the perspective afforded by his new religion, the justification of benefiting humanity, of benefiting the body politic, of benefiting the social order? Was this act, with a possible religious justification, an example of *imitato dei*? Was the official declaration of Christianity as a state religion a deliberate preparation for the trial and execution of his son? Alternatively, did the inspiration for it emerge only subsequently?

Little is known of Crispus, and the full background to his trial and death (if, indeed, there was a trial – he may even have been murdered). It is not even known in what manner the execution was performed – was it a crucifixion? I fully realize that there may be no clear answers to these questions. I fully realize that the questions themselves may be distasteful to some Christians. But I claim that there is a certain logic in the chronology of the events: Constantine's personal conversion (in the year 313); the tolerance of Christianity recognized by the Edict of Milan (313); the recognition of Crispus' status as a ruler (317); the Lord's Day Act (321); the defeat of Licinius (324); the official recognition of Christianity through the Edict of Nicaea (325); and the execution of Crispus (326).

There may be a simple explanation for these developments, based purely on chance. On the other hand, there may be a causative, cumulative connection among them: one that may be understood within the theoretical concept of a Rustum Complex (explaining Constantine's attitude and actions toward his son) and an empirical context of a belief in the fact and the meaning of the Crucifixion. In sum, the basis for a key historical event – the recognition of Christianity – may be related to an emotional personal connection made between the crucifixion of Christ and the fate of Crispus.

It may be claimed that such an interpretation does injustice not only to Christianity (for those who prefer its success to be linked to the beauty of its doctrine) but also to Constantine. Why utilize this one act of killing his son in order to deprecate or denigrate his larger achievement, of saving Christianity from persecution and contributing to the spread of monotheism throughout his empire? After all, Constantine is not the only leader to bear the historic responsibility for the death of his son; and he is not the only political/religious personality to have done so (as the examples of Jephthah and his daughter, or King David and his son Absalom, show).[42] Furthermore, there is always the possibility that Crispus had indeed been involved in a conspiratorial plan to overthrow his father, even relying on the very popularity that his military successes had enabled him to garner.

Fairness demands perhaps conceding the possibility that Constantine had acted out of a genuine desire to protect the state from political intrigue, and had even overcome any nepotistic inclinations to intervene on behalf of his son to avoid the meting out of the full measure of justice for his treasonable activities. It may even be assumed that a truly religious person, having recently converted to a monotheistic faith, would be more activated by the positive sentiments so eloquently expressed in the Sermon on the Mount than be motivated by the filial figure on the Cross as a temptation to commit murder.

However, while little is known of Crispus (and in later editions of his history, Eusebius deleted most of the references that had been included in the first edition, which was published when he was still alive), much is known of Constantine, his words and his works. Some of it from the adulatory works of Eusebius, others from full-scale biographies or references to him in histories. A modern, broad historical study of Asia Minor, written with a certain degree of skepticism, and at times even tongue-in-cheek cynicism, provides some fascinating insights into Constantine's character. Herbert Muller summarizes the approaches of modern historians who:

> ... are still debating the motives of Constantine the Great, the measure of his greatness, and the consequences of his handiwork. Chiefly they agree that the 'Thirteenth Apostle' was no saint, and that his legacy included a permanent confusion of the things that are Caesar's and the things that are God's. Still, his adoption of Christianity was epoch-making. In historical importance Constantine was indeed the Peer of the Apostles; so one must try to recover him from the pious fog in which Eusebius shrouded him.[43]

According to Muller, he was probably far more successful as a military commander than as a political leader, remarking that, initially, he was 'served well enough by his early patrons – Mars, Hercules, Jupiter, and especially the "Unconquered Sun"', and then 'became unconquerable when he shifted to Christ, before a battle outside Rome'.[44] As for the vision which he had of the Cross just prior to this battle, Muller concedes that it may well be authentic not because of anything unique, but because:

> His vision of the Cross was, after all, a common kind of experience; the gods habitually gave men cues in dreams and visions; and his vision had proved a true omen – he had won the battle. Thereafter his edicts and his official behavior testified to his gratitude.[45]

Muller justifies his casual approach to this momentous phenomenon in Constantine's life, with its subsequent far-reaching results, by stating simply that, 'There was always something of the pagan in Constantine.'

He then goes on to describe pithily the key facts of his religious faith:

> As a good Roman and a conscientious emperor, he would not
> simply scrap and scorn the faiths of his fathers; as an unsophisti-
> cated soldier he would naturally tend to confuse the 'Unconquered
> Sun' with his new God, and have difficulty grasping the nice
> theological distinctions about the nature of the Godhead. For he
> had not been instructed and converted by a missionary – God
> himself had given him a sufficient sign, without at once telling him
> that he was a jealous God who would resent any appearance of
> respect for the gods. Hence it is easy to point out lapses in the
> Christian emperor. He retained the title of Pontifex Maximas; he
> continued to issue coins in honor of his former patrons, especially
> Sol Invictus; in a decree making Sunday a day of rest he referred to
> it as 'the venerable day of the Sun' instead of the Lord's day; etc. It
> is still easier to demolish his claims to sainthood. He shocked his
> contemporaries by putting Lucinius to death after accepting his
> surrender and promising to spare his life. He embarrassed even his
> Christian eulogists by arranging for the murder of his wife Fausta
> and his son Crispus; though they were presumably guilty of some
> sin or crime. Eusebius was careful to delete all mention of them in
> the last edition of his *Church History*.[46]

In the end, Muller sums up that he was probably no worse than
others of his time, and that, in general, 'he was basically an earnest, well-
intentioned man'.[47] Yet, Muller himself deals only casually and *en
passant* with a basic fact: Constantine's filicidal action against Crispus,
and the murder of his wife, the step-mother of Crispus, after accepting
a presumption of guilt for an unspecified act. Quite possibly there was a
massive injustice perpetrated upon them; the full truth is beyond our
purview today. But it still leaves the fact of filicide, something which has
caused, according to Muller, embarrassment for Christian eulogists,
although the connection with the founder of their religion does not seem
to have occurred to them; for non-Christians, the parallels seemed, even
then, apparent. One person who does seem at least to have noticed the
importance of a filicidal act is one of Constantine's successors, Julian
(known by the appellation of 'the Apostate,' since he wanted the Roman
Empire to revert to paganism). As pointed out by T.G. Elliot in his book
on *The Christianity of Constantine the Great*, 'Julian the Apostate said
that Constantine had gone to Jesus to get forgiveness for murders of
Crispus and Fausta';[48] but Julian does not seem to have looked beyond
Constantine's need for attaining pardon, or argued the similarity

between the fate of his son and that of Jesus himself. According to Muller, it was suggested that there were pagans who, after the execution, 'represented the emperor as conscience-stricken, and as finding that the only way to wash away this sin, as they portrayed it, was to become a Christian and be baptized'.[49]

Recently, James Carroll has attempted to provide an explanation for the filicidal act by linking the personal feelings of Constantine with both the theological framework of Christianity and modern social science in the form of a Freudian perspective.[50] His analysis is of major importance, since it is an honest attempt by a Christian writer to empathize with the Jewish predicament. Beyond its scholarly depth, it also contains frank personal reflections of the author's genuine efforts to contribute to a *rapprochement* between the two monotheistic religions. Carroll's reference to the fate of Crispus, however, sadly reveals the depth of the chasm that still exists between them, certainly from the perspective of modern understanding and interpretation in relation to the meaning and message of the *Akedah*, with its interconnection with the Crucifixion.

Referring to the execution of Crispus, Carroll writes:

> A father who slays his son in righteousness ... one needn't be a Freudian to sense the new power that the myth of the Cross would have had over him. Evoking the binding of Isaac as it does, the story of the all-powerful father forced to put, at that moment, to death his son – but for a redemptive purpose – must have obsessed the emperor. If God can kill his son, so can God's co-regent. Not that either need be left with a feeling of triumph. So, of course, the emotional appeal to the crucifixion would have outweighed the glories of the Resurrection.[51]

The problematics of this short statement is that after the binding of Isaac, there was no consummation of an execution. Whereas Abraham may indeed have been 'forced' to arrive at the binding, no such obligation attached to Constantine, who had his son executed for purely secular reasons – with no righteousness or redemption involved, except inasmuch as he wished to personally re-enact God's sacrifice of His son. The idea of there being a co-regent with God is anathema to Judaism. Of course, it is Constantine's own conception being described, and not that of official Christianity. But Constantine is no minor figure in Christian history. Here, Carroll and I are in agreement as to his crucial role – hence the very title of his book, *Constantine's Sword*. And in the final sentence quoted – of the preference and precedence given to the 'emotional appeal of the Crucifixion' over the 'glories of the

Resurrection', this is precisely part of my argument, not just for a prominent historical figure, but for humanity at large.

As for the Freudian reference, one presumes that the intent is to refer to the Oedipus Complex, but, of course, there is nothing Oedipal in a filicidal act, and Carroll is not the first to make this error. Curiously, immediately before the quotation, Carroll does refer, in clear Oedipal terms, to the closeness between Constantine and his mother, Helena, who was peripherally involved in the palace intrigues leading to the deaths of Constantine's son and his wife. The Oedipal aspect in this context has nothing to do with the father–son relationship (of antagonism), but with the mother–son relationship (of untoward affection). Carroll writes that, after the deaths of these two family members, 'Helena assumed her sole place at her son's side';[52] here, of course, is a replica of Oedipus reigning with Jocasta, his mother, as queen.

Finally, reverting to Muller's work, there are two aspects of Constantine's religion that he discusses – his deathbed baptism and his faith. As for the former, he notes that the practice of deferring the baptism till the end of one's life seems to have been quite common, since there was then less likelihood of subsequent sins that could lead to damnation.[53] In terms of Constantine's faith, Muller explains:

> The all-important matter for the historian is the nature of Constantine's faith ... For him Christianity was a success religion. The God he habitually appealed to was a God of power – the 'Mighty One,' the 'Greatest God' – who promised his faithful servants victory on earth.

In sum, '... he regarded Christianity as a State cult, and was primarily concerned with the City of Earth, not with Augustine's City of God'.[54]

Beyond his own personal faith, he was called upon to resolve one of the early great controversies in the Church concerning the key factor of the respective status of the components of the Holy Trinity, a controversy stimulated by Arius, who 'preached the common-sense, scripturally sound, but theologically unsatisfying view that the Son was lesser than the Father who sent him'.[55] This controversy was eventually settled by the Edict of Nicaea, at the same time that Christianity was made the State Religion. Constantine not only convened this Council, but he also took an active part in its proceedings and influenced its final decision to reject Arianism: 'he forced through an agreement on a creed declaring that Jesus was of one essence with the Father, and anathematizing all who declared otherwise'.[56]

In intervening in this theological issue, Constantine was inevitably opening the way for State control of personal belief. This undermined the achievement of the earlier Edict of Milan, which had borne the promise of religious freedom for Christians and for Jews *vis-à-vis* the stronger pagan religions. In the future, his successors were to strictly enforce Christianity. The result was that 'persecution of pagans became more rigorous and systematic than any that Christians had ever suffered from, except briefly under Diocletian'.[57] In time, of course, similar controls were to be imposed on heretic Christians and Jews.

One final comment about Constantine. Beyond his contribution to the success of Christianity, the material monument to his power was the beautiful city, sitting astride two continents, that bore his name: Constantinople, today's Istanbul. It was here that one of the most magnificent churches in the world, the Haghia Sophia, was erected. This was later transformed into a mosque after the Ottoman Conquest and then, by order of Attaturk, made into a museum in the 1930s, which it remains to this day, an architectural masterpiece. His city was to be the New Rome, 'a genuinely Christian center'. Yet, 'Here again Constantine's intentions were obscured by some conventional pagan accessories, such as his temples to Tyche and the Mother of the Gods, a colossal statue of Apollo on which he substituted his own head as the Sun God.'[58]

The city itself was officially dedicated by name in the year 330; the foundations for the building of the western wall were laid in 326, the year in which Constantine had his son, Crispus, killed. The wall was built not far from the spot where Crispus had achieved his great victory on behalf of his father just two years earlier.

NOTES

1. Charles Norris Cochrane, *Christianity and Classical Culture: A Study of Thought from Augustus to Augustine* (New York: Oxford University Press, 1957), p. 212.
2. The meeting at Nicaea was the first comprehensive council of the Church; so its decisions were applied throughout the empire.
3. The reference to Brutus is not to the well-known individual involved in the assassination of Julius Caesar, but one of the founding figures of the city of Rome. *See* later reference to him in chapter 9, 'Kirkegaard'.
4. Cochrane, *Christianity and Classical Culture*, p. 207. It has been suggested that Fausta herself induced Constantine to kill Crispus, who was her stepson. However, she herself was also put to death by Constantine. If there was any amorous connection between Fausta and Crispus, then there are also, of course, some Oedipal elements (in the sexual aspect), as well as elements of the Rustum Complex in terms of the filicidal outcome.
5. Genesis, 34:7–20.
6. Cochrane, *Christianity and Classical Culture*, p. 207.
7. Eusebius, Bishop of Caeserea, *The Ecclesiastical History and the Martyrs of Palestine*, 2 Vols (trans. with Introduction and Notes by Hugh Jackson Lawlor and John E.L. Dulton) (London: SPCK, 1954).
8. Ibid., Vol. 1, p. 324.
9. Ibid., Vol. 2, p. 320.

10. Ibid., Vol. 1, pp. 324–5. It should be noted that Constantine had three other sons who, on his death in 337, inherited his kingdom by dividing it up amongst themselves.

11. *See* ibid.,Vol. 2, p. 2, where the translators discuss, in their Introduction, 'The Evolution of the Work'. They write that it:

> ... includes an account of the civil war between Constantine and Licinius. It records the death of the latter emperor and the festivities which followed it. It is clear therefore that the book was not finished till a considerable time after the estrangement between Constantine and Licinius, which took place in September 324. On the other hand, Crispus, the eldest son of Constantine, who was put to death in 326, was still alive when Eusebius wrote; and there is no allusion to the Council of Nicaea (June, 325), which could hardly have been ignored if it had already taken place.... Thus there can be little doubt that it was published at the end of 324 or early in 325.

12. Cochrane, *Christianity and Classical Culture*, p. 212, fn. 1.

13. Other artifacts were also claimed to have been found there, for instance the lance used to spear Jesus and the crown of thorns placed on his head.

14. Cochrane, *Christianity and Classical Culture*, p. 208.

15. Eusebius, *Ecclesiastical History*, Vol. 1, p. 320.

16. Ibid., p. 321.

17. Ibid.

18. Ibid.

19. Ibid.

20. Ibid., p. 323.

21. Exodus, 6:1 and 14:31.

22. Eusebius, *Ecclesiastical History*, Vol. 1, p. 324.

23. Cochrane, *Christianity and Classical Culture*, p. 179.

24. Ibid., p. 207.

25. This battle took place on 28 October 312, near Rome, at the Milvian Bridge (near the Cross in the sky was the inscription 'in hoc signo vinces'). This fact, of course, gives added significance to the very symbol of Christianity.

26. Hugo Rahner, *Greek Myths and Christian Mystery* (London: Burns and Oates, 1963).

27. Ibid., p. 104. As will be discussed in the next chapter, the debate as to the manner in which the date of Easter was to be determined led to the decision to attempt to distance Christianity from Judaism. *See* comment by W.H.C. Frend, *The Rise of Christianity*, discussing the Council of Nicaea, where he states: 'Independence from Judaism lay near to the emperor's heart' (Philadelphia, PA: Fortress Press, 1984). This is discussed in the next chapter.

28. Rahner, *Greek Myths*, p. 103.

29. Ibid., p. 104.

30. Ibid., p. 105.

31. Ibid.

32. Ibid., p. 106.

33. Ibid., at pp. 93–4:

> One thing stands out ... beyond any possibility of error or denial. The result of the Church's encounter with the sun-cult of antiquity was nothing less than the dethronement of Helias. There had never been even a suggestion of compromise. From the very beginning the Church had entered the Hellenic world with the clear and certain knowledge – knowledge that rested on biblical revelation – of a God who created the sun and the stars.

Rahner continues in this vein, but also has to cope with what he calls the 'homecoming of Helios', since there clearly was a degree of syncretism at work. Thus he claims, in discussing both the 'homecoming' and the 'dethronement' of Helios, that:

> The mysticism and symbolism which had been developed in Hellenistic devotion, were referred back to the concrete, historical and visible person of the man Jesus

Christ. But here too the Church is uncompromising and as she begins to take over images, words and ideas from the devotional life of the sun-worshipping Greeks, she interprets them in a manner that only has relevance to the historically clear-cut figure of her founder, Jesus of Nazareth; it is he who from the beginnings of Christian theology is 'the Sun of Righteousness' (Malachi, 4:2), the 'Dayspring from on high' (Luke, 1:78).

34. Ibid., p. 107.
35. Ibid.
36. Ibid., p. 108.
37. Ibid.
38. Ibid.
39. *See* Genesis 1, for this repetitive statement on the completion of each day.
40. Rahner, *Greek Myths*, p. 107.
41. *See* discussion in next two chapters, 'Easter' and 'Passover'.
42. Samuel II, 19:1. When being informed of Absalom's death, King David is mortified at the outcome of the battle and emits a plaintive cry: 'My son Absalom! Oh my son, my son Absalom! If only I had died instead of you! Oh Absalom, my son, my son!'
43. Herbert Muller, *The Loom of History* (New York: Harper and Brothers, 1958), p. 219.
44. Ibid., p. 220.
45. Ibid., p. 221.
46. Ibid., pp. 221–2.
47. Ibid., p. 222.
48. *See* T.G. Elliott, *The Christianity of Constantine the Great* (Scranton, NY: University of Scranton Press, 1996), p. 68.
49. Muller, *The Loom of History*, pp. 232–3.
50. James Carroll, *Constantine's Sword: The Church and the Jews* (Boston, MA: Houghton Mifflin/A Mariner Book, 2001).
51. Ibid., p. 203. Of course, it is true that much rabbinical thought, through the years, has interpreted the Binding of Isaac in similar terms to Carroll's approach. However, a different interpretation of the *Akedah*, based on modern ideas and concepts, does not undermine the essence of Judaism – on the contrary, I believe it enhances it, giving a more positive message through re-interpretation. In contrast, of course, reservations as to the meaning of the Crucifixion serve as a direct challenge to the very basis of Christianity.
52. Ibid., p. 203.
53. Muller, *The Loom of History*, p. 222n2.
54. Ibid., p. 223.
55. Ibid., p. 226.
56. Ibid. There is some evidence that Constantine later moderated his stance on this issue.
57. Ibid., p. 225.
58. Ibid., p. 231.

RELIGIOUS RITUALS

8
Easter

In earlier chapters, it was suggested that much of the writing in the New Testament, which initially consisted of the Four Gospels, attached prime (perhaps even sole) responsibility for the crucifixion of Jesus on the Jews in order to placate the Romans who, at that time, were the dominant power in Palestine and the surrounding area. Any attempt to make an accusation against the representative of the Roman Empire, Pontius Pilate, for his role in Jesus' death would have brought even more disfavor and calamity upon this new religion, for they would be attributing the death of their founder, with all the blame involved, to a leading official of the empire. It was far easier to blame the powerless Jews for insisting on the Crucifixion than to make the Romans the focus of Christian anger at the tragic end of their savior.

In this initial period, this theological approach was of little relevance in regard to the relationship between Jews and Christians. In political terms, the Jews had a far more potent enemy – the Roman Empire. It was this empire that had destroyed the Temple, the focus of their religion. So great was the anguish caused by this event that, despite tolerance by the Romans of the rabbis' efforts to save Judaism (by establishing synagogues and the foundations of a new communal life in lieu of the Temple sacrifices), some six decades later the Jews, with the blessing of the rabbis, attempted to drive out the Romans in a desperate, but futile, military campaign. Indeed, it was this action, and not the destruction of the Temple, that led to the real expulsion of the Jews from Palestine and their dispersion as a homeless people, throughout Europe and Asia, and later even farther afield.[1]

In general, it was the Christians who bore the brunt of Roman religious intolerance and power. However, the negative descriptions of Jewish complicity in Jesus' death took on a totally different complexion the moment that Christianity became recognized as the State Religion. From being a dubious belief system of a marginal group, itself struggling desperately to survive against the vicious policies of the Roman Empire, Christian theology became a political recipe for the persecution of those who were the Christ-killers, the descendants of the priests in the

Sanhedrin court and the public which had gathered at Golgotha to witness the execution. Thus, it was not Christian theology alone that was to be the real basis of Jewish suffering through rampant anti-Semitism, but the formal act of official recognition that was accorded the religion by Constantine.

Negative references to the Jews were interspersed throughout the New Testament. From the moment that they cried out to Pontius Pilate, 'Crucify him, crucify him', the responsibility for Jesus' death rested not only on a small élite group of priests (whose names and brief thumb-nail sketches appear, for instance, in an appendix to Walter Chandler's book on the trial),[2] but on the whole people. Pontius' gesture of possible pardon was rejected by Vox populi, the populace at large. Their descendants, therefore, were to bear the full burden of their ill-calculated decision, the mark of Cain was to be indelibly imprinted on all who remained adamant and obstinate in their continuous rejection of the truth that the Messiah had arrived to redeem mankind, and that he was Jesus Christ, the Son of God, and that they, the Children of Israel, were the betrayers of their Heavenly Father.

The story of the Crucifixion is the centerpiece of the New Testament, more important than the virgin birth (which is not even mentioned by two of the Evangelists), more important than Jesus' baptism, more important than the miracles he performed, the parables associated with his actions, perhaps even than the wisdom and humanity expressed in the Sermon on the Mount. From the Crucifixion came the Cross, the ever-present, widely recognized symbol of Christianity.

One of the two major Christian holidays, Easter, is dedicated to the story of Jesus' suffering on the Cross (his Passion). In Jerusalem to this day, a religious procession re-traces Jesus' steps, carrying the burden of his own Cross, along the Via Dolorosa. In Europe, pageants are performed in various places re-enacting the pathos of the story. In the Phillipines, one of the only basically Christian countries in Asia, a tradition has developed each Easter of young men impaling themselves on a cross to identify with Jesus' suffering, as he himself had suffered for humanity.

Historically, the passions aroused have often been disastrous for Jews. Easter, which overlaps with the Jewish holiday of Passover (with which it is irretrievably inter-connected because of the proximity of the Crucifixion to the Passover's celebration), has often been a trigger for increased acts of anti-Semitism, reaching their peak in the blood-libel that Jews kill a Christian child. According to some, this is done in order to use the blood for the making of Matzhoh, the unleavened bread that is a major culinary feature of the Jewish holiday; according to others, it

is a ritual repetition of the crucifixion of Jesus.[3] Despite the blatant lie
in this libelous story, it has appeared in many different places over the
centuries, ever since the first recorded instance in twelfth-century
Norwich in England.[4]

In his book, *The Foot of Pride* (a phrase taken from the Psalms), sub-
titled *The Pressure of Christendom on the People of Israel for 1900 Years*,
Malcolm Hay devotes a chapter to a succinct discussion of this phenomenon.[5] He ends the chapter, 'The Murderous Lie', with a prescient
quote from Cecil Roth, written in 1934, in whch he maintained that:

> Nazi propaganda in Germany issued periodical warnings to the
> general population to take special care of their children at Passover
> time in view of Jewish ritual requirements, and it would not be
> surprising if semi-official encouragement were to bring about in
> that country, in the near future, a major tragedy reminiscent of the
> Middle Ages at their worst.[6]

In the event, the tragedy was of course greater than any the Jews had
ever experienced in their centuries of victimhood. Furthermore, the
modern situation was *a priori* even worse, for, during the Middle Ages,
there had been Church leaders – particularly some Popes – who had
exerted their authority, even if often in vain, to put an end to the blood-
libel.

Nevertheless, whether with the silent connivance of Church authorities, or in violation of specific commands to desist, 'blood accusations',
according to Hay, 'became so frequent that it is difficult to make a
complete record. The number of human beings who were barbarously
put to death without trial on this grotesque charge will never be
known.'[7] At the same time, little attention has been paid to the obverse
side of the phenomenon – how many children were actually killed, and
who was responsible for these killings? In other words, were these total
fabrications, where Jews were not involved, and where there was even
no victim – no body had been found, no formal declaration of a missing
person had been lodged? Or, alternatively, were these instances where
young children had indeed been killed, but their assailants were never
apprehended and accused, to a large extent because unfounded
suspicions were levelled against the Jews? In the first recorded instance
of a blood-libel, a child had indeed been killed:

> A young boy named William had been found dead in a wood
> outside the town of Norwich. Some months later, Thomas of
> Monmonth accused the Jews of responsibility for the boy's death.

He said they had enticed the boy into a house, tortured him and crucified him.[8]

The story itself, which had been:

> ... concocted by a monk, a converted Jew ... was first put into writing by Thomas of Monmouth, a British monk of the Order of St Benedict, shortly before the preaching of the Second Crusade, in the middle of the twelfth century.[9]

It is of no little importance to stress that this first recorded blood-libel occurred between the First and Second Crusade, at a time when religious passions were inevitably at their highest.

The Christians, at Easter time, would be commemorating the resurrection of the Son of God three days after his crucifixion, which itself took place immediately prior to the onset of Passover. The Jews would be celebrating this latter holiday, which marked their freedom from slavery, as well as their formation into a clear semblance of a nation, as opposed to the more amorphous extended family that they had been until their exodus from Egypt. According to the description in the Bible, their exodus was made in haste, with no time for even preparing bread to take with them because of the lengthy period required for the bread to rise. As a result, one of the marked features of the festival is the eating of unleavened bread, made without yeast, which resembles crackers or wafers.[10] It is this special aspect of the festival that provided part of the rationale for the Christian accusation. The special kind of bread used during the Passover holiday, so it was claimed, required Christian blood.

An accusation of this kind is particularly paradoxical when applied to Jews, as the strict *kosher* rules of Jewish custom include a total ban on any blood in meat that is eaten. This is one of the reasons why the actual slaughter of an animal must be performed by a trained religious person (known as the *shochat*, the slaughterer), who also pronounces a blessing as part of the ceremony (performed today in modern abattoirs). Every effort is made to ensure that all blood is drained from the animal. Indeed, so severe is this ruling that if, on breaking open an egg, a spot of red is discerned, the custom is to throw the whole egg away. (There are, of course, other aspects of control over food, such as separating meat and milk, but these are of no concern here.) In contrast, a key feature of the Christian Eucharist is the partaking of wine which is thought to become the actual blood of Jesus. Similarly, the consuming of the bread or wafer represents the eating of his flesh – not symbolically, but actually.[11]

In a fascinating account of eating habits in late medieval Europe, Caroline Bynum notes how:

> Eating was ... an occasion for union with one's fellows and one's God, a commensality given particular intensity by the prototypical meal, the Eucharist, which seemed to hover in the background of any banquet. Because Jesus had fed the faithful not merely as servant and writer, preparer and multiplier of loaves and fishes, but as the very bread and wine itself, *to eat* was a powerful verb. It meant to consume, to assimilate, to become God. To eat God in the Eucharist was a kind of audacious deification, a becoming of the flesh, that, in its agony, fed and saved the world. Thus, to religious men and women, renunciation of ordinary food prepared the way for consuming (i.e. becoming) Christ, in Eucharist or in mystical union.[12]

How powerful the whole ceremony, as a solemn pageant, could be is described by Bynum in terms of the authoritative power of the clergy and the simple beliefs of their congregants. She writes that:

> In an atmosphere where confession and religious superiors controlled access to the Eucharist and stressed scrupulous awe-filled preparation, recipients naturally approached the elements in a spiritually and psychologically heightened state. When ... the priest, suddenly and to the accompaniment of incense and bells raised on high a thin, shimmering wafer of unleavened bread, embossed with the image of Christ, it is small wonder that the pious sometimes 'saw' Jesus.[13]

Bynum's casual passing reference to the wafer in the Eucharist as being unleavened bread obviously gives added meaning to the perceptions that Christians had of the Jewish festival of Passover at various times. If the wafer of unleavened bread for the Eucharist was, in essence, the body of Jesus, how easy it was to presume that the Jews, when making their own unleavened bread (their *Matzhoh*) for the holiday of Passover, and not believing in the divinity of Jesus or in the mystical capacity of the Eucharist, would – in lieu of their presumed innate incapacity to reach the same closeness to divinity – artificially inject the blood of a ritually killed child to their unleavened bread. A transference of understanding took place. What was an expression of deep religious faith for Christians became the basis for believing that those (the Jews) who lacked the ability to reach the same level of communion with God (through His son) would seek other means of achieving what the adherents of their rival religion accomplished on a regular basis, each time that they participated in the Eucharist. The fact that the Jews totally rejected any use of blood was ignored; it was presumed that a component of the wine that they drank and an ingredient in the *Matzhoh* that they ate was the blood and flesh of a slaughtered Christian child. The libel also ignored the fact that the eating of unleavened bread has no mystical overtones – the bread is not seen as a link with the divine, but as a memory of a historical event, the exodus.

Thus, even remonstrations by Popes and othe Church authorities had only a minor impact. The blood-libel appeared at regular intervals. Even in modern times, it re-emerges, and as noted at the beginning of the chapter, the Nazis did not hesitate to exploit the story for their own propaganda against the Jews. Since, today, it is clear that there never was any foundation for the lie, the question, in historical terms, becomes: what was the kernel of this story, who invented it, who maintained its longevity, who provided the rationalization – and why?

An American medieval historian, Gavin Langmuir, provides a possible answer to these questions.[14] The rationalization was directly related to the very irrationality of the claim as regards Jewish behavior; and this stemmed from a deeper irrationality – namely the central importance in Christianity of the Eucharist for communion with Jesus and his sad fate on the Cross. His thesis is insightful, novel and controversial.

Langmuir argues that, in medieval times, when the all-powerful Church insisted on its theological definition of the ceremony, many people found great difficulty in truly believing in the theory of transubstantiation;[15] but, perhaps out of fear for the consequences, or perhaps out of their own boundless faith, they refused to express these doubts openly. The explanation of the Eucharist seemed not to reflect reality, it seemed to be irrational, and much of Langmuir's book deals with irrational aspects of religious life, attempting to explain some of the background to anti-Semitism.[16] There was, at that stage, in the medieval period that he describes, no alternative Protestant movement (although there were a variety of 'heretical' groups and sects), there was no equivalent of a 'Jesus Seminar', carefully scrutinizing the Bible to divulge errors or misconceptions.[17] Besides which, there was a papal declaration from 1215 (during the period of the Crusades) that obligated belief in the doctrine of transubstantiation. In their subsequent frustration at what would today probably be defined as 'cognitive dissonance',[18] Christians turned on that minority group in their society, who were outside the framework of the Church and were thus not obliged to hold such beliefs;

Jews were beyond the pale and, as such, were spared the need to profess belief in something they did not genuinely believe in, or to regularly participate in a critically important ceremony whose basis they secretly challenged. The Jews thus bore the brunt of Christian cognitive dissonance, leading to compulsive behavior, expressed by an omnipresent and omnipowerful church which, in the early thirteenth century, also formally set in motion the investigative machinery of the Inquisition. In brief, Langmuir claims that:

> The belief that Jesus Christ was physically present in the consecrated bread and wine of the Eucharist had become the object of widespread doubt by the middle of the eleventh century, and the authorities of the Catholic religion responded by modifying the formulation of the belief, but they also prescribed in 1215 that Catholics had to believe it. Since the religious authorities had developed formidable means to repress open dissent by 1215, and since these were strengthened by the organization of the Inquisition starting in 1231, it became very dangerous to express doubts openly.[19]

Immediately before presenting this succinct summary of his thesis, Langmuir lays out the essence of his insight as to the hidden doubts of the ostensible believer, and links it directly to the phenomenon of anti-Semitism. While noting that, even in the social circumstances described, it was possible to 'remain conscious of ... doubts and agonize over them in solitude', nevertheless those who tried to 'avoid awareness of them by inhibiting their capacity for rational thinking ... lapse[d] into irrationality'.[20]

He then argues that, 'of all these reactions to doubt, the most important for a study of anti-Semitism is the one least likely to attract notice in history books: the repression of doubts by individuals who remained adherents of a religion'.[21] The inconsistency of outward belief and inner doubt was liable to lead to irrational behavior because of the emotional torment it might arouse. Thus:

> Many who could not escape awareness of the conflict felt their identity so threatened that they repressed their capacity to think rationally and empirically and projected their own nonrational meaning on realities so strongly that they perceived what they wanted to perceive.[22]

On the one hand, this might lead to outwardly harmless consequences (or even positive outcomes, as seen from a religious perspective), where the belief would actually be intensified, for instance:

> Desiring 'proof' that Christ was indeed physically present in
> Eucharist, some Christians 'saw' what they wanted to see: They
> 'saw' the consecrated wafer turn into flesh or blood; they 'saw' an
> infant on the altar; they 'saw' a child or thirty-year-old man on a
> cross.[23]

On the other hand, these perceptions or imaginings could lead to
negative behavior displayed toward Jews, for instance:

> By the later Middle Ages, after the institution of the feast of Corpus
> Christi in 1264, many also came to believe that Jews – who
> manifestly disbelieved in transubstantiation – tortured consecrated
> wafers in order to harm Christ, and that the wafer bled.[24]

Langmuir provides two concrete examples, from documentation, of
people in medieval times who gave some expression to their doubts, and
then states that he has a strong suspicion that 'the indications we have
are only the tip of an iceberg'.[25] He suggests that many people had
doubts, but only a few were prepared to incur the wrath of the Church.
As a result, there were many others who:

> ... neither resolved their doubts theologically nor took the beliefs
> they had been taught lightly. Instead, they defended their beliefs by
> imagining that the threats to their faith were external. They attrib-
> uted cosmic evil to other human beings – heretics, sorcerers,
> witches, and Jews. Not only did they regard these human beings as
> symbols of opposing beliefs; they also believed that they engaged in
> secret inhuman activities that attacked their Christ and undermined
> their society.[26]

Of course, amongst the four groups of people mentioned, the only
group whose identification was what would, in modern parlance, be
considered 'ethnic' (i.e., without reference to the individual as such but
only to his 'blood' connections) were the Jews. Langmuir poses the
problem of how the religious authorities themselves dealt with the
irrationality of their adherents – not necessarily the struggle with any
theological irrationality (for instance, the belief in the Eucharist, which
was the source of the problem), but the irrationality of the subsequent
beliefs in everyday life (for instance, the belief that Jews committed
ritual murders of Christian children). His summation of the issue is that:

The highest authorities did not explicitly prescribe irrational beliefs but supported some tacitly. Thus, bishops and priests supported the idea that, as a matter of empirical fact, Jews ritually crucified Christian children and they authorized shrines that institutionalized the idea.[27]

He adds that while Popes did not support the blood-libel, they often gave their approval to the shrines that were set up in memory of the children who had been allegedly killed by Jews.

Officially, then, the Church's approach was one of ambivalence: prospectively, to discourage any action being taken against Jews based on charges of ritual murder or host desecration, but retrospectively, after presumed proof had been obtained and Jews had been convicted and executed, of granting recognition to shrines set up in honor of the victims. Such recognition even afforded advantages to the populace at the local level. As Po-chia Hsia argues: 'When the new sites of Christian martyrdom drew pilgrims, when miracles attracted visitors, when sacrifices earned renown and wealth, the bond between piety and material well-being was firmly established.'[28]

Hsia's book provides several detailed descriptions of blood-libels regarding ritual murders and host desecrations during the period of the Reformation, including accounts of torture in order to elicit confessions, and a listing of the harsh punishments used to execute those accused, such as burning. He notes that the Reformation actually served as a positive turning-point, with a marked decrease in the instance of blood-libels. He also notes that, prior to this time, there had been almost no trials for infanticide, and almost no awareness of the fact of child murder, either in the family or in the neighborhood. The blood-libel had served as a convenient cover preventing any thorough investigation of ordinary crimes.[29]

In a chapter entitled 'Christianity Disenchanted', he describes this disenchantment in Weberian terms – that is, not disenchantment with Christianity itself, but a divesting of the religion of what Martin Luther and other Protestant leaders considered magic. He explains that 'stories about the transformation of the Eucharist in the child Jesus, the consecrated Host that bleeds, and the apparitions of Christ, were but "papist" lies'.[30] In the Protestant movements, the Eucharist was no longer a key ceremony, and as evidence mounted for the existence of infanticidal practices within the family and other forms of abuse practised against the vulnerable young, so emerged a growing awareness of a social reality that had till then been ignored, because the Jews had provided a convenient scapegoat. As Hsia explains the change:

Violence against children was not a preserve of the Jews; evil lurked in the hearts of all. Nor could one think of Jews as the chief servants of Satan when numerous examples of Christian men and women who abandoned or killed children could now be counted among the nefarious undertakings of the Devil.[31]

There is an interesting paradox here as, despite the many anti-Semitic statements in Luther's writings, his rejection of certain aspects of Catholic ritual may well have indirectly contributed to a diminution of one aspect of extreme anti-Semitic behavior: the blood-libel.

In addition to the change in religious orientation, there was also, according to Hsia, a major transformation in the jurisprudential structure, which gave greater assurance of the truth being divulged.[32] In his concluding chapter, Hsia sums up the overall situation within its religious context. He writes:

> The essential mentality underlying ritual murder discourse was the Christian belief in sacrifice, the dominant form of its representation being the story of Christ's Passion. In accusing Jews of child murders, and in extracting confessions from the suspects, the magistrates and the people thus created repetitions and variations on the theme of Christian sacrifice. The tortured Christian children, the bleeding little martyrs, and the abused Eucharist became symbols by which a society created its own moments and loci of sanctity. In acting out this sacred drama of human redemption, everyone was assured a role: the innocent Christian martyrs, the murderous Jews, the conscientious magistrates, the treacherous Christians who kidnapped and murdered children for money, and the entire Christian community, which participated both in witnessing the execution of the Jews and in receiving the fruits of divine redemption. The murdered children, like Christ became sacrificial gifts. The offering of their blood through the double sacrifice of Jewish murder and Christian vengeance was meant to create a bond of exchange between heaven and earth for assuring the incessant flow of divine grace.[33]

Nearly all instances of the blood-libel took place at Easter. There was a clear logic to this based on an underlying religious framework. Easter was the Christian holiday that commemorated the Crucifixion. Passover was the linked Jewish holiday, which had its own special customs that seemed to accentuate Christian suspicions: the making of *Matzhoh*, which so resembled the wafer used in the Eucharist; the special Seder meal that seemed so much to resemble the ceremony of communion, and which included the traditional four cups of wine to be drunk at designated stages of the ceremonial Seder.[34]

However, beyond the obvious religious connection, there was a further factor that has been almost totally ignored in historical accounts of the blood-libel: what might be termed its geographical, or perhaps more accurately its climatological, component. Easter and Passover are both recognized as festivals of spring, celebrating the resurgence of life in nature, the longer days and brighter suns, the emergence from the depths of winter darkness and dampness. This obviously provided a parallel for Christians with the theme of the resurrected life (and the popular Easter eggs are a symbolic expression of renewed life). For Jews, too, the mere fact of having to prepare special utensils, which are used only during the Passover week, provided a useful background for a thorough 'spring'-cleaning (and the eating of eggs at the beginning of the Seder meal is also customary).

The factual impact of this connection with the season of spring, in terms of the blood-libel, leads to a conjecture as to a non-religious reason for the prevalence of such cases during this time of the year. During the long, dark days of winter, without the electricity, easy transportation and entertainment facilities of modern life, the tendency would be to spend much time within the confines of one's house, especially in the more northern climes, where most cases of blood-libel seemed to be concentrated. The violent death of a child, through accident, through carelessness, through criminal intent, could be covered up because of the limitations on outside activities. Neighbors would not notice the absence of a child, since there would be little reason to be spending time outdoors. With the advent of spring, the fate of a dead child could no longer be concealed. Furthermore, the very fact of the cramped conditions in which a family was obligated to pass the long winter days and nights was liable to create the internal tensions that might suddenly erupt in violence, even of a fatal nature.

If the family bore responsibility through negligence or through criminality for the death, the blood-libel would provide a tempting explanation for the disappearance of the child, or for the discovery of its corpse. At that time, there was a lack of two key factors that exist at present: the accumulation of forensic knowledge, and the awareness of the extent of child abuse within the family, or even in neighborhood settings (and, in this regard, it is perhaps only in the last three decades that perceptive research has revealed this aspect of the hidden dynamics of family life).[35] The very fact of the initial difficulties in recent times in making both experts and the public aware of the phenomenon of child abuse, as the evidence for its prevalence began to filter through, by virtue of pioneering research in the 1960s and 1970s of the twentieth century,[36] provides support for the thesis I am submitting. (The early research in this area was part of the empirical evidence that led to the formulation of the Rustum Complex as a direct contrast to the Oedipus Complex.[37]) The conjunction of spring replacing winter with the religious holidays of Easter and Passover created a constellation that encouraged the spread of the blood-libel. With the passage of time, there is little prospect of being able to determine what happened several hundred years ago in widely scattered parts of the world, but I believe that a full understanding of the blood-libel and the manifestations of anti-Semitism would be greatly enhanced by the concept of the Rustum Complex (or the Laius Complex),[38] which provides a modern theoretical framework for the comprehension of this unfortunate phenomenon in the history of Christian–Jewish relations.

However, Christian theologians were also intent on drawing a distinction between the two holidays in order to emphasize the autonomous nature of the new religion. This was effected by a manipulation of the manner of calculating the cyclical process. As W. Frend notes, 'The fixing of the date of Easter, independent of Jewish calculations of 14 Nissan, was the emperor's second reason for summoning the Council' (of Nicaea) with the intention, *inter alia* of 'abandon[ing] the Jewish date'.[39]

Hugo Rahner, who presented such a convoluted explanation of the move from Saturday to Sunday,[40] linking the rising of the sun to the resurrection of Jesus, provides a similar analysis of the manner in which, at least in calendarical terms, Easter became disassociated from Passover. This was no minor change and it occasioned lengthy debate. As Rahner describes the opposing stances, 'The Christians of Asia Minor, relying on the tradition received from John, insisted on celebrating Easter on the day which the Jews, on the basis of astronomical observations, reckoned to be the fourteenth of Nissan.'[41] (This is the seventh month of the year as reckoned from Rosh Hashana, the Jewish New Year; but, also, it is sometimes referred to (including in the Bible) as the first month; probably because of its connection with spring and re-awakening. 'But,' Rahner continues:

> this went counter to the practice that had grown up over almost the whole of the empire. Here ... the times were so fixed that the day of the resurrection – the next day but one, that is to say, after that commemorating Christ's death – fell on the day of Helios; in a word, it fell on the day which we still call Sunday and which from the very beginning had been a day of celebration.[42]

A similar approach is adopted by Stephen Wilson, in discussing 'Patterns of Christian Worship'.[43] In two interrelated discussions, he deals first with the move 'from Sabbath to Sunday', and then with the change 'from Passover to Easter'.[44] In both instances he refers to the need to seek separation from the Jewish observances, while yet sensing the need to retain some minimum degree of relevance (for the Sabbath is mentioned in the Ten Commandments, and Jesus' passion and resurrection take place at Passover). While he lays less stress on the connection to the pagan worship of the sun than is expressed in Rahner's work, Wilson does refer to a work by S. Bacchiochi,[45] who, in Wilson's summation of his thesis, 'argues that (Sunday) was introduced to exploit the associations of the pagan day of the sun'.[46] He then adds that, 'This was done in Rome under the bishop Sixtus (*c.* 115–25 CE) at the same time as the shift from Passover to Easter.'[47]

As for the later shift, Wilson has no doubt that in considering 'the dating, the form, or the rationale for the Christian Easter, there seems to be an underlying anti-Jewish motif'.[48] Thus, according to him:

> The Pasch ... presented the Church with a particularly thorny problem as it strove to establish an identity distinct from Judaism. Chronological coincidence, ritual indebtedness, and supersessionary convictions combined to present a complex situation. The earliest and simplest move, found among the Quartodecimans, was to reverse the ritual pattern – fasting when the Jews feasted and celebrating joyfully when they ate unleavened bread. The shift to Sunday from the 14th of Nissan was a more overt break.[49]

He concludes, 'Passover Easter was, at the best of times, a sensitive issue whenever Jews and Christians came into contact ... Hovering all the while was the potentially explosive issue of Jewish responsibility for Jesus' death.'[50]

Thus, whereas Christmas has a regular date, Easter is determined by complicated computation based on the lunar calendar (which is the basis of all Jewish holidays) and adjusted so that the holiday can be celebrated on a Friday (Good Friday) and a Sunday (Easter Sunday). Interestingly enough, Rahner himself, true to his theme of the 'Christian Mystery of Sun and Moon',[51] goes on to claim that this conflict around the determination of the suitable day 'may be regarded as the second phase of the encounter between Christianity and the ancient sun-cults'.[52] For Rahner, the importance of making Sunday the day for commemorating the Resurrection at Easter provided a useful link into Passover while, at the same time, as others have noticed, ensuring autonomy for the new religion. In addition to the holy day, Sunday, in the

> ... pagan planetary week, it would also give such consecration to
> the Jewish Pasch into which Jesus had so firmly built his own
> redemptive work that the two could no longer be separated. Thus,
> not only the *dies Solis*, but the cycle of the solar year should do
> their service to the true sun, Christ.[53]

However, it should be mentioned that the day is determined more by
lunar than solar considerations; the solar aspect is linked to the idea, as
noted, of spring. In this context, Rahner quotes from an anonymous
preacher in the fifth century:

> Now the germinating power of the earth breaks forth ... The whole
> of nature, which till this moment had had the semblance of death,
> celebrates the resurrection together with her Lord ... The round
> earth and the vaulted sky join in a common song of joy to Christ,
> God and man, who brought peace to heaven and earth.[54]

Rahner struggles, as he had done in his analysis for the rationale of
Sunday being the weekly holy day instead of Saturday, to explain the
manner in which Easter is determined, which effectively loosens the link
with Judaism but retains the link with the pagan worship of the sun and
moon:

> Transposed ... into this Hellenic reckoning of time ... Jesus died on
> the day of Venus, lay in his grave on the day of Saturn, and arose
> from the dead on the day of Helios. Jesus arose on the middle day
> of the month whose beginning fell in the Roman Martius which, be
> it noted, was in the Roman empire also the first month of the year.[55]
> He arose on the day on which, in the waxing light of Helios as he
> began to move towards his summer zenith, his sister star, Selene,
> irradiated by his light, stood before her brother and bridegroom.
> Because of this, the coincidence that Christ rose on the day of
> Helios gains even deeper significance. How deeply such thoughts
> engrossed the minds of the first Christians when they received the
> institution of the Pasch, now filled with a new Christian meaning,
> from their brethren that had come out of pious Jewry – all this is
> made plain by the long argument over the date of Easter.[56]

Thus, a Christian holiday that is so obviously closely intertwined with
the parallel Jewish holiday (unfortunately, as shown, to the detriment of

Jewish victims of the blood-libel) is described, in a modern, learned discourse, in a book that has the imprimatur of the Catholic Church, in terms that link it to ideas that were prevalent in pre-Christian Hellenic culture. The Friday death is seen as a sunset, the Sunday Resurrection as akin to the rising sun. The full syncretism is summarized by Rahner:

> This Pasch from the death on the cross to the life of the resurrection – in Christian symbolism Pasch always denotes the 'passover' from death to life – was fashioned by the ancient Church in the liturgy of the Easter vigil into a marvellous sun mystery.[57]

In Jewish tradition, the basis of the Pasch, which in Hebrew means 'passover', is the memory of the exodus from Egypt, specifically that the first-born Israelite male children were saved from the tenth plague when the angel of death *passed over* their houses.

NOTES

1. *See* Gedaliah Alon, *The Jews in Their Land in the Talmudic Age (70–640 CE)* (Cambridge: Harvard University Press, 1989); *see* chapter 23, 'The Gathering Storm', and chapter 24, 'The Bar Kokhba War'. He writes of an estimate of casualties 'at more than half-a-million', and adds that 'The loss in population must have been further compounded by extensive emigration, both forced and voluntary' (p. 643).
2. *See* Walter M. Chandler, *The Trial of Jesus: From a Lawyer's Standpoint: Vol. 2, The Roman Trial* (Buffalo, NY: William S. Hein and Co., 1983), Appendix 1, p. 291, 'Characters of the Sanhedrists Who Tried Jesus'. Basing his material on an earlier French account by Lémann, Chandler writes:

   > The members of the Sanhedrin that judged Christ were 71 in number, and were divided into three chambers; but we must know the names, acts, and moral characters of these judges.

   About 40 short biographical sketches are given. Chandler's book is discussed in chapter 3 above, 'Crucifixion'.
3. For an excellent discussion of the comparative aspects of the two holidays, see Paul F. Bradshaw and Lawrence A. Hoffman (eds), *Passover and Easter: Origin and History to Modern Times* (Notre Dame, IN: University of Notre Dame Press, 1999). This is Vol. 5 in a series on 'Two Liturgical Traditions'. Vol. 6 also deals with these two holidays, and is subtitled, *The Symbolic Structuring of Sacred Seasons*; it deals *inter alia* with a similar connection between the Christian holiday of Pentecost and the Jewish holiday of Shavuot (also known in some English translations as Pentecost, from the reference to the 50 days between the two holidays, similar to the Christian counting from Easter).
4. *See* A. Jerrop and M.R. James, *Life of Saint William of Norwich* (1896).
5. Malcolm Hay, *The Foot of Pride: The Pressure of Christiandom on the People of Israel for 1900 Years* (Boston: Beacon Press, 1951).
6. Ibid., p. 139.
7. Ibid., p. 127. Hay also writes (p. 122), 'This accusation of kidnapping little children, killing them after torture, and using their blood for a religious rite, proved to be the most powerful instrument of hate propaganda that has ever been invented.'
8. Ibid., p. 122.
9. Ibid.

10. *See* Joseph Tabory, 'Towards a History of the Paschal Meal', in Bradshaw and Hoffman (eds), *Passover and Easter*, p. 62.
11. *See* description in Frances Young, *Sacrifice and the Death of Christ* (London: SCM Press Ltd, 1983), p. 62:

> *The Eucharist*: (A) communion-sacrifice was the characteristic Christian cult-act, namely the Eucharist. This was understood to be communion in the body and blood of Christ, both sharing food in his presence and feeding on him as the bread of life. In other words, both types of communion-sacrifice have contributed ideas. Notice, however, that it is the body and blood of Christ which are shared. The unique feature of the Eucharist as a communion-sacrifice was that the victim was not slaughtered and eaten; rather the sharing of bread and wine was a memorial of Christ's sacrifice. Thus it was intimately connected with the sacrifice of Christ, and the communion meant participation in the benefits of his redemptive death. In fact, the Eucharist refuses to be classified neatly, since it was a sacrifice of praise and thanksgiving offered by the Church in response to redemption in Christ, as well as a re-enactment of his sacrifice and a participation in its benefits. In a sense all types of sacrifice met in this liturgical act, which focused the sacrificial worship of the Church on the sacrificial death of Christ.

12. Caroline Walker Bynum, *Holy Feast and Holy Fast* (Berkeley, CA: University of California Press, 1987), p. 3. *See also* description by Hyman Maccoby in his book, *The Mythmaker: Paul and the Invention of Christianity* (London: Weidenfeld and Nicolson, 1988), chapter 11, 'Paul and the Eucharist'; *see also* reference to this work in the context of sacrifice in the final chapter, 'Moriah'.
13. Bynum, *Holy Feast and Holy Fast*, p. 60.
14. Gavin I. Langmuir, *History, Religion and Antisemitism* (Berkeley, CA: University of California Press, 1990); a Centennial Book, published with the cooperation of the Center for Medieval and Renaissance Studies, UCLA.
15. The definitions of transubstantiation in the *Random House Dictionary of the English Language* are:

> 1. The changing of one substance into another. 2. *Theol* (in the Eucharist) the conversion of the whole substance of the bread and wine into the body and blood of Christ, only the external appearance of bread and wine remaining (a doctrine of the Roman Catholic Church).

16. *See*, especially, Langmuir, *History, Religion and Antisemitism*, chapters 3, 'Rationalization and Explanation'; 8, 'Nonrational Thinking'; 12, 'Religious Doubt'; 13, 'Religious Irrationality'. *See also* the fascinating study by Pietro Redondi in his biography of Galileo. He devotes a full chapter to 'The dispute over the Eucharist'. The belief in transubstantiation raised certain problems for physical science: for instance, the material significance of such concepts as color, odor and taste. According to Redondi:

> In the seventeenth century ... 'color, odor, and taste' were cultural terms that designated before all else the daily experience of the Eucharistic miracle. They were words of the theological language and of everyday religious life.
> Pietro Redondi, *Galileo Heretic* (Princeton, NJ:
> Princeton University Press, 1987), p. 226.

17. For ongoing debates on the meaning of the biblical text, dating back to the first centuries of Christianity, see the fascinating study by Bart D. Ehrman, *The Orthodox Corruption of Scripture: The Effect of Early Christological Controversies on the Text of the New Testament* (New York: Oxford University Press, 1993). Generally, minority views were declared heretical, with sometimes dire consequences. By the time of the medieval period discussed by Langmuir, and before the Reformation, the Church had established a degree of monolithic control, which would have made it all the more difficult for individuals or groups to give expression to doubts or to raise alternative approaches. This is also the period of the greatest expression of anti-Semitism, and these empirical facts lend support to Langmuir's thesis.

18. *See* Leon Festinger, *A Theory of Cognitive Dissonance* (Stanford, CA: Stanford University, 1957).
19. Langmuir, *History, Religion and Antisemitism*, p. 259. For a description confirming the depth of this belief in the modern world, see Alan W. Watts, *Myth and Ritual in Christianity* (Boston, MA: Beacon Press, 1968). In discussing 'The Passion', he writes that: 'The great feasts and fasts of the calendar commemorate the mythological aspects of the life of Christ – his great world-saving actions rather than his teachings or miracles for the healing of individuals.' He explains that:

> In the Mass ... we represent the crux of the whole Myth: the bread and wine which we are, because we eat it, becomes by Sacrifice the Body and Blood (i.e. Life) of Christ. And this, in turn, we eat again so that it becomes us, making our body and blood Christ's. This is why the myth so properly insists that the Mass is much more than a *mere* symbol: the bread and wine become in actuality and not alone in figure the very Christ. It is precisely in the almost magical character of the Catholic Mass that its whole truth lies, and all attempts to rationalize the Mystery deprive it of its real point. (p. 149) [emphasis in original]

20. Langmuir, *History, Religion and Antisemitism*, p. 258.
21. Ibid., p. 259.
22. Ibid., p. 260.
23. Ibid., pp. 260–1.
24. Ibid., p. 261.
25. Ibid., p. 262.
26. Ibid., p. 263.
27. Ibid., p. 266.
28. R. Po-chia Hsia, *The Myth of Ritual Murder: Jews and Magic in Reformation Germany* (New Haven, CT: Yale University Press, 1988), p. 227.
29. Ibid., pp. 152–4. On p. 153 there is a table showing the number of executions for infanticide in Nurenberg for each decade over a 200-year period.
30. Ibid., p. 147.
31. Ibid., p. 159.
32 Ibid., *see* especially pp. 198–203, sub-title 'Law *versus* Religion'.
33. Ibid., pp. 226–7.
34. *See* Lawrence A. Hoffman, 'The Passover Meal in Jewish Tradition', in Bradshaw and Hoffman (eds), *Passover and Easter*, p. 8.
35. *See* my discussion in *Generations Apart: Adult Hostility to Youth (*New York: McGraw-Hill, 1981), especially chapter 9, 'Family Cares'.
36. Ibid., chapter 7, 'Children of All Ages'.
37. Ibid., part 2, 'The Uses of the Oedipus Complex', and part 3, 'The Rustum Complex'.
38. Ibid., chapter 2, 'The Myths of Generational Conflict'.
39. W.H.C. Frend, *The Rise of Christianity* (Philadelphia, PA: Fortress Press, 1984), p. 499.
40. *See* discussion in previous chapter, 'Constantine', of the work of Hugo Rahner, *Greek Myths and Christian Mystery* (London: Burns and Oates, 1963).
41. Ibid., p. 111. The supporters of this approach using the Jewish date of the 14th of Nissan, were known as the Quartodecimans.
42. Ibid.
43. Stephen G. Wilson, *Related Strangers: Jews and Christians 70–170 CE* (Minneapolis, MI: Fortress Press, 1995), chapter 8, 'Patterns of Christian Worship', p. 222.
44. Ibid., pp. 230–5, under sub-heading 'From Sabbath to Sunday'; and pp. 235–41, under sub-heading 'From Passover to Easter'.
45. S. Bacchiochi, *From Sabbath to Sunday* (Rome: Pontifical Gregorian University Press, 1977).
46. Wilson, *Related Strangers*, p. 234.
47. Ibid.
48. Ibid., p. 240.

49. Ibid.
50. Ibid., p. 241. Wilson's summary of the dispute between Jews and Christians over the two holidays includes the fact of 'the denial of the legality of the Jewish Passover' and 'outright vilification' (p. 230). In sum, the basic points of conflict are (p. 240):

   1. The true meaning of the Passover is to be found in the sacrifice of Jesus as the Paschal lamb.
   2. Pasch is for Christians a weekly (i.e. Eucharistic), as well as an annual, feast.
   3. The Jews cannot legally celebrate Passover because Jerusalem is destroyed.
   4. The precise date of Pasch is insignificant, because for Christians, the key day is always Friday, in remembrance of Jesus' Passion.

51. Rahner, *Greek Myths*, chapter 4.
52. Ibid., p. 111.
53. Ibid., p. 109.
54. Ibid., pp. 111–12.
55. As noted before, although the Jewish New Year is celebrated during September, there are biblical references to the month of Nissan (generally about April) as being the first month of the year.
56. Rahner, *Greek Myths*, p. 110.
57. Ibid., p. 119.

9

Passover

Passover is a religious holiday, but it is no less a celebration of a national event with universal connotations: the manumission of the Jewish people (then known as the Israelites or Children of Israel) from slavery. It also marks their emergence on the world stage as a people or nation, one which, at its formation, bore both the religious message of monotheism and the secular message of freedom. The exodus out of Egypt, the 40 years of wandering in the desert, the reception of the Ten Commandments at Mount Sinai, and the entry into the Promised Land are all symbolic metaphors that are deeply embedded in world culture through the impact of the successor religions, Christianity and Islam. As already discussed, the holiday of Easter is inextricably connected with it, despite all efforts to sever the link. The Last Supper is often even, possibly incorrectly, perceived as being the Seder meal, the special celebratory repast at which Jews celebrate their miraculous delivery from years of servitude.

As for the connection between the total context of the Crucifixion and Resurrection and the historical event of the Exodus, Madeleine Boucher claims that:

> For Christians Jesus' death and resurrection is the moment in history which is the point of departure for the new Exodus. If the miracle of the loaves points to the Last Supper, a Passover meal, it is not unreasonable to infer that it suggests also its context, the passion. Christians know that at both meals the bread which is broken and distributed that those who partake may have life is Jesus' body.[1]

She then adds the 'sea miracle' which 'suggest[s] the resurrection' and is linked to 'the biblical symbol of water'. Thus, with the strongest linkage being between Easter and Passover, she concludes that 'the relation between the two miracles' is that 'the breaking of the bread, symbol of Jesus' death, precedes the victory over waters, symbol of the resurrection'.[2]

Yet, the name given to this festival is related to none of the above-mentioned factors: not to the Exodus itself, not to the Ten Commandments or to the wandering in the desert (for which there are separate festivals of Shavuot and Sukkot), nor even to the final return to Canaan, but to the deliverance of the Israelite children from the cruel fate which befell the first born of the Egyptians when God inflicted the tenth and final plague on the overlords of the Israelites after an intractable Pharaoh had refused to voluntarily let His people go. The Israelites were commanded to put a sign on the entrance to their houses: blood from a lamb, smeared on the two posts and the crossbar of the front door of each house. That sign was to be a protective device, so that, as described in the Bible, 'the Lord will pass over the door, and will not suffer the destroyer to come into your house to smite you'.[3] The redemption of children (the first-born in each family) was to be incorporated into the name of the festival; the use of a lamb was also inevitably a reminder of the *Akedah*, where a ram had been substituted for Isaac.

The word for passing over in Hebrew is formed from the root PSCh (Pesach) and this is, naturally, the Hebrew name for the festival; this root is also the basis for the word 'paschal' in reference to Easter. More particularly, the term 'paschal' is used in reference to Jesus, most particularly in 'Christ, the paschal lamb, sacrificed for us.'[4] As Paul Bradshaw explains in his description of 'The Origins of Easter':

> The image of Christ as the Passover lamb is found in I Corinthians 5:7, and also underlies John's Gospel. There Jesus is identified as 'The Lamb of God' near the beginning (1:36), and then is said to have died on the cross on the day of the preparation of the Passover (i.e. 14 Nissan) at the hour when the lambs for the feast were being slaughtered (19:14). In addition, the soldiers are said to have refrained from breaking the legs of the dead Jesus and so fulfilled the scripture requiring that no bone of the Passover lamb be broken (19:32–6; cf. Exod., 12:46; Num., 9:12).[5]

In essence, the sacrifice of the lamb was the basis of the redemption of the Israelites; in similar fashion, the sacrifice of Jesus was the basis of the redemption of mankind.

The special, singular feature of Passover is the Seder meal, preceded by the reading of the *Haggadah*, which is a re-telling of the Exodus with the performance of certain rituals. Of particular interest is the fact that the *Haggadah* itself makes no mention whatsoever of Moses.[6] Here is perhaps a subtle expression of a key distinction between Judaism and

Christianity. The dominant character in Jewish history, whose major achievement was to take his people out of slavery and lead them to the frontiers of the Promised Land, is ignored in the ceremonial recital of this key event during the festival commemorating his exploit. In a way, this perhaps reflects the fact that Judaism revolves around a people, being essentially an ethnic religion; whereas, in contrast, Christianity revolves around an individual, although as a missionary faith it is all-embracing in its membership affiliations.

This is a crucial difference. In theory at least, the exclusivity of a religion in ethnic terms (the Jews as a 'chosen people') allows for tolerance towards others; thus, according to Jewish tradition, non-Jews are required only to keep the seven 'Noahide' commandments, namely those of the ten that are universal in nature and not specifically related to the Jewish people as such: for instance, not to kill, not to steal, not to covet anothers' possessions. In contrast, a universalist missionary religion tends to be, paradoxically, exclusive in its approach, specifically because of its universalistic aims. It is exclusive in the sense of its claims to eternal truth with no accepted alternatives, and this leads to a narrow exclusivity which lies at the basis of much anti-Semitism, as European Jews were, for many long centuries ,the only significant, noticeable non-Christian group, the one minority group that refused to be converted and to be incorporated into the religion of the majority, the group that – in modern terms – insisted on the right to the advantages and beauty of a pluralistic society.

However, from a Jewish perspective – disregarding the Crucifixion – there is an interesting connection between Jesus and Moses which is directly related to the theme of this book, namely the similar dangers confronting both of these religious leaders at the time of their birth. These dangers are also similar to the circumstances surrounding other religious leaders, such as Krishna in Hindu tradition, or Zeus in Greek culture.[7]

The only one of the four Evangelists who deals with what seems to be an important aspects of Jesus' life is Matthew. Immediately after describing the virgin birth, the naming of the infant son, and the visit of the wise men who had told King Herod of the 'star in the east' as a sign of the birth of the 'King of the Jews', he recounts how 'the angel of the Lord appeared to Joseph in a dream' and told him to flee to Egypt with 'the young child and his mother ... for Herod will seek the young child to destroy him'.[8] When their disappearance became known to Herod, who had apparently wished to kill the potential usurper said to be 'the King of the Jews', in a fit of vengeful anger he 'slew all the children that were in Bethlehem, and in all the courts thereof, from two years old and under'.[9] Only after being informed of Herod's death does the family of Jesus return from Egypt.

This story has obvious close parallels to the circumstances surrounding Moses' birth. At the time, all the male children of the Israelites were to be killed; but Moses, as a young infant, was hidden, first in his parents' home and then in the bulrushes, where he was discovered by Pharaoh's daughter who saved him and later took him into her own house where she brought him up as her child.[10] There is also an obvious link (if inverse) to the story of Oedipus, who was saved by shepherds after being abandoned by his royal parents; and perhaps even to that of Sohrab, who was also 'abandoned', at least figuratively, by his father.[11]

These instances of infanticide form a useful background to David Bakan's contention that a major underlying theme of the Bible is its message of generational reconciliation:[12] in essence, that the parental generation (the one with power, both physical and political) should use its wisdom to provide proper nurturance for the succeeding generation. Both the Old Testament and the New Testament refer directly to the vulnerability of young children; both the *Akedah* and the Crucifixion deal with this issue. In Pharaoh's Egypt and Herod's Bethlehem, hosts of young children were ruthlessly disposed of; in the *Akedah*, Abraham struggled with his conscience; and through the Crucifixion, Christian theology had claimed that God had sacrificed His son for the benefit of humanity.

But this is important not only for generational contact, but also for the nature of the relations between the founding religion of Judaism, and the successor religion of Christianity. The essence of my theme is that an awareness of this fact is essential for a fuller understanding of the intricately complicated relations between these religions. Thus, although there are many explanations given for the ubiquitous expressions of anti-Semitism, it is not just the initial fact of the Crucifixion that set up the conditions for anti-Semitism, but the memory of it became a key factor in sustaining the phenomenon over the years until its ultimate tragic denouement in the Holocaust. The negative qualities attributed to Jews – their role as moneylenders, their wealth, their arrogance, their strange manners – were not the causative reasons for anti-Semitism, but only the rationalizations for it.

Two factors were linked together by the Gospels: the empirical claim that the Jews were directly responsible for the death of Jesus, and the theological claim that God had sacrificed His son to redeem the sins of humanity. Logically, these two claims could have cancelled each other out, as far as the Jews were concerned, for even though they had rejected the Messiah, they could well have been the recipients of Christian gratitude for being the agents by which God's beneficence was made available. I have, in the first chapter,[13] posed the question as to what would have been the theological course of history if no such catalytic agents had provided the empirical facts behind the theological theory. This is a hypothetical 'what if' query. Given the essential irrationality of anti-Semitism – or, to place it in broader terms, of racism – it is possible that other reasons would have been found for focusing senseless hatred on the Jews, because, it should not be forgotten, they were the most convenient scapegoats as a recognizable minority group in the pre-modern, pre-democratic age. However, I would argue that the consistency and the intensity of Christian anti-Semitism are a direct consequence of the ever-present Cross and the shadow it has cast over the fate of the Jewish people.

Within the framework of this generational hypothesis, there is a further factor that should be noted, a philological factor, similar to the earlier discussion of the underlying meaning of the 'Son of Man'. The Jewish people in biblical times are referred to as Israelites, or as the Children of Israel, not Jews. Thus far I have mainly used the first term, and deliberately so. At this stage, I wish to suggest that, according to the thesis of this book, there is a significance – perhaps hidden and subtle, but nevertheless very real and consequential – to the phrase 'Children of Israel'.

The name Israel is linked to the person of Jacob, the grandchild of Abraham, who is considered to be the original patriarch of the Jewish people. While most references to Jacob use his given name at birth (which is significant because it is connected to the fact that he was the younger of the twins born to Isaac and Rebecca),[14] he undergoes a name-change that is linked to his momentous meeting with an unknown person, generally believed to be an angel, although the Hebrew text uses the word for a man. However, at the end of a struggle between the two of them, the man tells him that from that moment on, his name shall no longer be Jacob, but Israel, 'for thou hast striven with God and with men, and hast prevailed'.[15] Jacob himself presumes that he has 'seen God face to face'.[16] (This is perhaps the closest that the Old Testament comes to a mysterious entity who possesses at one and the same time both divine and human qualities.)

However, despite the fact that it was clearly said to Jacob that 'Thy name shall be called no more Jacob, but Israel',[17] the Bible itself continues to refer to Jacob by his original name, until the next fateful meeting that he has when he is re-united with his son, Joseph, in Egypt. From which moment onwards, the two names are used interchangeably, sometimes even in the same verse, or even the same sentence, as in Genesis, 49:2: 'Hear, ye sons of Jacob; and hearken unto Israel, your father.' More significantly, on his deathbed he is referred to as Jacob, and then immediately afterwards, when his body is to be embalmed, he is called Israel.[18]

At the beginning of the second book of the Bible, Exodus, an outline is presented of Jacob's family, 'the names of the sons of Israel, who came into Egypt with Jacob': this is in the first verse. A few sentences later, after mentioning the death of both Joseph 'and all his brethren', the Bible immediately (in verse 7) refers to the 'Children of Israel', not in the context of the immediate progeny of Jacob (his sons and grandsons), but in a larger 'ethnic' context, 'And the children of Israel were fruitful, and increased abundantly.' At this point, a possible translation is 'Israelites'. In any event, it is clear that this is no longer a familial reference, but an ethnic one, dealing with the people of Israel into the next generations. In English versions of the Bible, due regard is given to this fact by the use of the word 'sons' when referring to the 12 boys who were born to Jacob, and then switching to the use of the word 'children', when referring to the later generations. However, what must be stressed is that, in contrast to English and most European languages, Hebrew makes no distinction between 'sons' and 'children'. Hebrew in that period, and today, has no separate word for 'children', the masculine form of 'son' is used even when referring to girls.

Arising out of this simple fact is a deeper link that must be noticed, and that has far-reaching implications. It was noted earlier that the term in Hebrew for a person may be either *Adam*, from the first person mentioned in the Bible, or *Ben Adam*, that is, a 'son of Adam'.[19] In a similar fashion, the same word 'Ben', which means 'son', is used to refer to the Israelites: however, it is never used in the singular, but only in the plural, changing the meaning from 'son of' to 'children of'.

The biblical use of the phrase 'Children of Israel' is clearly archaic; the first time the word 'Jew' is used is in the Book of Esther, which was written at a much later period during the dispersal of the Jews after the destruction of the first Temple.[20] There is no example in the English language (or in most European languages) to a people (whether as a nation or a group) referred to in a biblical manner as 'Children of ...'. Yet, in Hebrew the individual form *Ben Adam* (a person) can be generalized – thus *bnei* (in the plural) is widely used to refer to people as such (*Bnei-Adam*) as well as in many other contexts. This linguistic possibility does not exist in English, or most other Romance or Germanic languages.

In modern Hebrew, this use still comes completely naturally, and has no archaic or biblical overtones. Thus, there is a youth movement called *Bnei-Akivah* and a soccer team called *Bnei Yehuda*. Young people living in a kibbutz are referred to as *bnei-kibbutz*, while those who are town people may be referred to as *bnei-ha'ir* (which means 'city' or 'town'). People who are lucky may be referred to as *bnei-mazal*, and the fact that people are mortal will elicit the term *bnei-mavet* (the world *mavet* means death – compare to the Latin root 'mort', which forms the basis of the word 'mortal'). In the *Haggadah* itself, a contrast is drawn at the beginning of the ceremony between the Jews having once been slaves and now being free people: that is, *bnei-chorin*, the word *chorin* denoting freedom. A literal translation would therefore be 'the children of freedom'.

Arising out of this excursus – and seen in the context of an underlying Rustum Complex – I would suggest that the biblical references to the 'Children of Israel' have a potentially devastating impact on the image associated with the Jews, accentuated by the fact that these 'children' had also turned against the Heavenly Father when He sent His son to earth as the Messiah. Freudian analysis has used the Oedipus Complex to explain anti-Semitism in generational terms (and examples of such argumentation will be presented in a later chapter on 'Freud'),[21] the argument being that Judaism is the 'father-religion' and Christianity is the 'son-religion'. The Rustum Complex presents a contrasting psychological explanation for the phenomenon of anti-Semitism: the constant references to the 'Children of Israel' in the Bible and in later theological discussions or direct preaching have the effect of subtly emphasizing the sort of problematical or negative qualities in Jews as a people that are often – in the Rustum Complex – attributed to the young.

I am aware of the fact that this thesis is dependent on two controversial factors: the relevance of the Rustum Complex (or, for that matter, the Laius Complex) in and of itself; and the implications, if accepted, for the varied manifestations of anti-Semitism over the years and in different places. Against any reservations in connection with the thesis, I would argue:

1. The fact of child abuse within the family has only recently been acknowledged.[22] A full explanation is still not to hand; the idea of the Rustum Complex (or the Laius Complex) is merely an attempt to contribute to such understanding, and was originally based on the perceived need to provide a balance to the overwhelming impact of the idea of the Oedipus Complex.
2. The whole phenomenon of anti-Semitism (or of related general ideas of racism or xenophobia) is based on irrational sentiments and motivations.[23] Like other authors, I trace, in this book, many of these expressions back to the biased description of the crucial facts relating to the Crucifixion. Within this overall framework – of irrationality

and bias, of mystery and mysticism, of syncretic influences and forced interpretations, of concocted lies in connection with blood-libels and convoluted descriptions (by Jews no less than Christians) relating to the *Akedah*, of senseless violence during the crusades and ruthless repression into the modern age – some measure of understanding may be gleaned from a philological explanation of the term 'the Children of Israel', and the possible existence of hostile feelings toward the young as defined and described in the Rustum Complex.

This obviously does not provide a full explanation for this pheno-menon, but it may well contribute a certain degree of understanding to something that is basically beyond understanding, but that has wrought untold tragedy – at the personal and national level – to the Jewish people. This phenomenon culminated in the Holocaust, in which the 'Children of Israel' were led to their death in carefully designed and organized death camps. Among the victims were a million children.

Beyond the historical tragedy of the Jewish people in history – a consequence, basically, of religious conflict – the contribution of the Jewish people to secular progress has also been denied. Hans Kohn, in a fascinating discussion in the opening pages of his book on nationalism,[24] has suggested that the very idea of democracy was conceived not by the Greeks alone, but by two ancient peoples: the Israelites, mainly through the prophets and their canonical recognition, being the second people. Chronologically, this would, of course, actually make them the first: the forerunners of the Greeks.

In any event, as noted at the beginning of this chapter, the message embodied in the story of the exodus from Egypt, and commemorated in the festival of the Passover, is a universal one: of freedom, for the individual and for the nation. As noted in another context in an earlier chapter, this freedom was not limited to the Israelites alone, but to a mixed group of people who joined them at the last moment. The Bible deals only cryptically with this factor, twice referring, in a few words, to these 'hangers-on' or 'camp followers'.[25] The presumption may well be that other oppressed or deprived groups in Egypt at that time took the opportunity afforded them by the success of the Israelites in throwing off the yoke of slavery, and joined them in their march to freedom.

However, the story of the Exodus is not time-bound; its message has echoed on through the ages and served as an inspiration for peoples, mainly Christian, who have identified with the cry of 'let my people go' and used it to claim that same freedom for themselves. As Michael Walzer explains:

The Exodus is an account of deliverance or liberation expressed in religious terms, but it is also a secular, that is, a this-worldly and historical account. Most important, it is a realistic account, in which miracles play a part but which is not itself miraculous.[26]

Walzer, a Jewish writer, ends his book dealing with the biblical theme of the Exodus from the perspective of a modern social scientist and historian, with a reference to 'contemporary liberation theologians' for whom there is 'a constant thrust toward political messianism' with 'a strong sense of this-worldly complexity'.[27] Noting this ambiguity in Christian eschatology, Walzer concludes that:

Liberation is not a movement from our fallen state to the messianic kingdom but from 'the slavery, exploitation, and alienation of Egypt' to a land where the people can live 'with human dignity'. The movement takes place in historical time; it is the hard and continuous work of men and women.[28]

He adds that, in symbolic terms, 'pharaonic oppression, deliverance, Sinai and Canaan are still with us, powerful memories shaping our perceptions of the political world ... This is a central theme in Western thought, always present though elaborated in many different ways.'[29]

Judaism is an ethnic religion. This is different to Christianity, but in some respects similar to Islam, with its concept of an Umah, a people.[30] The Jews are members of both a religious community and (especially for secular Jews) an ethnic nation (now complicated by the establishment of the State of Israel, as the majority of Jews still live outside of Israel and will probably do so for the foreseeable future). However, deeply embedded in Judaism are a number of universal messages, many of them initial gropings toward concepts of freedom, dignity, democracy and justice, interspersed with more primitive ideas sanctioning harsh measures in war, or severe punishments for individual violations of divine commandments.

Even the positive commandments can become watered-down. For instance, the many references to being just and fair to strangers have been interpreted by most branches of Jewish orthodoxy and ultra-orthodoxy as referring only to a stranger who becomes a convert. This seems a clear violation of the original intent, with its stress repeated several times in different places in the Bible, of the fact that the reason for such consideration was specifically because the Jews had been strangers in the land of Egypt where, despite terrible tribulations, they steadfastly retained their identity and did not 'convert' to the belief-system of the surrounding environment (although both Joseph and Moses married non-Israelite women).

Indeed, if there is an unseen hand in history, or some divine purpose, then it seems to me that being exposed to the suffering of slavery in Egypt fundamentally shaped Judaism. Certainly, from a reflective and retrospective perspective, the memory of slavery, preserved over thousands of years through the family ceremony of the Seder meal, preceded by the reading of the *Haggadah*, is an essential part – or rather, certainly should be – of the Jewish collective psyche (something that is not always achieved in the State of Israel, either in terms of resolving internal social problems, or in its obtuse attitude to the legitimate aspirations of the Palestinian people).[31] Nevertheless, Jews as individuals have been prominent in liberation struggles throughout the world, and the Zionist movement itself, in its earliest years, included many aspirations for social justice; for instance, the kibbutz movement, with its egalitarianism and communal framework.

Moses, then, is not the founding father of Judaism in the same way that Jesus is of Christianity and Muhammed of Islam. Furthermore, there is no direct reference to him in the traditional text of the *Haggadah*, but his presence is felt, his impact is extensive, and his symbolic role in both Jewish and universal history is unique. Moses, having married a non-Israelite, specially chose the name of Gershom for one of his sons because it is derived from the word for stranger, *ger*,[32] as a reminder of having been strangers – and slaves – in Egypt. Here, the universality of Judaism is seen at the individual level.

But the final message left by the life and works of Moses – the reluctant leader, the lonely law-giver, the righteous rebel striking down the Egyptian taskmaster[33] – comes indirectly, through his death and burial. Despite his success in taking the Israelites out of Egypt and through the desert, he is denied entry into the Promised Land, and his burial place is unknown.[34] This seems to be more than just a hint that the essence of human endeavor is in the striving: that the Promised Land is a lodestar and not necessarily a realizable reality; a source of inspiration but not a blueprint for living; and that death has an inevitability and finality that cannot be overcome, not by pilgrimages to shrines nor the sacredness of sepulchres. The memory of a great leader should be just that: a memory, and not a memorial.

The reward for one's deeds is, then, not necessarily immediately attainable, but the results may be enjoyed by later generations; and the preservation of the memory of the person is not linked to the place of burial, but to the inspiration still derived from his works and words. Moses lies somewhere in the desert; no stream of pilgrims visit his grave, he is not mentioned by Jews reading the *Haggadah* at the Seder table, nor is he divine or eternal, neither the product of a messianic line, nor the founder of a royal or a priestlydynasty. He is only a mortal, with human faults, who served his people well at a crucial moment in their history.

NOTES

1. Madeleine Boucher, *The Mysterious Parable: A Literary Study* (Washington, DC: Catholic Biblical Quarterly, 1977), pp. 74–5.
2. Ibid., p. 75. The 'sea miracle' is a reference to the parting of the waters at the Red Sea.
3. Exodus, 12:23.
4. *See* Paul F. Bradshaw and Lawrence A. Hoffman (eds), *Passover and Easter: Origin and History to Modern Times* (Notre Dame: University of Notre Dame Press, 1999), p. 82, where Bradshaw writes that, 'The original focus of the celebration was not on the resurrection of Christ but rather on Christ, the Passover lamb, sacrificed for us.'
5. Ibid. For a perceptive analysis of the two festivals by an Israeli writer, see Israel J. Yuval, 'Easter and Passover As Early Jewish–Christian Dialogue', in Bradshaw and Hoffman (eds), *Passover and Easter*, p. 98. On p. 106, he writes:

   > It would seem that a new story requires new meaning for old symbols. The three symbols of Passover, *pesach*, *matsah*, and *maror* (paschal lamb, unleavened bread, and bitter herbs) were awarded different meanings in each of the two religions. Christianity identified the *pesach* with Jesus, the lamb of God (*agnus dei*). *Matsah* was the body of the Savior (*corpus Christi*), a remembrance of the bread of the Last Supper, and *maror* became symbolic of the suffering of the Savior (*passio domini*) or of the punishment awaiting the people of Israel for what they did to their Messiah.

   See also comment by Allan Watts that:

   > The Mass represents a true sacrifice, in that Christ submitted deliberately and willingly to his crucifixion, which took place at the very moment when the Jews were sacrificing the Passover Lamb at the Temple. The reason why the new Christ-sacrifice redeems and the old passover-sacrifice does not is that the Victim of the former is *willing*, the performer of a self-sacrifice, at once Priest and Offering.
   >   *Myth and Ritual in Christianity* (Boston, MA: Beacon Press, 1968), p. 147
   >   [emphasis in original].

6. For an interesting analysis of the *Haggadah*, *see* Carole B. Balin, 'The Modern Transformation of the Ancient Passover Haggadah', in Bradshaw and Hoffman (eds), *Passover and Easter*, p. 189. Interestingly, she does not mention the absence of Moses in the *Haggadot*, though some newer versions do mention his role. She mentions just one unusual *Haggadah*, where Moses is mentioned as a protector of animals (including lambs) and not as leader or liberator.
7. For Hindu tradition, *see* David D. Shulman, *The Hungry God: Hindu Tales of Filicide and Devotion* (Chicago, IL: University of Chicago Press, 1993); for Zeus, *see* discussion in earlier chapters 5 and 6 ('Rustum' and 'Oedipus').
8. Matthew, 2:13. In this connection, it might be mentioned that Luke, who together with Matthew mentions the virgin birth but makes no mention of any period spent in Egypt immediately after the birth, does make a reference to a family visit to Jerusalem at Passover, which took place 12 years later. Luke is the only Evangelist to mention this visit, or even the fact that 'his parents went to Jerusalem every year at the feast of the passover'. On this occasion, Jesus went to the Temple on his own, without informing his parents, who looked for him for three days, until they found him, 'in the temple, sitting in the midst of the doctors, both hearing them, and asking them questions. And all that heard him were astonished at his understanding and answers' (Luke, 2:46–7).
9. Matthew, 2:16.
10. Exodus, 2:1-10. The regulation by the Pharaoh was an instruction to the 'Hebrew

midwives' called Shiphrah and Puah: 'When ye do the office of a midwife to the Hebrew women, ye shall look upon the birthstool; if it be a son, then ye shall kill him; but if it be a daughter, then she shall live' (Exodus, 1:16). It should be mentioned that the midwives (the first women in the Bible to be mentioned by name in their own right and not as the wife of ... , or the mother of ...) reacted with civil disobedience, as 'the midwives feared God, and did not as the King of Egypt commanded them, but saved the men-children alive' (Exodus, 1:17). I have used their civil disobedience as an example in a Hebrew book dealing with conscientious disobedience; *Kol Ha-Kavod (The Voice of Honor)* (Tel Aviv: Ramot/Tel Aviv University, 1996).

11. In the case of Oedipus, his parents, Laius and Jocasta, abandoned him to his death; in the case of Rustum, his father left home before his birth, went on combat, and never returned home. Believing that a daughter had been born, he subsequently showed no interest in the child's welfare and development.

12. *See*, in general, David Bakan's work in this area: 'Paternity in the Judeo-Christian Tradition', *The Human Context* (4 (1972), p. 354; *Disease, Pain and Suffering: Toward a Psychology of Suffering* (Chicago, IL: University of Chicago Press, 1968); and *The Duality of Human Existence: An Essay on Psychology and Religion* (Chicago, IL: Rand McNally, 1966).

13. See p.6.

14. The name 'Jacob' is based on the stem for the Hebrew word meaning 'to follow', indicating that he was the second twin to be born.

15. Genesis, 32:29.

16. Genesis, 32:31.

17. Genesis, 32:29.

18. Genesis, 49:33 and Genesis 50:2.

19. See chapter 4, 'Messiah', at pp. 74–8.

20. The reference is to Mordechai as a Jew.

21. *See* chapters 5, 6 and 11: 'Rustum', 'Oedipus' and 'Freud'.

22. *See* discussion in chapter 5, 'Rustum'.

23. *See* especially Gavin Langmuir, *History, Religion, and Antisemitism* (Berkeley, CA: University of California Press, 1990).

24. Hans Kohn, *The Idea of Nationalism: A Study in its Origins and Background* (New York: Collier Books, 1967), at pp. 27–40.

25. See Exodus, 12:38: 'And a mixed multitude went up also with them.'

26. Michael Walzer, *Exodus and Revolution* (New York: Basic Books, 1985), p. 9.

27. Ibid., pp. 148–9.

28. Ibid., p. 149.

29. Ibid.

30. The concept of *Umah* conjures up the idea of peoplehood originally shared among Arabs; later, as Islam spread, it incorporated all of the faithful without reference to ethnic identity.

31. I have discussed Israeli policy critically, within the context of biblical themes; *see* my Hebrew book, *Weeds in the Garden of Eden: Biblical Narratives and Israeli Chronicles* (Tel Aviv: Papyrus/Tel Aviv University, 2002), esp. chapter 5 dealing with peace.

32. See Exodus, 18:3; of the two sons, 'The name of the one was Gershom; for he said: "I have been a stranger in a strange land".'

33. See Exodus, 2:11–12.

34. Deuteronomy, 34:6, 'He was buried in the valley in the land of Moab over against Beth-peor; and no man knoweth of his sepulchre unto this day.'

MODERN MIMESIS

10
Kierkegaard

While religions, as noted, deal with eternal verities and cosmological concepts, they are understood through the prism of an individual's singular perceptions in terms of a personal life-story, with its psychological influences, historical contexts, societal affiliations and philosophical reflections. Part of the beauty of biblical stories is their power to evoke close identification with the leading figures and their capacity to arouse the feeling of sharing vicariously in the drama being recounted.

This is particularly so in the case of Christianity, especially as regards the suffering of Jesus on the Cross. Western art is replete with expressions of this critical moment in human history, from the rigidly stylistic icons of the Orthodox Church to the dramatic symbolism embodied in the original approaches of a Christian artist such as Salvador Dali (who paints from a unique perspective, showing the Crucifixion as seen from above), or a Jewish artist, such as Marc Chagall (who attempts to relate the Passion of Jesus to the persecution of his people, the Jews).[1] Similarly, modern literature has used the theme of Jesus' life, culminating in the Crucifixion, as a basis for further conjectures, for instance, in the work of Noble Laureates, the Greek author, Nicolas Kazantzakis, and the Portuguese author, José Saramago, in their provocative works, *The Last Temptation of Christ* and *The Gospel According to Jesus Christ*, respectively.[2]

This focus on Jesus is understandable and inevitable, given his dominant role in Christianity; in fact, the New Testament is concerned mainly with embellishments on the original descriptions contained in the four Gospels. In this sense, the Old Testament provides a far greater variety, and while in Judaism itself artistic expressions were historically limited, given the prohibition on graven images (which led to an inhibition against any form of artistic representation), both Jewish and Christian writers have drawn incessantly on biblical themes – from stories of the pre-Israelite episodes of the Garden of Eden, the Tower of Babel, The Deluge and Noah's Ark, and the various dramas described in the lives of the Patriarchs and Matriarchs, through the critical period of Moses' activities and achievements to the political struggles, military battles and family rifts of judges and kings, priests and prophets.

The story that has quite possibly elicited the most extensive response, in both art and literature, is the Sacrifice of Isaac (or, in the more accurate Hebrew terminology, the Binding of Isaac). One of the most poignant of such expressions is the poem by the talented but doomed British poet, Wilfred Owen, who, from the battlefields of Europe during the First World War, emitted a cry on behalf of his generation to those to whom their fate had been entrusted:

> Behold! Caught in the thicket by its horns
> A ram, offer the ram of pride instead
> But the old man would not do so
> But slew his son,
> And half the seed of Europe
> One by One.

Owen himself was killed not long afterwards in the closing days of the war.[3]

This theme of generational differentiation, of the young being the victims of an older generation's human failure, political machinations and military arrogance, is also deeply embedded in the culture of modern Israel, where talented writers and artists[4] express their own cry of frustration, anger and powerlessness against the vortex of violence into which they have been born, and into which they are inducted, given the ongoing struggle between the state and its neighbors, and the recurrent wars and continual skirmishes which have resulted.

Social scientists and philosophers have also been wont to elucidate their own independentant theoretical frameworks by judicious use of relevant biblical passages. Sometimes, this is done by strict adherence to the original material, at other times, by allowing imaginative musings to elaborate on the original structure. This latter approach is nowhere more marked than in some of Sigmund Freud's presentations where, in an attempt to demonstrate the universality of the Oedipal theme, he was prepared even to 're-write' the basic format, with the primal crime not being the fratricide of Cain killing Abel (right at the beginning of Genesis), nor even the attempted filicide of Abraham vis-à-vis his son, Isaac, but a revamped version of the story of Moses. In Freud's version, he is not a prophet or political leader, but The Patriarch of the Israelites (replacing Abraham); he does not end his life in a tranquil death, as described in the Bible, but in a violent killing carried out by his sons. All this in order to make the Bible's ancient narrative compatible with Freud's own novel theory.[5]

This aspect of Freuds' work, and its impact on later social scientific analyses, will be discussed in the next chapter; in this chapter, the focus will be on one of the best-known works by a leading modern philosopher: Soren Kierkegaard's short but important book, *Fear and Trembling*.[6] In less than 100 pages, the great Danish philosopher probes deeply into his understanding of the story of the *Akedah*; while seeking its universal message, he also exposes much that is hidden in the deepest recesses of his own soul and psyche. The book itself is an attempt at a modern interpretation of a bygone tale but, through the pertinent observation of his English translator, Walter Lowrie, a deeper and more accurate understanding of Kierkegaard's reflections may be gained.

Lowrie, who is also a biographer[7] of Kierkegaard, has carefully and intensively examined his private *Journals*, in which he kept a fairly detailed diary exposing his innermost thoughts. It transpires that his book, *Fear and Trembling* – widely considered one of the major modern contributions to an understanding of the *Akedah* – was written during a crisis in his personal life, and that much of its tone, content, and argumentation is reflective of this.

Two of his major books were published simultaneously, on 16 October 1843, *Fear and Trembling* and *Repetition*, and 'both recount his desperate struggle in renouncing every hope of earthly happiness when he gave up the prospect of marriage with the woman he loved'.[8] During the frantic writing of these two works (both completed within a few months), he still retained a desperate hope that his love for the woman of his choice, Regina, might yet be requited. This ambivalence is reflected in the writing; as noted by Lowrie: 'We know that while he was writing these two works the struggle to attain resignation was complicated by the hope that he might yet make Regina his wife.'[9]

While these hopes apparently infiltrated *Repetition*, which, thus, later required some re-writing when the hopes were finally and irretrievably dashed, they were carefully hidden in *Fear and Trembling*, which 'maintained itself throughout on so sublime a plane that no change had to be made in it; for it never was the chief point in the story that he might get Regina back as Abraham received Isaac alive'.[10]

Lowrie then quotes from an entry in Kierkegaard's *Journal*[11] that contains clear references to the personal aspect of both of these books; where the author confides that, 'the law of delicacy, according to which an author has a right to use what he himself has experienced, is that he is never to utter verity but is to keep verity for himself and only let it be refracted in various ways'.[12] To which Lowrie comments that in:

> *Fear and Trembling* there was no risk that anybody else might recognize Regina under the figure of Isaac ... The white light of

truth is here so thoroughly refracted that even the reader who has
such acquaintance with S.K.'s story as his contemporaries did not
have may need to be told that Abraham's sacrifice of Isaac is a
symbol of S.K.'s sacrifice of the dearest thing he had on earth.[13]

According to Lowrie, even in his diary Kierkegaard makes only one
direct reference to the impact that his personal life had on his philosophical analysis of the *Akedah*. This involves attributing evil intent to
Abraham, possibly in order for Kierkegaard himself to find some escape
from his own dilemma; instead of blaming the object of his love for the
breakdown of relations, he sees himself as being at fault, in a sense, of
course, being enabled thereby to retain his respect and affection for her.
He ponders, 'suppose that Abraham's previous life was not blameless,
and might let him now mumble under his breath that it was God's
punishment', and that 'he must assist God in making the punishment as
heavy as possible. I suppose,' he adds:

> that at first Abraham looked upon Isaac with all his fatherly love,
> his venerable countenance, his broken heart ... he exhorts him to
> bear his fate with patience, he has let him darkly understand that
> he the father suffered from it still more. However, that was of no
> avail.[14]

At this stage, a transformation takes place, and another aspect of
Abraham's personality is revealed. Kierkegaard writes (for himself alone)
a description entirely at odds with the Abraham whom he presents to the
public in his book:

> Then I think that Abraham has for an instant turned away from
> him, and when again he turned toward him he was unrecognizable
> to Isaac, his eyes were wild, his venerable locks had risen like the
> locks of furies above his head. He seized Isaac by the throat, he
> drew the knife, he said: 'Thou didst believe it was for God's sake I
> would do this, thou are mistaken. I am an idolater, this desire has
> again awakened in my soul, I want to murder thee, this is my desire.
> I am worse than any cannibal; despair thou foolish boy who didst
> imagine that I was thy father, I am thy murderer, and this is my
> desire.'[15]

Kierkegaard then has Abraham whispering softly to himself that it is
preferable to represent himself as 'a monster, that he curses me for being
his father' than that Isaac should know the full truth behind the planned

sacrifice, namely that 'it was God who *imposed the temptation*',[16] [emphasis added] as this might lead to Isaac's loss of faith and reason, and to him supplanting the curse against his father for the planned killing with a curse against God.

These ruminations are hidden from the reader of Kierkegaard's classic analysis of the *Akedah*, but they obviously reveal a real and meaningful background to the book. The book is generally considered to be a paeon of praise to God. He uses Abraham's absolute faith as the peg on which to develop the religious theme – faith in God and belief in His benevolence – but the book also has ominous human overtones. Indeed, there is a triangular interaction; Abraham as father toward his son, Isaac; God in dialogue with his faithful servant, Abraham, patriarch of the Jewish people; and Kierkegaard's monologue with himself about his belief in God, his identification with Abraham in his cruel dilemma, and his own love for Regina, which is on the point of being eclipsed forever because of her announced betrothal to another man.

The revealing private thoughts of Kierkegaard may well help us to understand some of Abraham's own internal dialogue (as I tried to do in the earlier chapter on the *Akedah*), for Abraham kept no diary. The test imposed on him was described by a third person. We know mainly of Abraham's outer actions, almost nothing of his inner emotions; we know of his dialogue, first with God, then with God's messenger, but nothing of Abraham's monologue with himself, which surely took place during his three-day journey: reservations as to the mission he was embarked on, challenges as to the divine command imposed on him, questions as to his own immediate and obedient response. What was Abraham himself going through at that time – striving desperately between opposing options, ranging from the belief that he was proving his faith through to considering the possibility of reneging on his commitment and returning home, to feeling that he actually wanted to go through with the command to the end? This ambivalence is an implicit, essential part of the story.

Indeed, for Kierkegaard, Abraham is not merely being put to the test, not merely being required to provide proof of his belief ('test' and 'proof' are the commonly-used translations of the original Hebrew word, *Nisah*), but he is being exposed to what Kierkegaard refers to in his *Journal* as a 'temptation'. This word – an archaic and dated translation from the Hebrew and today clearly an anachronism – is used not only in Kierkegaard's private *Journal*, but is also the term that Kierkegaard (and of course his translator) uses in the book itself. Kierkegaard refers not only to a 'test' but also to a 'temptation' to which Abraham is exposed. Herein is a revealing aspect of his analysis, no less significant than the journal in leading to an understanding of hidden meanings: was Abraham being tested or was he being tempted? For Kierkegaard, the solution is to suggest that what was for Abraham (given his special character) only a test could, for others, be a temptation. This differentiation requires explanation and once again, as was done in earlier chapters, a linguistic exploration of the manner in which the original Hebrew has been translated into modern European languages, specifically Danish and English, will help clarify the issue.

In the earlier chapter on the *Akedah*, I argued that there could be no certainty as to the nature of the test to which Abraham was being subjected. Yet, Kierkegaard refers throughout the book not to a test alone, but also to a temptation. The implication is that what was being required of Abraham was to commit an act that a reader might consider he was actually quite willing to perform – hence the term 'temptation'. This ambiguous situation arises because the English language has, in the course of the last millenium, undergone much transformation. Versions of the Bible from several hundred years ago, such as the King James, often use archaic forms (such as 'thou' and 'ye'), and use translations that convey slightly different meanings to what is now understood. These are slowly being replaced in more modern translations.

In an earlier age, the word 'temptation' conjured up the concept of trial or testing. Today, that aspect of the meaning is archaic, and presumably not even known. But it is the word used on occasion by Lowrie, where Kierkegaard refers to the word *Nisah* in Hebrew, which means 'test' or 'trial'. From the context, it is clear that this same kind of differentiation was also made in the Danish version used by Kierkegaard.

The implication of using the words 'test' as 'temptation' is that the person upon whom the demand to perform a certain act is made (in this case, the sacrifice of a son), is not reluctant to do so, but eager, even though aware of its dire consequences. On this basis, Kierkegaard draws a distinction between the fact that God's demand on Abraham would indeed have constituted a test for him, because of Abraham's positive qualities; whereas for others who lacked his character, the demand might be a temptation, especially for those harboring possible negative intentions against their offspring. In one simple sentence, Kierkegaard clarifies the situation as he perceives it: 'If he does not love like Abraham, then every thought of offering Isaac would be not a trial but a base temptation (*Anfechtung*).'[17] (It should be noted that Strong's Concordance of the Bible[18] from 1965 uses the word 'tempt' in Genesis 22:1, whereas the Soncino Bible uses the word 'prove' and notes the difference from the authorized version, suggesting that something which tempts 'is that which puts to the test'.)

Kierkegaard's sentiment, quoted above, is not a casual, marginal statement. It is an essential part of Kierkegaard's overall approach, which must now be examined. He states that:

> If it should fall to my lot to talk on the subject, I would begin by showing what a pious and God-fearing man Abraham was, worthy to be called God's elect. Only upon such a man is imposed such a test. But where is there such a man? Next I would describe how Abraham loved Isaac. To this end I would pray all good spirits to come to my aid, that my speech be as glowing as paternal love is. I hope that I should be able to describe it in such a way that there would not be many a father in the realm and territories of the King who would dare to affirm that he loved his son in such a way.[19]

Kierkegaard then completes this paragraph with the previously quoted sentence which contrasts a 'trial' with 'a base temptation'.[20]

It must be stressed: when the word 'temptation' was used in the English translation several hundred years ago, it was an accurate rendering of the English for test or trial. But, given the change in language, it is no longer a suitable word.

In any event, as if to stress the ambiguity of the terminology – and of the story itself – there are also places where Kierkegaard uses both words in tandem, without any attempt to suggest a distinction between them. Thus he writes:

> In the story of Abraham we find ... a paradox. His relation to Isaac, ethically expressed, is this, that the father should love the son. This ethical relation is reduced to a relative position in contrast with the absolute relation to God. To the question 'why' Abraham has no answer except that it is a *trial*, a *temptation*, terms, which ... express the unit of the two points of view; that it is *for God's sake and for his own sake*.[21] [emphasis added].

Taking the analysis way beyond concerns with Abraham's behavior, Kierkegaard then goes on to put the story in its overall social context, dealing not only with the facts as they are recounted but also with the manner in which the story is likely to be perceived. He writes:

> Can one then speak plainly about Abraham without incurring the danger that an individual might in bewilderment go ahead and do likewise? If I dare not to speak freely, I will be completely silent about Abraham, above all I will not disparage him in such a way that precisely thereby he becomes a pitfall for the weak.[22]

Here we have a hint at the internal conversation Kierkegaard conducted with himself in his diary, and finally, at the end of this specific passage, he makes a revealing statement: 'it is only by faith one attains likeness to Abraham, not by murder'.[23]

Here, there is a clear expression of Kierkegaard's penetrating insight as to what is ultimately involved in the story of the *Akedah*, where a killing might be carried out in the name of a religious belief. However, Kierkegaard is unable to expand this insight into a larger sociological or psychological perspective concerning potential hostility toward the young, because his analysis is hidebound by his own personal feelings at that time (as described by Lowrie), his own intense identification with the figure of Abraham, and his own religiosity which, for all his creative abilities, was still attuned to standard interpretations of biblical stories and themes.

Determined to present Abraham – and, in effect, God – in a positive light in terms of the demand that God has imposed on him, Kierkegaard attempts valiantly (but, I would suggest, in vain) to clarify the distinction between Abraham's action and the way in which lesser human beings understand the story. Some will read it and be tempted to emulate it (as described in at least one murder case),[24] or at least to use it as a model or as a justification in countless cases of child abuse. Kierkegaard justifies sacrifice when motivated by faith.

Only on one occasion in the book does Kierkegaard make a passing comment on the fact that, in the final analysis, Isaac was not sacrificed. As in much commentary on the Bible, Kierkegaard is intent on developing his laudatory approach to Abraham, based Abraham's his desire to carry out God's will, and not based on the fact that, at the last moment he refrained from doing so. He writes:

> When faith is eliminated by becoming null or nothing, then there remains only the crude fact that Abraham wanted to murder Isaac; which is easy enough for anyone to imitate who has not faith, the faith, that is to say, which makes it hard for him.[25]

However, even Kierkegaard is not immune from expressing the more brutal aspects of the *Akedah* in positive terms; he does this when comparing Abraham's action to that of other notable figures who killed their own children (for acceptable reasons, according to Kierkegaard although these killers lacked the extra noble qualities of Abraham). His examples, by their very inappropriateness, reveal, no less than his *Journal*, his inability to resolve the awful dilemma posed by the story of the *Akedah*; a dilemma that is apparent in his focus on the beginning of the story, the demand for a sacrifice, while he basically ignores its climax, which is the saving of Isaac. This focus is an inevitable consequence of a deeply committed religious perspective, just as it was – and is – in rabbinical interpretation in the Jewish tradition, and in canonical interpretation in the Christian tradition. It is, in many ways, to paraphrase Shakespeare, a case of protesting too much, of investing tremendous intellectual energy in explaining and justifying a divine command that is actually horrible to contemplate. The weakness of the case is shown by the examples of similar actions by others, particularly the manner in which they are presented.

In discussing the filicidal actions of Agamemnon from Greek mythology, Jephthah from the Bible, and Brutus from the early years of Roman history, Kierkegaard waxes enthusiastic in a way that is clearly inappropriate to the facts and partly irrelevant to the point he is trying to make about Abraham's beliefs and character. He writes:

> When Agamemnon, Jephthah, Brutus at the decisive moment heroically overcome their pain, have heroically lost the beloved and have merely to accomplish the outward sacrifice, then there never will be a noble soul in the world who will not shed tears of compassion for their pain and of admiration for their exploit. If, on the other hand, these three men at the decisive moment were to adjoin to their heroic conduct this little word, 'But for all that, it will not come to pass', who then would understand them?[26]

Yet, of course, for Abraham it did not 'come to pass'.

More significantly, these filicides were based either on *quid pro quo* bargains struck by the fathers (in the case of Agamemnon and Jephthah), or on an act of exploitation of parental power (in the case of Brutus). The example of Brutus is particularly inept as it arose from a political conflict. The Brutus referred to is a consul in Rome in its early days (not to be confused with the infamous assassin of Julius Caesar), and his sons were put to death for partaking in an alleged conspiracy against him. Kierkegaard describes his action in superlatives, due not to religious faith but to the nigh-sacred nature of legal requirements. He claims that:

> When a son is forgetful of his duty, when the state entrusts the father with the sword of justice, when the laws require punishment at the hand of the father, then will the father heroically forget that the guilty one is his son, he will magnanimously conceal his pain, but there will not be a single one among the people, not even the son, who will not admire the father, and whenever the law of Rome

is interpreted, it will be remembered that many interpreted it more learnedly, but none so gloriously as Brutus.[27]

The problem is slightly more complex (within a religious framework) in the other two instances, for here, vows had been made: in return for a military victory, a sacrifice is promised. In the case of Agamemnon, the sacrifice was required by the deity in payment for the favorable conditions that had been created for victory; and so Kierkegaard writes that Agamemnon 'will magnanimously conceal his pain' since 'for the welfare of the whole [nation] he was willing to sacrifice her, his daughter, the lovely young maiden'.[28] Jephthah, as described in the Book of Judges, made a rash vow to sacrifice the first living thing to exit his house if he returned from battle a victor. Despite this recklessness, given the high likelihood that his daughter (or some other member of the family) would rush out to greet him on his triumphant return, Kierkegaard writes of how:

> Every free-born man will understand, and every stout-hearted woman will admire Jephtha, and every maiden in Israel will wish to act as did his daughter. For what good would it do if Jephtha were victorious by reason of his vow if he did not keep it?[29]

In all these instances, Kierkegaard justifies the act, and they serve as models for his claim of higher principles. Yet, even so, there is a utilitarian bargain involved or a practical political consideration. This is lacking in Abraham's case, and so Kierkegaard argues that his act is on an even higher ethical plain; according to Kierkegaard:

> By his act he overstepped the ethical entirely and possessed a higher telos outside of it ... It was not for the sake of saving a people, not to maintain the idea of the state, that Abraham did this, and not in order to reconcile angry deities ... Therefore, whereas the tragic hero is great by reason of his moral virtue, Abraham is great by reason of a purely personal virtue.[30]

It is the non-utilitarian aspect of Abraham's act that makes it so significant. If, unlike the case of Agamemnon, Jephthah and Brutus, there is no bargain being kept, no political aim being furthered, no vow being consummated, why should Abraham respond to God's demand? This is specifically the question that Kierkegaard poses after dealing so eloquently with the fate of the sons and daughters of the three characters he chose for comparative purposes. 'Why then,' he asks:

did Abraham do it? For God's sake, and (in complete identity with this) for his own sake. He did it for God's sake because God required this proof of his faith; for his own sake he did it in order that he might furnish the proof. The unity of these two points of view is perfectly expressed by the word which had always been used to characterize this situation: it is a trial, a temptation (Fristelse). A temptation – but what does that mean? What ordinarily tempts a man is that which would keep him from doing his duty, but in this case the temptation itself is the ethical ... which would keep him from doing God's will.[31]

For the most part, Kierkegaard ignores the fact that the climax of the story is not the sacrifice of Isaac, by God's peremptory dictate, but the saving of Isaac, by the timely intervention of the angel. In his only reference to this fact, Kierkegaard poses only the question, 'If Abraham had actually sacrificed Isaac, would he then have been less justified?'[32]

But the issue, ultimately, is not about how to judge Abraham, but how to interpret his conduct. In order to avoid any intimation of problematical behavior, Kierkegaard elevates Abraham to a level that the average person cannot reach. Even those, like Agamemnon, Jephthah and Brutus, who may perhaps be praised for their willingness to keep a vow or to implement the law even against their own offspring, are still – specifically because of their motives – lacking in those unique qualities possessed by Abraham. Yet, one may ask, is the average person capable of making and understanding these subtle distinctions? For, in any case, even these three utilitarian actors are, in Kierkegaard's analysis, deserving of praise, despite the lesser quality of their act in relation to Abraham.

What does all this mean in everyday terms for the daily, mundane, but crucial, problems of generational contact, including of child abuse? What does this mean for understanding Constantine's execution of Crispus? As a recognized saint, is he comparable to Abraham, or only to Brutus, who put his sons to death because of alleged treason? And what does all this mean in terms of understanding the willingness of a divine being to sacrifice his son, also for the larger good, not just of the body politic, but of all humanity?

Geza Vermes, a Jewish writer, who has published several books dealing with the theological conjunctions between Christianity and Judaism, uses Paul's perceptions of the *Akedah* to explain its importance for the subsequent Crucifixion.[33] Paul's analysis links in with that of Kierkegaard; Vermes writes that:

For Paul, the Akedah prophesized a higher truth, a divine mystery revealed in Christ, in that although man was able to attain such heights of love and self-surrender, God did even greater things to show his love for man. The father was ready to offer His only son, and the son consented to his own sacrifice so that man might be deified ... the Akedah prefigures Redemption by Christ ... the Savior is Christ, not Isaac. The power of salvation is not the Binding of Isaac, but the Sacrifice of Christ.[34]

Thus, the killing of a son can be understood on four differet levels: at the lowest level, mentioned by Kierkegaard, it is murder, something which is far more widespread than any official figures over the centuries can reveal; it then becomes justified in special cases, such as where fidelity to a vow or the law is the value being expressed (*vide* Agamemnon, Jephthah and Brutus); in a unique case, such as the *Akedah*, it shows the willingness of a 'God-fearing man' who was 'worthy to be called God's elect', for 'only on such a man is imposed such a test'[35] (in which case, of course, it is a test and not a temptation); finally, it expresses the willingness of God to have His son sacrificed for the redemption of humanity.

Strangely, Kierkegaard refers only to the first three instances: the connection between the *Akedah* and the Crucifixion forms no part of his thesis, despite the connections between them, as mentioned in the New Testament itself, and in countless interpretations. But, while Jesus is barely mentioned in this book, and the Crucifixion not at all, his mother is: 'Who was ever so great,' is Kierkegaard's query, 'as that blessed woman, the Mother of God, the Virgin Mary?'[36] She was 'highly favored amongst women', but she was not spared 'the distress, the dread, the paradox'. Like Abraham, 'she has no need of worldly admiration'; neither is she a heroine any more than he is a hero, 'but both of them became greater than such, not at all because they were exempted from distress and torment and paradox, but they became great through these'.[37] Specifically for Mary, beyond the privilege that was her fortunate fate:

> One forgets the dread, the distress, the paradox. Was it so easy a matter not to be mistaken? Was it not dreadful that this man who walks among the others – was it not dreadful that He was God? Was it not dreadful to sit at table with Him?[38]

So their unique greatness is derived from their intimate involvement (in different ways) with divinity: Abraham, through constant dialogue as the first person to proclaim the Oneness of God; Mary, through direct physical contact. This is the peak of sublime description. It is almost as though, if Abraham had not been subjected to this test of his faith, his life and work would be worthless, his message to the world of monotheism would have gone unheeded, his status as Patriarch of the Jewish people would be irrelevant.

Yet, for all its sublime aspirations, Kierkegaard's book is a reflection of his own life's dilemmas. Having dealt extensively with Abraham in relation to the *Akedah*, he embarks on an excursus, of which the initial question, posed as a sub-heading, is, 'Was Abraham ethically defensible in keeping silent about his purpose before Sarah ... [The reference is to the unknown character of Eleazar, and is likely to confuse the reader. He is not mentioned specifically in the Bible as being present at the event of the *Akedah*, and his name was introduced much later by rabbinical interpretation. The only characters who would be known by all readers are Sarah and Isaac, and for the purposes of my argument, this is all that is needed] before Isaac?'[39] For the next 30 pages, we are treated to a rambling discussion, with no mention of any of the four people around whom the question revolves; and when they are finally mentioned, Kierkegaard disposes of the issue in eight pages. However, this is a real and meaningful issue, as Israel Charny[40] has shown. He attributes some of the responsibility to Sarah, who is a silent bystander/witness but should have had some sensitivity as to the turmoil going through her husband's head and heart; indeed, she dies immediately afterwards, though it is not clear whether she was ever apprised of the dramatic events at Moriah.

In this 30-page diversion, Kierkegaard hints at facts that Lowrie's work has clarified for all: keeping silent is the problem. Ignoring the biblical story, he deals with various literary figures (for example, Faust), real personages (for example, Socrates), biblical characters (from the Book of Tobit, part of the Jewish Apochrophyl writings), and a mythical creature (a merman).[41] Near the beginning of his complicated analysis, Kierkegaard states the need to explain the role of silence in human relations, both from an ethical and an aesthetical perspective. Thus he begins with an incomplete sentence: 'A couple of examples.'[42] The first example that he gives is of:

> A girl ... secretly in love with a man, although they have not definitely avowed their love to one another. Her parents compel her to marry another ... she obeys her parents, she conceals her love 'so as not to make the other unhappy, and no one will ever know what she suffers.' – A young man is able by a single word to

get possession of the object of his longings and his restless dreams. This little word, however, will compromise, yea, perhaps (who knows?) bring to ruin a whole family, he resolves magnanimously to remain in his concealment. 'The girl shall never get to know it, so that she may perhaps become happy by giving her hand to another.' What a pity that these two persons, both of whom were concealed from their respective beloveds, were also concealed from one another, otherwise a remarkable higher unity might have been brought about.[43]

Kierkegaard then moves on to an involved explanation as to the difference (arising out of silence or concealment) between aesthetics and ethics. The aesthetic would allow for a 'happy ending' with their marriage, 'by the help of chance';[44] but ethics, lacking chance, requires action, and in lieu of such action, the actors will have a 'secret (which) they hold at their own peril'.[45]

Given the revelations that Lowrie provides as to the personal background to the writing of this book – one of the most popular he ever wrote ('in greater demand than any other works of Kierkegaard')[46] – can there be any doubt as to what his intention was, at the most intimate, personal level, in providing this example, or when elsewhere he writes that:

A young savior falls in love with a princess and the whole content of his life consists in this love, and yet the situation is such that it is impossible for it to be realized, impossible for it to be translated from ideality into reality.[47]

Nevertheless, finally applying this lengthy diversion on the topic of silence (which comprises a full third of the book) to Abraham, Kierkegaard explains that Abraham himself did not speak, and his silence is, according to Kierkegaard, 'an offense to aesthetics, for aesthetics can well understand that I sacrifice myself, but not that I sacrifice another for my own sake'.[48] Abraham's speech is directed to God; to Isaac, he says only one sentence in reply to a query – as Kierkegaard points out – 'God will provide Himself the lamb for the burnt offering, my son.'[49] Even this, according to Kierkegaard, was difficult for him to say.[50] And even then it is a conundrum, for the use of 'lamb' may be metaphorical. He is certainly not lying. After all, in Christianity, the theme of the *Akedah* has been used, together with the Passover lamb, to refer to Jesus on the Cross.

It is not at all clear why Kierkegaard makes no reference to the Crucifixion, no reference to a deep theme in Christianity linking the two critical events, no attempt to compare the sacrifice of Isaac with the sacrifice of Jesus, in any part of the book. After all, here, too, God is silent, quiescent. There is no response to the plaintive 'Lama Azavtani?' (Why have you forsaken me?')

There is, however, a quizzical reference to a story that Kierkegaard squeezes into his discussion of the ethical aspects of Abraham's silence. He writes that, 'When Amor leaves Psyche he says to her, "Thou shalt give birth to a child which will be a divine infant if thou dost keep silence, but a human being if thou dost reveal the secret".'[51] Mary, as far as we know, did keep silent, and indeed, some of Jesus' siblings did not accept his leadership or role as Messiah[52] (perhaps because of sibling rivalry). Was this perhaps the dread, the paradox, from which Mary suffered? – that she was unable to divulge even to her own children the unique status of her oldest son and the special manner in which he had been conceived?

Is this, perhaps, also a burning question for Kierkegaard? He keeps silent about his rejected love (except for a diary entry); he writes a book about the *Akedah*, which ends with a complex discussion on silence; he makes a link between the Patriarch Abraham and the Virgin Mary and how both are silent on crucial issues affecting them; he makes passing mention of a marginal story in which a divine child will be born if the mother preserves silence as to her secret knowledge of his status, but that if the secret is revealed, divinity will be foregone. And he keeps silent about Jesus himself and his crucifixion, despite the clear connection with the *Akedah*, which so many others have discussed.

Fear and Trembling is more than a deep and impressive philosophical analysis that has been widely acclaimed; it is also a deep personal, reflexive monologue, to which the public has become privy only through Lowrie's revelations. It is a mimesis: an acting out of a personal crisis through its interconnection with a favored biblical character.[53] When first published, Kierkegaard's silence included his use of a pseudonym to guard his identity – to strengthen his 'silence' even more through anonymity: the ostensible author was given as – most significantly – Johannes de Silentio. The use of this pseudonym was not unique to *Fear and Trembling*; Kierkegaard used it on a number of occasions for his other books, especially his earlier ones.

In a book written shortly after *Fear and Trembling*, Kierkegaard focuses on Jesus. This book was also published anonymously (and, in some modern editions, published in one volume, together with *Fear and Trembling*). In this work, *The Sickness Unto Death*, Kierkegaard tried to resolve this issue of the choice between divinity and humaneness (as mentioned in Amor and Psyche). He writes that, 'In paganism man made

God a man (Man-God); in Chritianity God makes himself man (the God-Man).'[54] Once again, Kierkegaard writes of love and sacrifice, with possible further personal implications. He claims that God has 'infinite love of His compassionate grace', but that 'He made nevertheless one stipulation, He can do no other.'[55] That stipulation is not to cause offense by denying His truth, which includes the recognition of His son. Kierkegaard writes that:

> This precisely is the sorrow in Christ: 'He can do no other'. He can humble Himself, take the form of a servant, suffer and die for man, invite all to come unto Him, sacrifice every day of His life and every hour of the day, and sacrifice His life – but the possibility of the offense He cannot take away.[56]

Linked to this is the fact that, 'The greatest possible human misery, greater even than sin, is to be offended in Christ and remain offended.'[57] Yet offending is itself a sin. As Kierkegaard explained: 'The sin of abandoning Christianity as a falsehood and a lie is offensive warfare ... Sin against the Holy Ghost is the positive form of offense.'[58] This position has far-reaching implications for Jews. They are the ones who, by definition, have given offense. This is particularly so since no:

> ... doctrine on earth brought God and man so near together as has Christianity; neither could anyone else do it, only God himself can ... Neither has any doctrine ever so carefully defended itself against the most shocking of all blasphemies, that after God had taken this step it should then be taken in vain.[59]

After all, 'God came to the world, let himself be born, suffers and dies; and this suffering God almost begs and entreats ... man to accept the help which is offered to him.'[60]

The outsiders *par excellence* to this situation are quite clearly the Jews; and for this sin there is, *à la* Kierkegaard, no recompense. Paradoxically, but also most significantly, Kierkegaard claims that, 'The sin of dispensing of the forgiveness of sins is offense'; to which he immediately adds that:

> The Jews were quite right in being offended at Christ because He would forgive sins. It requires a singularly high degree of dullness ... in case a man is not a believer ... not to be offended at the fact that a man would forgive sins.[61]

The double negative is confusing, but the insinuation is clear. Jews are not prone to forgiving (despite the fact that their major holiday is the Fast of the Day of Atonement, asking God for forgiveness for sins committed, singly and collectively, as well as to seek forgiveness from family, friends, associates and neighbors, at least theoretically).[62] On the other hand, Christianity, according to Kierkegaard, is capable of forgiving all sins: except the ultimate one of denying the divinity of Jesus, a sin that all Jews, of course, automatically commit.

Kierkegaard was not writing in the Middle Ages, nor under the control of any papal imprimatur. He was a leading philosopher of the nineteenth century and an honored forerunner of modern existentialism. Yet he presents a modern version of the inevitability of Jewish sin and its unforgiveability. This is based on the original refusal of Jews to recognize Jesus as the Son of God. The Cross does indeed throw a very long shadow.

In the next chapter, we shall examine how the use of generational concepts have affected modern anti-Semitism through reference to the work of a Jewish psychoanalyst, Sigmund Freud, one of the dominant personalities of the twentieth century. Part of this anti-Semitism was to be a concretization of the inability to forgive the Jews for their obstinacy; with no capacity to forgive, the consequences were to be devastatingly fatal.

Neither of the above books by Kierkegaard deals with Jews or with anti-Semitism. Kierkegaard himself has never been accused of anti-Semitism, either in his writings or in his conduct. For that reason, his passing comment about the Jews takes on added pertinence. Because of its marginality, it is even more revealing. Kierkegaard is not trying to argue a point, to denigrate the Jews, to present them in a negative light, to instill anger or hatred in his readers. No: he is only making a statement of 'fact', presumably incontrovertible, requiring no explanation or annotation – that is, Jews lack the capacity to forgive, and therefore fail to appreciate this quality in Jesus. Through Jesus, forgiveness can be attained for all sins, with the exception of one cardinal sin: the failure or refusal to recognize the divinity of Jesus. That, according to Kierkegaard, is unforgivable, because it is to deny the very greatness of God in deciding to share the experience of being human, to be born, to live, to suffer, to die.

In many parts of the world, especially in Asia (which contains half the world's population), people do not believe in the divinity of Jesus, although they may well recognize his many outstanding qualities. But in Europe itself, the most significant group of people who, as a collective, proclaim their disbelief, are the Jews. And they do so not as outsiders but as a people into whose midst Jesus was born; as the descendants of those who were given the first chance, and the choice, of recognizing Jesus' divinity and accepting him as the Messiah. In rejecting him they, in a sense, undermine a divine plan, the magnificent and magnanimous gesture on the part of God to participate – at a unique time in history – in the everyday life of His Chosen People. This is an unforgivable sin, and entails for Jews the eternal brand of the Mark of Cain: they are to be hounded and harassed down the corridors of history, for they are a constant reminder of the humiliation and suffering of Jesus on the Cross, and of the initial failure of his movement and of the barrier they represent (by their persistent refusal to acknowledge their error) to an eschatologically better world.

All this is contained implicitly in Kierkegaard's casual comments – on different pages, yet inextricably linked – on the Jews' inability to forgive, and on Christian willingness to forgive everything except the inability to recognize the divinity of Jesus Christ. This is what is known as 'the Jewish problem', but in essence it is a Christian problem, for Jewish denial is the other side of Christian faith. Faith often involves overcoming doubt, and Jews are a constant reminder of doubt when what is required is the deep faith that Abraham possessed when responding positively to God's demand. There is broad consensus in rabbinical and canonical theology that what was at stake in the story of the *Akedah* was a test of Abraham's faith.

The *Akedah* is the prologue to the Crucifixion. Yet, Kierkegaard's discussion of the *Akedah* – perhaps the best known and most quoted of all modern interpretations – makes no mention of the Crucifixion and only one of Jesus himself. Abraham is important for Kierkegaard for two reasons: for the proof of his faith in God and for his absolute love for his son, Isaac. Without that love, there is no test of faith; there is only a temptation.

The question is, then for how many people is the story of the *Akedah* a test, and for how many a temptation, a vicarious mimetic identification with the ambivalence of being a parent, with the ambiguity of one's relations with one's progeny?

Kierkegaard himself never married; he died in his forties, just 12 years after writing *Fear and Trembling*. He confronted the issue of marital love in his own life, which eluded him, but the issue of parental love – of parental care, devotion, concerns, aspirations – only in his penetrating analysis of Abraham the father at the *Akedah*. In light of this, what would be Kierkegaard's personal understanding of the meaning of the Cross, and how would he relate to the Heavenly Father who sacrificed his son for humanity's sake? For that matter, what would be his attitude to the filicidal act, not of a biblical character, but of a key figure in the history of Christianity – Constantine? Is he, by the standards of Kierkegaard's analysis, to be condoned as Brutus, one of his predecessors, was – for having met the test of ignoring the familial connection in order to apparently further a political goal? Or was Constantine merely succumbing to temptation? Or, in his own mimesis, re-enacting the two biblical dramas? On these issues Kierkegaard is silent. Perhaps there is something in the idea of a divine being sacrificing his son that is troublesome; something that is somehow related to his own intensive analysis of Abraham in his role as a father in the story of the *Akedah*?

In *Sickness Unto Death*, he makes many references to Jesus, including to his suffering and his death, but nowhere is there mention of the Crucifixion, or of the Cross. Such references are very rare throughout his writings. A minor exception is a sentence in his *Journal* which reads, 'He spared Abraham's first-born and only tested the patriarch's faith, he spared not his only begotten son.'[63] Elsewhere in his *Journal* he presents his own version of what might have transpired at Moriah; Abraham, in this instance, does not heed the divine intervention and so we read (in his private material not incorporated into *Fear and Trembling*): 'And he drew his knife – and he thrust it into Isaac.' He then continues (with an indirect reference to resurrection):

> At that moment Jehovah in visible form stood beside Abraham and said: 'Old man, old man, what have you done? Did you not hear what I said?' ... But Abraham replied ... 'No Lord I did not hear it' ... Then Jehovah brought Isaac back to life.[64]

Having re-written this dramatic episode for his own personal edification, Kierkegaard goes on to explain how Judaism and Christianity differ in their interpretation. He suggests that, 'In the Christian view Isaac actually is sacrificed – but then eternity. In Judaism it is only a test – Abraham keeps Isaac.'[65] Isaac is apparently sacrificed, in the Christian view, because Jesus is sacrificed.

Most revealing of all, however, are his personal reminiscences of how he was introduced to the Crucifixion as a child; and there is veiled criticism of his own father, even though written in the third person. In his book, *Training in Christianity*, he describes a child (himself) being shown a picture of the Crucifixion, without an adequate explanation of who or what it represented, until the child is told that this crucified man was the Savior of the world, but he has no clear conception of what that means. Elsewhere, he writes of knowing Jesus, not through his works and parables, but only through the picture of the Crucifixion: 'Although only a child,' he writes, 'he was already of old age, an old man.' It seems that for him too, the Cross threw a shadow over the child unable to fathom its message – but was this only a memory of childhood, or also a veiled hint of adult frustration: a coded expression of incomprehension, or even of reservation as to its meaning and message?

Many of his writings contain stringent attacks upon what Kierkegaard terms 'Christendom', which is basically established Christianity, in contrast to the real Christianity, which is linked directly to the words and actions of Jesus.[66] Some of the criticism even focuses on official representatives of the church with whom Kierkegaard had personal contact. Yet, as a major modern philosopher, much of whose work revolved around religious issues Kierkegaard is surprisingly reticent about some of the key, unique issues, which form the basis of Christian theology: the issues which relate to generational contacts, and which form the basis of the contentions made in this book.

Kierkegaard addresses the matter of the divinity of Jesus and his virgin birth on one occasion in his *Journal*. He presents an interesting argumentation, one ignored by most Christian writers, and one which, I suggest, basically begs the question. The divinity of Jesus is significant for its uniqueness; this is a monotheistic religion, in which the one God has only one begotten son. On this basis, Kierkegaard refers to other examples, and peremptorily rejects their validity, using their presumably false claims to strengthen the truth of Jesus' special status. Thus, he writes:

> The thesis that it cannot be true that Christ was born of a virgin because something similar is said of Hercules, etc., and in Indian mythology etc., which is not true, is rather curious, since in a certain respect the opposite conclusion seems more correct; precisely because they say this about so many other great men for whom it was not true – for this very reason it must be true of Christ, for the fact that it has been said so often points to man's need for it.[67]

Indeed, it does, but the question remains whether the claim for Jesus is a reflection of a true reality, or a reflection of a widely felt need. Kierkegaard kept his argument on this score within the recesses of his diary and did not share it publicly in his written work. For him, it was quite possibly convincing; and, perhaps, it would also be convincing for believing Christians. But for outsiders – the point must be made – it is wholly unconvincing. The issue of Jesus' divinity is not just whether it is factually correct, but whether it is unique in the annals of human history. Why should Matthew the Evangelist be considered more convincing than authors from Greek or Indian culture who preceded him? And why did Mark, the first Evangelist, ignore the crucial detail about the virgin birth in his writing on the life of Jesus? In this regard, one might note that on another occasion in his *Journal*, Kierkegaard does discuss the issue of the virgin birth in terms of Jewish incapacity to believe in it, in contrast to a greater willingness on the part of pagans. He writes, 'That Jesus was born of a virgin – this would not decisively scandalize pagans, but to Judaism this must be really offensive.'[68]

As Kierkegaard, in *Fear and Trembling*, raises the issue of the silence of its leading character, Abraham, *vis-à-vis* those closest and dearest to him, it is surely legitimate to question Kierkegaard's own silence on the issue of the Crucifixion and its meaning in the context of his understanding of the *Akedah*. Is there a problem arising out of the conjunction of 'trial' and 'temptation'? Are there deeper reflections that he did not even dare to confide to his *Journal*? Why is he so expansive on the *Akedah* and so silent on the Crucifixion? We do not know. We will never know. Kierkegaard prefers his silence and preserves it for posterity. His pseudonym, Johannes de Silentio, is very apt.[69] As we know, he hid from his readers any personal hints, despite the impact that his personal feelings seem to have had; only the *Journal* enables us to fathom some of the hidden meanings, although there seems to be no hidden text regarding the Crucifixion. Kierkegaard is, on this matter, silent. Kierkegaard de Silentio.

Had Kierkegaard lived beyond his 42 years, he may well have wished to deal with these issues. Having conceded this, it may nevertheless be suggested that Kierkegaard's problems lay not with what he defined as Christendom, or a failed Church, or with the officialdom of Christianity, but with its theology. In that sense, it was easier to write about the *Akedah* than about the Crucifixion. It was also easier to write under a pseudonym in much of his work – and not just *Fear and Trembling* – as this allowed him to suggest that he was expressing 'their' views and not necessarily his: that he was only the 'publisher'. It is not possible, therefore, to know exactly what Kierkegaard's real views were: did he agree with Johannes de Silentio, or did he differ from him?

Murray Rae has dealt with 'Kierkegaard's vision of the Incarnation' in a recent book.[70] This focuses mainly on 'Philosophical Fragments',[71] and he refers constantly not just to Kierkegaard, but to one of the pseudonyms that he used, Climacus, almost as though Kierkegaard and 'Climacus' were separate individuals. Most significantly, he writes that:

For Kierkegaard the incarnation lies at the very centre of Christian faith. And yet belief in the doctrine of the incarnation does not constitute Christian faith. Faith is a matter of personal response to, and trust in the God-Man who confronts us with the challenge to follow him ... such a requirement confronts those who seek an objective certainty concerning the being of the God-Man and who are unable, therefore, to place their trust in him.[72]

Rae's book is interesting and complex, although often complicated by the interchange between Kierkegaard and Climacus; but it seems to me that the essence of this book is crystallized in Rae's critical reference to the work of John Hick.[73] In leading up to his discussion, Rae notes that:

On the face of it, at least, Christians are those who confess that in Jesus Christ the nature and purpose of God is disclosed to humankind. Doctrinally, this disclosure of God in Jesus has been expressed by speaking of Jesus as God Incarnate ... To confess the creed of the Christian Church is to claim that the one who has given us life now comes among us to share it.

This, I would contend is the traditional Christian position, but ... there are increasing numbers of theologians who insist that it is naive to speak of Jesus in this way. The doctrine of the incarnation, they say, is in need of revision. It must be updated and brought into line with what we know of the world. Christianity must change its shape in order to win acceptance in a world which has outgrown the allegedly primitive mentality of earlier times.[74]

Hick's appraisal is an antithesis, according to Rae, of Kierkegaard's approach. But Kierkegaard, it seems to me, is nowhere as clear in his references to God-Man as Hick is in his denial of an Incarnate God. But this interrelationship between Hick and Kierkegaard leaves one with an impression far different from what Rae intended – namely that Kierkegaard might have had similar doubts which he failed to articulate. Is his detailed discussion of the *Akedah* (with its excursus on the issue of silence) really an attempt to understand why the only begotten son of a benevolent God should be sacrificed? Is the praise heaped on Abraham – and Agamemnon, Jephthah and Brutus – a cover for the questions that Kierkegaard failed to ask about God? For the divinity of Jesus – which Kierkegaard discusses in terms of the God-Man – is mainly necessary to explain the Crucifixion and the sacrifice of the son; but Kierkegaard delves deeply into Abraham's action with Isaac and ignores God's passivity *vis-à-vis* Jesus' plight, as well as the subsequent explanation provided for His inaction. These questions take on added significance considering the ambivalence underlying some of Kierkegaard's major books, especially those written using a pseudonym.

Most commentators on Kierkegaard ignore this underlying fact, but the full measure of the resulting ambiguity in Kierkegaard's work is discussed in Rae's book. Although focussing on another of Kierkegaard's books, *Philosophical Fragments*, the implications for *Fear and Trembling* are clear. Rae takes issue with those Kierkegaard scholars who do not see any need to probe a distinction between the writer, Kierkegaard, and his 'fictional' counterpart, the author of his book. Rae sums up the situation by stating that in his own book dealing with incarnation, he will:

> ... conform to Kierkegaard's own request that we should do him the courtesy of not presuming his agreement with any of the views which are met with in the pseudonyms. Such agreement as may exist nevertheless must be discussed rather than presumed.[75]

In respect of the incarnation, is Kierkegaard also silent, or does he speak through his pseudonym? There is, I submit, no definite answer.

Confirmation of Rae's approach to the pseudonymous writings is provided by a book devoted specifically to this topic. The intriguing title is *Kierkegaard: Godly Deceiver*, and the author, Holmes Hartshorne, also sub-titled the book, *The Nature and Meaning of his Pseudonymous Writings*. In his opening sentence, he explains that, 'One of the most distinctive feature of Kierkegaard's literary work is the large number of his books which were written pseudonymously.'[76] He adds that, 'Ostensibly, these books are not by Kierkegaard at all; their authorship is ascribed to such characters as Johannes de Silentio or Judge William or Johannes Climacus.'[77] Of particular import is Kierkegaard's own assertion at the end of his work, *Concluding Unscientific Postscript*, where he writes that, 'In the pseudonymous works, there is not a single word that is mine ... I am just as far from being Johannes de Silentio in *Fear and Trembling* as I am from being the knight of faith he depicts.'[78] Hartshorne suggests that Kierkegaard was far more serious in placing this distance between himself and his 'fictional' authors than his interpreters have recognized. Hartshorne's own solution to this strange literary situation is to suggest that Kierkegaard's books are examples of irony – a topic that interested him from his early work in an academic dissertation on irony in Socrates' writings.

Irony, however, is only one aspect of his work; it was Kierkegaard's tactic – borrowed from Socrates – 'To deceive the reader into the truth'.[79]

Two other 'formative factors' in his writing were melancholy and Christianity. The former was clearly a reflection of his personality (and also a key factor in the break-up of his relationship with Regina); the latter was the essence of his belief system.[80] The three are, however, closely interrelated; it is quite likely that the irony in his work, and the melancholy in his nature, were a consequence of the dilemmas he sensed when confronting Christianity. Outwardly, he expressed this – with little irony, in fact with outright vehemence – in his critique of Christendom. Inwardly, he was involved in a struggle to maintain and express his faith in Christianity. In this sense, the topic of Abraham provided a wonderful example; but dealing with the willingness of Abraham to sacrifice his beloved son raised serious questions as to the problematics of such faith, and also reflected a similar willingness on the part of God to sacrifice His son.

If this be so, the diversionary discussion in *Fear and Trembling* becomes more understandable and more pertinent. In this discussion of the story of the *Akedah*, Kierkegaard was intent on struggling with his emotions and with the meaning of Abraham's action, but was also concerned to conceal the full background to his writing. Hence the pseudonym; hence the discussion of Abraham's silence.

According to Lowrie, these hidden factors had to do with the final breakdown of his relationship with Regina, and the references to Abraham and his love for Isaac, the object of the planned sacrifice, were indirect references to his own situation. Yet, an alternative – or perhaps an additional – possibility may be raised: that Kierkegaard was struggling with his religious beliefs, in particular as concerning the issue of the Crucifixion and the message contained therein of God's sacrifice of His son, which was akin to Abraham's willingness to do likewise. It may be suggested that Kierkegaard was confronting God's action towards Jesus via a discussion of Abraham's action towards his son, Isaac. Else why would he totally ignore the obvious connection, so often incorporated into Christian theology?

Although *Fear and Trembling* deals ostensibly with the depth of Abraham's faith, it was possibly really concerned with the extent of Kierkegaard's doubt. In this sense, perhaps Kierkegaard was a prototype of the modern religious person; he may well have been way ahead of his time, a forerunner of the 'Jesus Seminar', and of questioning theologians, such as Hick. But, even more so, as an early existentialist, he may have inadvertently encountered the truth – that, in the final analysis, especially in a secular world, the essence of religion is not unquestioning faith but probing doubt; it is not the pat, standard answers of organized religion (what he called 'Christendom') but the endless questioning of a Sisyphistic search for the unknowable; it is not the finality of a sacrificed son but the ongoing journey to Moriah, or Golgotha, or whatever mountain-top – Sinai, Olympus – serves as the beacon and symbol for a particular society.

NOTES

1. Chagall's picture has been used, on several occasions, as a cover illustration on books dealing with the connections between Jesus and the Jews; *see*, for instance, Susannah Heschel, *Abraham Geiger and the Jewish Jesus* (Chicago, IL: University of Chicago Press, 1998).
2. Nicolas Kazanzakis, *The Last Temptation of Christ* (London: Faber and Faber, 1961); and José Saramago, *The Gospel According to Jesus Christ* (London: Harvill, 1993).
3. The poem is quoted in full in Louis Berman, *The Akedah: The Binding of Isaac* (Northvale, NJ: Jason Avonson, 1947), p. 202.
4. Ibid., chapter 23, 'The Akedah in Music and Literature', and chapter 24, 'The Akedah in Art'.
5. Sigmund Freud, *Moses and Monotheism* (London: Hogarth Press, 1939).
6. Soren Kierkegaard, *Fear and Trembling* (Princeton, NJ: Princeton University Press, 1941).
7. Walter Lowrie, *Kierkegaard* (Oxford: Oxford University Press, 1938).
8. Translator's Introduction to *Fear and Trembling*, p. 9. *See also Repetition: An Essay in Experimental Psychology* (Princeton, NJ: Princeton University Press, 1941).
9. Kierkegaard, *Fear and Trembling*, p. 9. Lowrie writes the name Regina in its accepted English form, but some writers use the Danish form, Regine.
10. Ibid., pp. 9–10.
11. *See* Howard Hong and Edna Hong (eds/trans), *The Journals of Soren Kierkegaard: A Selection* (Oxford: Oxford University Press, 1938).
12. As quoted in Kierkegaard, *Fear and Trembling*, p. 10.
13. Ibid.
14. Ibid., p. 11.
15. Ibid.
16. Ibid.
17. Ibid., p. 42.
18. James Strong, *The Exhaustive Concordance of the Bible* (New York: Abingdon Press, 1965). An interesting analysis of the use of the word 'temptation' is provided in a book where the word appears in its very title: *see* Susan R. Garrett, *The Temptations of Jesus in Mark's Gospel* (Grand Rapids, MI: William B. Eerdmans Publishing, 1998). In the opening sentence she writes:

> The first Christians remembered Jesus as one who had faced and endured temptation ... Matthew, Mark, and Luke all depict Jesus as tested by Satan in the wilderness. From the early Christian's perspective, the tempting or testing of Jesus would not have seemed unusual or offensive. (p. 1)

Later, she explains a bit of the problematics in the word by noting that:

> Modern English usage does not make a strong connection between trials of affliction and trials of seduction. English speakers often interpret suffering as a 'test' of faith, but view seductive persons or things as 'temptations', which they regard as fundamentally different. (p. 5)

19. Kierkegaard, *Fear and Trembling*, p. 42.
20. *See* quote at footnote 17 on the previous page.
21. Kierkegaard, *Fear and Trembling*, p. 81.
22. Ibid., p. 42.
23. Ibid.

24. *See* Carol Delaney, *Abraham on Trial: The Legacy of Biblical Myth* (Princeton, NJ: Princeton University Press, 1998).
25. Kierkegaard, *Fear and Trembling*, p. 41.
26. Ibid., p. 69.
27. Ibid., pp. 68–9.
28. Ibid., p. 68.
29. Ibid. It should be noted that there are later extrapolations on the text, which suggest that in the end she was not killed; just as there are extrapolations on the *Akedah* that suggest Isaac was killed.
30. Ibid., pp. 69–70.
31. Ibid., p. 70. On each occasion that the word temptation (in English) appears, the Danish word appears in parenthesis; and three different words are used, with *anfechtung* being the most frequent (see, for example, p. 71). Thus, there may be subtle distinctions in Kierkegaard's work that are lost in translation, but, to the best of my understanding, these have no effect on the argument.
32. Ibid., p. 74.
33. Geza Vermes, *Scripture and Tradition in Judaism: Haggadic Studies* (Leiden: E.J. Brill, 1961).
34. Ibid., p. 220.
35. Kierkegaard, *Fear and Trembling*, p. 42.
36. Ibid., p. 75.
37. Ibid., pp. 75–6.
38. Ibid., p. 76.
39. Ibid., p. 91.
40. Israel Charny, 'And Abraham went to Slay Isaac: A Parable of Killer, Victim, and Bystander in the Family', *Journal of Ecumenical Studies*, 10 (1973), p. 304.
41. Kierkegaard, *Fear and Trembling*: for Faust (p. 117), for Socrates (p. 126), for Tobit (p. 111), for the merman (p. 103).
42. Ibid., p. 94.
43. Ibid., pp. 94–5.
44. Ibid., p. 95.
45. Ibid., p. 96.
46. Ibid., p. 5 (translator's note).
47. Ibid., p. 52.
48. Ibid., p. 122. Lowrie, the translator, notes that the word 'aesthetics' has a slightly different meaning in the original Danish.
49. Ibid., p. 128.
50. Ibid., p. 127.
51. Ibid., p. 97.
52. *See*, for instance, earlier reference (chapter 3) to Ernest Renan, *The Life of Jesus* (1863), chapter 2, 'Infancy and Youth of Jesus', esp. pp. 84–5.
53. *See also* discussion of mimesis in chapter 2, '*Akedah*'.
54. Soren Kierkegaard, *The Sickness Unto Death* (Princeton, NJ: Princeton University Press, 1941), p. 257. This book was published in one volume with *Fear and Trembling*.
55. Ibid., p. 257.
56. Ibid.
57. Ibid.
58. Ibid., p. 256.
59. Ibid., p. 248.
60. Ibid., p. 216.
61. Ibid., p. 247.
62. *See*, for instance, Philip Goodman, *The Yom Kippur Anthology* (Philadelphia, PA: The Jewish Publication Society, 1971).
63. *Soren Kierkegaard's Journals and Papers*, Vol. 1, Howard V. Hong and Edna H. Hong (eds/trans) (Bloomington, IN: Indiana University Press, 1967), p. 127, entry no. 298 (9 September 1836).

64. Ibid., Vol. 2, p. 508, entry no. 2223 (1853).
65. Ibid.
66. *See*, for instance, Soren Kierkegaard, *Attack on Christendom* (Princeton, NJ: Princeton University Press, 1944).
67. Hong and Hong (eds/trans), *Journals*, Vol. 1, p. 124, entry no. 276 (13 September 1839).
68. Ibid., Vol. 2, p. 510, entry no. 2227 (1854).
69. Kierkegaard uses pseudonyms in many of his works, especially the earlier ones, each of them chosen to hint at a larger theme in the work. Kierkegaard often treats these personaes as though they were actual people, separate from him and with different views.
70. Murray A. Rae, *Kierkegaard's Vision of the Incarnation: By Faith Transformed* (Oxford: Clarendon Press, 1997).
71. Soren Kierkegaard, *Philosophical Fragments* (Princeton, NJ: Princeton University Press, 1936).
72. Rae, *Kierkegaard's Vision of the Incarnation*, p. 68.
73. See John Hick (ed.), *The Myth of God Incarnate* (London: SCM Press, 1977). *See also* Hick, 'Trinity and Incarnation in the Light of Religious Pluralism', in J. Hick and E. Meltzer (eds), *Three Faiths – One God: A Jewish, Christian, Muslim Encounter* (London: Macmillan, 1989), p. 197. At p. 209, Hick writes: 'I have been suggesting that we should not insist that Jesus was literally God incarnate, but should see him as a human being who was so startlingly open and responsive to God's presence that God was working through him for the salvation of many.'
74. Rae, *Kierkegaard's Vision of the Incarnation*, pp. 173–4.
75. Ibid., p. 5.
76. M. Holmes Hartshorne, *Kierkegaard: Godly Deceiver: The Nature and Meaning of his Pseudonymous Writings* (New York: Columbia University Press, 1990).
77. Ibid., p. 1.
78. Soren Kierkegaard, *Concluding Unscientific Postscript* (Princeton, NJ: Princeton University Press, 1941), n.p.
79. Kierkegaard, *Fear and Trembling*, p. xv.
80. Ibid., p. 28. Hartshorne writes that of the three – irony, melancholy and Christianity – 'The most enduring and also the most powerful was Christianity' (p. 28).

11

Freud

Just as Kierkegaard, who was a Christian but barely concerned himself with the Crucifixion, despite its clear relevance for his analysis of the *Akedah*, Sigmund Freud, as a Jew, barely mentioned the *Akedah* despite its clear relevance to generational interaction, which formed such an important aspect of his overall work, through his focus on the Oedipus Complex. In the case of Kierkegaard, I have argued that his lapse in this regard may well reflect doubts that plagued him as to the meaning attributed to the Crucifixion by Christian theology. In the case of Freud, there also seems to be an ulterior motive, linked not to theological doubts, however, but to scientific assertion, or what is really ideological propensity.

The story of the *Akedah* does not fit in comfortably with the Oedipal theme, which is so central to Freud's work. As noted in an earlier chapter, Freud never made any concerted effort in one comprehensive book to present his radical and important thesis regarding child hostility towards parents (more specifically father to son, arising out of sexual rivalry for the love of the mother/wife), but the essence of this idea permeates almost all of his work.[1] A reasonable assumption is that Freud, who was not averse to using biblical themes, deliberately ignored the *Akedah*, as it was, in its description of a father sacrificing his son, in direct conflict with his Oedipal thesis.

On one occasion, Freud makes a passing comment that one of his patients explained to him his troubles in maintaining belief in a God who would command a father to sacrifice his son.[2] But that is the limit of his awareness of a problem requiring treatment, and certainly having possible direct implications for the patient's relations with either his own father or (if he was a father himself) with his son.

Freud's reticence with regard to one of the major biblical stories (and one that deals with a clash of generations, which so intrigued him in the Oedipus story) cannot be seen as a minor or insignificant lapse on his part, as on a number of occasions he embarked on ambitious projects that were bound up with biblical themes. The most notable of such projects is his fascinating but controversial account of Moses' life, and the manner in which he fulfilled his role as the bearer of the message of monotheism to the Children of Israel in the desert.[3] So intent was he on finding universal applications for the original Greek myth on which he based his Oedipal theory that (in his own manufactured account) he replaces Moses' tranquil death in the desert, near the border of the Holy Land, with a violent death at the hands of his younger followers.

Furthermore, Moses is presented not just as a religious and political leader, or a prophet, but as the father figure of the Israelites, thereby replacing, of course, Abraham, the key figure in the story of the *Akedah*. This particular role is assigned to Moses in order to set up a situation in which his followers (now seen as 'sons') rise up and put him to death. In doing so, Freud claims that the Israelites were only re-enacting the primal crime, which he had himself described (in another manufactured account) about a quarter of a century earlier in *Totem and Taboo*.[4] In this book, he presented his own version of a hypothesized event in which a horde of young sons came together to kill and devour their father in order to supplant the patriarchal generation. Not content with such a patricidal act, the sons then acted as 'Cannibal savages' who 'devoured their victim as well as killing him'. This cannibalism turns, according to Freud, into a 'totem meal, which is perhaps mankind's earliest festival' and becomes 'a repetition and a commemoration of this memorable and criminal deed, which was the beginning of so many things – of social organization, of moral restrictions and of religion'.[5]

This basic event, 'with which civilization began ... has not allowed mankind a moment's rest'.[6] Indeed, it provides the prototype for the foundation of two monotheistic religions. In re-writing Moses' fate, Freud suggests that the Israelites were reluctant to accept his message of monotheism – an idea that he had borrowed from Egyptian religion through Pharaoh Ikhanaton – and so they rebelled against him.[7] Freud then claims that 'fate had brought the great deed and misdeed of primaeval days, the killing of the father, closer to the Jewish people by causing them to repeat it on the person of Moses, an outstanding father figure'.[8]

However, this act evoked a later response: of 'remorse for the murder of Moses' which in turn 'provided the stimulus for the wishful fantasy of the Messiah'.[9] This leads Freud on to a further conclusion that it is not surprising that 'the violent killing of another great man became the starting point for the Christian religion'.[10] It is of no little interest to note that, in this instance – in directly linking the fate of Moses and Jesus – Freud refers to the latter as a 'great man', this presumably in an attempt to hint at him being a possible father figure and to escape (within the context of the thesis being presented) the inconvenient definition of the death as being that of the *Son* of God. Furthermore, it was no doubt difficult for Freud to present Jesus as a father figure, given the young age at which he was crucified (in his early thirties) and the fact that he never married and so did not have any children. The father figure was thus difficult to conjure up in such circumstances, and so Freud chooses the image of a 'great man'.

Elsewhere, however, in *Totem and Taboo*, Freud does acknowledge the fact that it is the son who is the victim. However, ignoring any possibility of linking this fact to the *Akedah* (that he so elegantly avoids mentioning), Freud enters into a dialectical explanation that fits neatly into the Oedipal scheme. He writes:

> There can be no doubt that in the Christian myth the original sin was against God, the Father. If, however, Christ redeemed mankind from the burden of original sin by the sacrifice of his own life, we are driven to conclude that the sin was a murder. The Law of Talion, which is so deeply rooted in human feelings, lays it down that a murder can only be expiated by guilt. And if this sacrifice of a life brought about atonement with God, the Father, the crime to be expiated can only have been the murder of the father.
>
> In the Christian doctrine, therefore, men were acknowledging in the most undisguised manner the guilty primeval deed, since they formed the fullest atonement for it in the sacrifice of this one son.[11]

In the course of this argument, Freud takes care to avoid any reference to any paternal participation in the fatal act: thus, it is the 'son' who sacrifices 'his own life', not the 'father', who is involved in a voluntary gesture of sacrifice on behalf of mankind. The question also arises as to why this particular fatal act should not be seen as an independent crime without an antecedent, since, within the Bible itself, there is no earlier act of patricide as Freud intimates. The only 'evidence' of such an act is not in the Bible but in Freud's own writing, where he describes, as mentioned, a totally conjectural situation – a figment of his own imagination – in which the sons rebel, kill and devour their father. This is the crime, according to Freud, for which the crucifixion of Jesus provides expiation. This is surely carrying biblical exegesis way beyond anything that even rabbinical or canonical 'creativity' had conjured up in the past.[12]

Freud is, perhaps, entitled to speculate in order to substantiate his ideas, but in drawing upon the Bible as a basis, there are certain logical ground rules by which the commentator must abide. There is no room for a hypothesis of a primal crime in which sons kill a father, when the earliest passages of the Bible provide vivid examples of other primal crimes; in terms of fatalities, it is fratricide (Cain killing Abel) and not patricide that is the evil deed. Also, it is widely recognized that the original sin was the eating of forbidden fruit.

As for the link between Moses and Jesus, Moses was indeed a father, but little is known of his two sons beyond the explanation of the names that they were given.[13] There is no intention to create a dynasty, as in terms of generational continuation; this is reserved for the priestly caste, that is, the descendants of Moses' brother, Aharon. He was the priest appointed to look after the Holy Ark, a function that was also assigned to his sons. However, two of them were killed, simultaneously and mysteriously,[14] when they acted negligently whilst performing their sacred duties – presumably this was the result of God's intervention, and thus is an early example of the sacrifice of sons within a religious context.

The fictional extrapolation by Freud when discussing the primal crime is, I believe, of major import, because, in its very extremity in setting up a 'make-believe' primal world, for which there is neither a biblical account nor scientific evidence, it provides proof of the manner in which belief-systems intrude on scientific research, and in which academic theories affect the presentation and interpretation of religious writings.

The sociology of knowledge in the past, and critical theory in the present, provide ample warnings of the manner in which what seems to be objective analysis may be merely a reflection of the writer's personal predilections, or a consequence of his social affiliations.[15] For instance, being religious or not obviously affects the manner in which the Bible is read and understood; being Jewish or Christian affects the manner in which key events (such as the Crucifixion) are explained; being male or female (or a feminist or a sexist) may affect one's reading of what is known as the Fall, when Eve is understood to have succumbed to temptation;[16] being young or old (in fact or in spirit) may affect the understanding of the *Akedah*.

In my book, *Generations Apart*, I noted the fact that, in generational conflict, almost all the analyses have been made by the older generation, since the younger, for the most part, lack the capacity to do the necessary research and writing – and by the time that such capacity was achieved, they had often passed from the younger category to the older, and so the question was posed of 'Who Speaks for the Young?'[17] At the most personal level, there is wide agreement that Freud's work was affected by his coming to terms with the death of his father – which occurred at a time when he was beginning to struggle with the issue, in psycho-analytical terms, of generational contact – and conflict. Specifically, he was moving from his initial musings on a 'seduction theory' (where the older generation seduce the younger) to the linked but inverse theory where (in the case of male children) incestuous yearnings for the love of the mother lead to patricidal urges against the father as the potential rival for that love.[18] These feelings have to be confronted and curbed – at an early age, between four and six – as part of the normal process of socialization, and failure to do so leads to behavioral problems in the future.

Many writers on Freud have suggested that the insight that led to this theory emerged as a result of his depressive state (lasting several years) brought on by the death of his father.[19] However, it is likely that a more significant factor in Freud's life was that four of his children were actually within the crucial Oedipal phase (ages four to six, when the crisis should be resolved); however, biographers and interpreters of his theoretical framework ignore this factor.[20]

In terms of his depressive state, such a reaction to his father's death seems unlikely, since his father died at the ripe old age of 80, when Freud himself (much younger than his siblings, by as much as 20 years) was himself already 40. That is, Freud had been blessed with a father who lived a decade beyond the biblical figure of three score years and ten, and he himself was in middle age, at the threshold of his great career. Why would the death of his father have brought on such an extreme reaction – a depression lasting several years?

In terms of a depression within the family context, two other possibilities seem far more likely, but have been ignored. First, as mentioned, Freud, as the first person to become intellectually aware of the existence (universal, at that) of an Oedipus Complex, had to cope simultaneously with the fact that his own children (with their presumed incestuous and patricidal thoughts) were going through this critical phase in their lives (unless, of course, he blocked out any personal ramifications). Second, as an intellectual who later expressed his skepticism about the nature of religious beliefs in his book, *The Future of an Illusion*,[21] he was faced with a challenging dilemma as a Jew. Jewish custom declares a period of mourning for the death of a parent in which, for 11 months a son is obliged to say the mourner's prayer (*kadish*) at the three daily services, morning, afternoon and evening. Did Freud comply with this burdensome ritual, despite his indifference to religious customs – and if so, how did he cope with this disparity between his intellectual awareness of the illusionary nature of religion and his daily observance of a religious custom? Or, alternatively, did he forego this daily religious ritual – and, if so, how did this affect his feelings of betrayal towards his lately deceased father? In effect, he was confronted with an insoluble dilemma, and it is quite likely that it was his guilt and/or frustration that caused his depressive state, and might even have triggered some of his thinking about the Oedipus Complex.

Thus, those who have argued for a connection between the fact of his father's death and the theory of the Oedipus Complex may indeed be correct in suggesting the connection, but at fault in their interpretation of the roots of its origin. It may have been his disloyalty to his father at this time that not only caused the depression but also led to the assignment of blame to the son in the Oedipus Complex, rather than his own memories of childhood hostility as is generally presumed.

These are not irrelevant considerations, as there are few modern thinkers for whom the connection between a theoretical framework and their personal background is so important. (For instance, Freud even relates some of his own dreams in his early work on *The Interpretation of Dreams*.)[22] In addition, Freud's understanding of religion rests on generational factors; he states that the belief in abstract concepts such as God is a consequence of illusions arising from childhood experience, as when faced with uncertainty or danger, an adult is likely to invoke memories of childhood, with its fantasies and lack of logic. Formal religion is therefore really a collective response, similar to that of any child struggling with neurotic feelings.[23]

Leading off from this is, of course, the manner in which Freud relates to biblical themes – and more important, given his exceptional status – the impact that his ideas have had on other thinkers and their attempts to use a Freudian perspective to interpret both the Bible and social reality.[24] If Freud's basic assumptions are questionable, then consequent interpretations must be meticulously examined; furthermore, where the Oedipal aspect appears strongly, the possibility should be explored of understanding the same phenomenon from a diametrically opposite perspective: that provided by the Rustum Complex.

If, for instance, some aspects of anti-Semitism, which are rooted in religion, are now understood within the framework of the Oedipus Complex, it is quite possible that an opposite approach – that of the Rustum Complex – might provide greater and better clarification. For – as already noted in earlier chapters – the Bible abounds with generational themes, and Freud and other authors often refer to Judaism and Christianity in generational terms: of 'father' and 'son' religions, or 'mother' and 'daughter' religions. Whether one's perspective is that of the Oedipus Complex or that of the Rustum Complex (or Laius Complex) is liable to have a tremendous impact on the manner in which many biblical stories are understood – and most particularly, of course,

those of the *Akedah* and the Crucifixion, where the generational theme
is a primary factor, and where the consequences (intended and planned
in the *Akedah*, and actualized in the Crucifixion) are so extreme.

In a work devoted to the issue of the psychoanalytic aspects of what
he calls 'The Dogma of Christ', Erich Fromm, a Jewish writer, explains
that:

> The transformation which Christianity, especially the concept of
> Christ and of his relation to God the Father, underwent from its
> early days down to this era, must be understood primarily in the
> light of this social change and of the psychic change conditioned by
> it, and of the new sociological function which Christianity had to
> assume.[25]

Fromm claims that the success of Christianity was not attributable to the
fact that in its original, pure form it won over so many adherents in the
Roman Empire to its belief-system, but to the fact that the religion was
adapted in order to make it more palatable: thus, 'the original religion
was transformed into another one', but the Church took care to conceal
'this transformation'.[26]

Part of this change related to its new status, from a religion of the
oppressed to a religion of the rulers, and from a change from reluctance
to accept the authority of the state to actually incorporating state
authority into the religion.[27] Thus, perhaps, forming what Kierkegaard
referred to as 'Christendom'.[28] This led, according to Fromm, to a new
dogma of Jesus, in which (in words that were stressed): '*The decisive
element was the change from the idea of man becoming God to that of
God becoming man.*'[29]

Having succinctly described this complex process, Fromm then
presents a more detailed explanation of its key factors, invoking a direct
reference to Oedipus. He writes:

> Since the new concept of the Son, who was indeed a second person
> beside God, yet one with him, changed the tension between God
> and his son into harmony, and since it avoided the concept that a
> man could become God, it eliminated from the formula the revolu-
> tionary character of the older doctrine, namely, hostility to the
> father. The Oedipus crime contained in the old formula, the
> displacement of the father by the son, was eliminated in the new
> Christianity. The father remained untouched in his position. Now,
> however, it was not a man, but his only begotten Son, existing
> before all creation, who was beside him. Jesus himself became God

without dethroning God because he had always been a component of God.[30]

After presenting this explanation, Fromm poses a question as to why Christianity, within this perspective, should have succeeded, especially in contrast to its 'great competition ... the emperor cult'.[31] He asks specifically, 'Why did Christianity and not the emperor cult succeed in becoming the established state religion of the Roman Empire?' To which he answers, 'Because Christianity had a quality that made it superior for the social function it was intended to fulfill, namely, faith in the crucified Son of God.'[32] It was easier, according to Fromm, for the 'suffering and oppressed masses' to identify with Jesus; not, as in pagan religions, 'in order to dethrone the father in fantasy, but in order to enjoy his love and grace. The idea that a man became a God [for instance, with the emperors declaring themselves to be pagan gods] was a symbol of aggressive, active, hostile-to-the-father tendencies. The idea that God became a man was transformed into a symbol of the tender, passive tie to the father.'[33]

Fromm goes on to explain the ease with which identification with God was possible, because hostility to Him as Father had been eliminated by the shared status of Father and Son. However, the problem remained as to what to do with 'aggressive impulses' that 'could not have disappeared'.[34] Fromm suggests that the solution to this quandary lies in the fact that the stress in religious dogma was no longer 'on the overthrow of the father, but on the self-annihilation of the son'.[35] While such an outcome might seem potentially undesirable, Fromm concludes (rather lamely) that aggression being directed against the self would provide 'an outlet that was harmless for social stability'.[36] Basically, the rulers (presumably both religious and secular) were able to exploit this theological process to their advantage. They themselves could identify with the 'suffering Jesus' and thereby receive penance for any negative acts on their part toward the masses, while the latter, for their part, could also find solace for their own suffering by remembering that Jesus, too, had suffered, indeed on their behalf.

This basic change in the conceptualization of the Church came about at Nicaea, where, in Fromm's description, it was asserted that Jesus 'became the pre-existent only-begotten Son of God, of one nature with him and yet a second person beside him'.[37] Fromm makes no reference here to the role of Constantine in effecting this transformation, while simultaneously declaring Christianity to be the State Religion and then, within a year, acting out the sacrifice of a son by having his own son tried, sentenced to death and executed.[38]

Within Fromm's explanation, it is of interest to note the distinction he draws between the fate of Jesus and other young dying gods in contemporary pagan religions; they remained only as sons, without attaining the same relationship with their divine fathers that had been vouchsafed to Jesus. Thus, gods, such as 'Attis, Adonis and Osiris', retained an 'unconscious hostility to the father-god',[39] whereas in Christianity, due to the oneness of God and Jesus, the hostility disappeared: 'Jesus eventually became God without overthrowing God because he was always God.'[40]

This process, as described by Fromm, involves a certain amount of co-optation. Since there is an interconnection between a divine being and the ruling class, by presenting the son in this manner and suggesting parity between the two, the ruling class were able to fend off any criticism or challenge. Through the suffering of Jesus, the masses would be able to find comfort for their own suffering and would therefore moderate their anger against the rulers. Fromm claims that the Church succeeded in inducing passive attitudes in the populace, which persisted until the Reformation. 'Protestantism,' he claims, 'turned back to the father-god', and this permitted 'an active attitude on the part of the masses'.[41] His thesis also covers the role assigned to the Virgin Mary, and the role of the Great Mother in contrast to a Heavenly Father.[42] However, it ends at this point, and therefore all the implications arising from the growth of Protestantism are not dealt with.

What Fromm is suggesting is that strong sociological and personal forces were brought under control within the western world by the basically lulling effect caused by a novel approach to religious matters. The novelty was not in the idea of monotheism (since Judaism had obviously preceded Christianity, and at that time Jews were spread throughout the Roman Empire and were then not averse to converting others), nor in the idea of a young dying god who becomes resurrected (since other examples existed), but of a combination of these two ideas, linked to the exalted status of the son, who was considered on a par with the Heavenly Father. The enhanced status of the son provided both psychological and sociological relief, the former in terms of personal and familial relations (for instance, between father and son), the latter in terms of societal and political factors (for instance, between rulers and ruled). If, in theoretical and theological terms, there is a direct link from the *Akedah* to the Crucifixion, in practical and political terms there is, according to Fromm (building on Freud), a direct link from Oedipus to Jesus, from the fatal meeting at the crossroads near Thebes to the fatal event at Golgotha.

Within this Freudian perspective, and its implications for theology, the question arises as to what would be the impact of a generational conflict that stemmed not from hostility of the son toward the father, but from the father toward the son, from the parents toward the children, from the older generation toward the younger. What is the Freudian meaning behind a divine son who is crucified in an act of redemption for humanity, who becomes resurrected, and then disappears into Heaven where he is given equal status with his Father, but whose divinity is rejected by those who believe in a Heavenly Father without an interceding son?

If there is a real social problem of potential parental hostility, then the comforting Freudian description provided by Fromm becomes only partially acceptable, as there is also the opposite social phenomenon of filial hostility. A divine son who is considered equal with his Heavenly Father might – even if only because of clever political manipulation by a ruling and priestly class – lead to a tranquil social and political comity (at least in theory). But, within this same theoretical framework (of generations and religion), what is the consequence of adult hostility? Could such hostility find a convenient outlet in the belief that a Heavenly Father wished to sacrifice His son, and was this point so critical that, prior to the Crucifixion, He had directed the first person to be fully apprised of His Presence to sacrifice his own son on a mountain top? Could the kind of considerations that possibly, led to Constantine's filicidal action explain why Christianity was attractive to the masses? Alternatively, far from Christianity providing parity between the generations (through a Heavenly Father and a Divine Son), the critical factor might well have been that the Heavenly Father sanctioned, by the act of sacrifice, hostile actions against a younger generation.

Indeed, this may be one of the key issues differentiating Christianity from Judaism. Did the Crucifixion put an end to generational conflict or did it exacerbate it? In any event, history hardly provides support for Fromm's thesis, for violence has persisted. In Christian societies, the masses have not exactly acted according to Fromm's peaceful description; they have not always been successfully co-opted. In fact, at a number of key moments in history (for instance, England in 1649 and France in 1789), when there was the vague concept of the 'divine right of kings', deicide was practiced. Furthermore, internecine warfare between Catholics and Protestants was a regular feature of European history.

But, most particularly, violence justified on religious grounds was focused on the Jews: as those who had rejected the Messiah as the Son of God; as the Children of Israel who had betrayed the trust reposed in them by their Heavenly Father; as the Chosen People who had forfeited their right to retain their original exalted status. All of this is an integral part of western civilization, and of the central role of Christianity in this civilization. In the last millenium, the violence ranges over the bloody massacres that accompanied the Crusades, to the ruthless persecution of the Inquisition, to the pogroms in Eastern Europe, and to the recurrent blood-libels: all culminating in the tragedy of the Holocaust.

These expressions of anti-Semitism have been exposed to Freudian analysis, in which the adherents of the son-religion are presumed to give expression to their Oedipal urges against the members of the father-religion. As expressed by one of the most typical examples of such analyses, there is a direct road that leads from Golgotha to Auschwitz.[43] David Bakan, in a book dealing with the infanticidal impulse, notes, in the Preface to his book, that:

> The genius of the twentieth century is related to its resolve to pursue truth relentlessly. The mind of the twentieth century, *the century of psychoanalysis on the one hand and the Nazi concentration camps on the other*, appreciates that virtue is not served by not looking at evil.[44] [emphasis added]

Israel Charny, an Israeli psychologist, has claimed that the profession of psychology is at fault not only for not having a satisfactory explanation for the human evil perpetrated in the Holocaust, but for not having even invested the necessary thought, energy and resources to fathoming the causative underpinnings of its perpetration.[45] Zigmund Baumann has made a similar critique of his profession, sociology;[46] while in a recent study, Stephen Haynes has carried out a perceptive and comprehensive study of responses to the Holocaust, and in particular the challenge that it poses for Christian theology.[47] Psychoanalysis has made some effort to probe deeply into the hidden causes of the Holocaust, going beyond traditional explanations of anti-Semitism, but it remains far too hidebound by its Freudian framework.

I do not intend attempting in this chapter to probe deeply into the ultimate mystery of how the Holocaust was possible: of how a leading nation of European civilization could lapse into such debauchery. But, inasmuch as Oedipal ideas have been canvassed in terms of the son-religion oppressing the father-religion, let me suggest that an alternative approach might be usefully examined, in which the Children of Israel would be seen as a legitimate target for repressive measures partly as a delayed punishment for their earlier crime of killing the Son of God, partly because the terminology of the 'Children of Israel' sets up a social situation into which hostile feelings toward the young can be channeled.

In order to appreciate the possibility of such considerations, it might be noted that, even within the Jewish community, theological explanations have been given for the tragedy that befell the Jews. Fundamentalist Ultra-Orthodox groups, struggling to understand how God could have forsaken His people, have attempted to resolve the dilemma by claiming that the tragedy can be seen as a punishment for the behavior of secular Jews who are therefore delinquent in observing the commandments, or of Zionist Jews who are arrogant in their desire to pre-empt the advent of the Messiah.[48] Ideas such as these occasionally erupt into fierce debate between Ultra-Orthodox rabbis and secular politicians within Israel; such arguments inevitably evoke vigorous, and even vicious, responses from their opponents.

As mentioned in an earlier chapter, anti-Semitism (like xenophobia and racism) is basically illogical, and therefore there is not necessarily a logical explanation for it. In this sense, psychoanalysis has certain advantages: it offers explanations relating to the unconscious, the irrational and the emotional. All this is well and good for its ability to contribute to some understanding of what is, in the final analysis, really incomprehensible, but it is undermined by its over-reliance on the Oedipal perspective. The Rustum Complex – which suggests the damage done by an older generation to a younger one – may provide useful insights for understanding the manner in which rationalizations are provided for a Heavenly Father punishing the aberrant 'children' of his 'Chosen People'; or for the displacement of suppressed and unconscious hostility to the young finding substitute expression in harming the 'Children of Israel', especially given the linguistic problematics of such a term, as was discussed in the earlier chapter on 'Passover'.

Indeed, in order to understand the subtle manner in which anti-Jewish sentiments are often expressed, one might note not the actions of rabid anti-Semites, but the measured tones of scholarly writing. One notable example is found in the work of John Cuddihy, who blames the Jews for undermining western civilization and introducing rudeness into what is essentially a genteel culture.[49] This is found, according to Cuddihy, not just in the behavior of Jews, but in the writings of some of the leading Jewish scholars: the three whom he deals with are Freud, Karl Marx and the French anthropologist, Lévi-Strauss. In mounting an attack on the civility that is the mark of western civilization, they are, he claims, invidiously undermining its foundations, each one in a different manner, but all as representative of their Jewish background (though their own Jewishness was mainly nominal, and for Marx, son of converted Jews, practically non-existent). At the same time, Jewish intellectuals act as 'apologists of Jewry', to make 'Jewry less disreputable'.[50]

The western civilization that Cuddihy wishes to save from the ravages inflicted by outsider Jews is the one civilization that – according to Arnold Toynbee in his monumental, 10-volume *Study of History*[51] – is not doomed like all its predecessors to disappear, but is destined for an endless future. This is not due to its scientific acumen, technological achievements, military prowess or cultural vitality, but to the power of its universal Church, and to the uniqueness of its Savior. Toynbee's work is a *tour de force*, comparing the birth, growth, rise and fall of civilizations; it assigns the Jewish people (together with a few other deviant groups) to the title of a 'fossil' people, that have survived beyond their capacity to contribute to mankind.[52]

In a key chapter, Toynbee poses the question of whether creative individuals may save the civilizations that they belong to from disintegration. For him:

> The source of action is never the society itself but always an individual ... the action which is an act of creation is always performed by a soul which is in some sense a superhuman genius; that the genius expresses himself, like every living soul, through action upon his fellows; that in any society the creative personalities are always a small minority; and that the action of the genius upon souls of common clay operates occasionally through the perfect method of direct illumination but usually through the second-best expedient of a kind of social drill which enlists the faculty of mimesis (or imitation) in the souls of the uncreative rank and file and thereby enables them to perform mechanically an evolution which they could not have performed on their own initiative.[53]

Creative individuals contribute to the growth of a civilization and they emerge out of a creative minority; but in a state of almost inevitable disintegration, the minorities tend to lose their creativity and become merely a dominant group, while the creative individuals may well join the opposition. Thus:

> The secession of the proletariat, which is the essential feature of disintegration, has itself been achieved under the leadership of creative personalities for whose activity there is now no scope except in the organization of opposition to the incubus of the uncreative 'powers that be'.[54]

The question, then, is whether, from this perspective, the civilization can be saved: whether a savior may arise. 'Such saviors will be of diverse types, according to the nature of the remedy that they seek to apply to the social disease.'[55] Amongst these several groups of potential saviors will be the 'savior who points the way to transfiguration' and 'who will appear as a god incarnate in a man'.[56] After examining the savior 'with the sword', the savior 'with the Time Machine', and the savior in the guise of a 'Philosopher Masked by a King', Toynbee discusses in great detail 'The God Incarnate in a Man'.[57] Toynbee notes that these:

> ... are the demigods born of human mothers by a superhuman sire – a Heracles, an Asklepios, an Orpheus, to mention only Greek examples. These half-divine beings in human flesh seek by their labors in various ways to lighten the lot of man, and in the punishments inflicted on them by jealous gods they share the sufferings of the mortals whom they serve. The demigod – and this is his glory – is subject, like men, to death, and behind the figure of the dying demigod there looms the greater figure of a very god who dies for different worlds under diverse names.

Then follows a list of the deaths of seven such gods, including the death 'for a Christian World as Christ'.[58]

Toynbee immediately poses the question of a dying god who appears in different places and at different times. 'Who is this god,' he asks, 'of many epiphanies but only one Passion?'; and then reflects, 'In what spirit does the Dying God go to his death?' It is impossible to know the ultimate meaning of the god's dying without knowledge of 'the feelings and motives'. For instance, 'Does the Dying God die by compulsion or by choice? With generosity or bitterness? Out of love or in despair?' Only by gaining answers to these questions will it be possible to achieve 'a spiritual communion'.[59] In many ways echoing Kierkegaard's praise for sacrificing a son without reservations,[60] Toynbee provides one example – of Orpheus – where he declares that, 'the goddess who was Orpheus' mother would never have let Orpheus die if she could have helped it'.[61] Quoting from the Greek poetry describing Orpheus' death, he claims that it is possible to compare the perfect sacrifice with the imperfect. Thus, 'in Calliope's lovely lamentation for the death of Orpheus, there is a jarring note of bitterness which strikes, and shocks, a Christian ear'.[62] Toynbee then quotes from the elegy on the *Death of Orpheus*, written by Antipater of Sidon about 120 years before the crucifixion of Jesus, 'Why do we mortals make lament over the deaths of our sons, seeing that the Gods themselves have not power to keep Death from laying his hand upon their children.'[63] Toynbee claims that such an approach is 'like a cloud that veils the Sun', since it 'takes the light out of Orpheus' death'.[64]

However, for Toynbee, this Greek poem 'is answered in another and greater masterpiece: "For God so loved the World, that he gave his only-begotten son, that whosoever believeth in Him should not perish but have everlasting life"'.[65] Here, according to Toynbee, is an ultimate truth: a dividing line between the mythical dying gods of other civilizations and the dying god of western, Christian civilization. Quoting the poet Shelley, he writes, 'The One remains, the many change and pass.'[66] In this search for creative individuals as saviors of a civilization, failure was a foregone conclusion for those whose creativity was only expressed by the sword, or in philosophy, or through weaving utopian dreams: thus, only 'gods were left in the running'.[67] And, of these gods, only one could succeed, for:

> At the final ordeal of death, few, even of these would-be savior gods, have dared to put their title to the test by plunging into the icy river. And now, as we stand and gaze with our eyes fixed upon the farther shore, a single figure rises from the flood and straightaway fills the whole horizon. There is the Savior.[68]

This is not written by a preacher, eager to excite his congregants, but at a crucial point in one of the major academic treatises of the twentieth century. Western civilization will apparently be the one exception to the normal process of civilizations. It will be saved from inevitable decay and demise. Just as the Crucifixion offers the promise of eternity to the individual, so Christianity is the sustaining religion for western civilization.

One wonders how one of the most creative individuals of the twentieth century, Freud, would have responded to this optimistic appraisal of an endless future, given his own pessimistic assessment in his book, *Civilization and its Discontents*, written not long before.[69] Of course, in terms of Toynbee's analysis, Freud would be an example *par excellence* of one of those creative individuals who join and lead the opposition. Would Freud be considered a member of a creative minority – Jewish, intellectual, central European, medical profession – or merely an example of the last gasps of a fossil people? Freud's work is clearly problematic – partly due to its over-emphasis on the power of a story in which a son inadvertently kills his father – but its originality and its comprehensive embrace cannot but evoke admiration.

Toynbee's work is also original and comprehensive, and has earned him a distinguished place among historians and social scientists. But it, too, is problematic. Specialists have called attention to its defects in the area of their expertise, while Jewish scholars[70] have challenged Toynbee

on his description of the Jews as a fossil people and their biblical tales as
being no more than Syriac myths, as well as for his one-sided treatment
of the Israeli–Arab conflict. But the major problem with his work – from
the perspective of this book – is its emphasis on the power of a story in
which a god willingly sacrifices his son, with assurance of eternal life for
the individual and for the civilization, as a unique event in history. The
actual event of a sacrifice of a son is, as Toynbee notes, not unique; it is
the willingness to do so – without reservations, without regrets – that is
attributed to God that makes it unique. For those who do not believe in
myths of this description, or in the fact of a divine Son of God, but who
are aware of the power of myth as well as of the suffering, in many
places, in many periods, of the young, Toynbee's description is also
problematic and disturbing.

These thoughts lead us back not just to the Crucifixion, but also to
the *Akedah*, and to Mount Moriah. This is the place where Isaac was
almost sacrificed; the place where, in the Temple that arose there many
generations later, animal sacrifices were offered up to God; the Temple
that Jesus claimed would disappear and re-appear; the Temple that was
destroyed four decades after the Crucifixion of Jesus. Mount Moriah,
situated in the heart of Jerusalem; Mount Moriah, the present site of
two magnificent mosques.

NOTES

1. In general, *see* my references to Freud's work from the perspective of the Oedipus
   Complex, in Leon Sheleff, *Generations Apart: Adult Hostility to Youth* (New York:
   McGraw-Hill, 1981); especially in part 1: 'Oedipus at the Crossroads', pp. 3–94, and part
   2: 'The Uses of the Oedipus Complex', pp. 95–176.
2. *See* Freud's case study of the 'Wolf Man', *From the History of an Infantile Neurosis*
   (London: Hogarth Press, 1918).
3. Sigmund Freud, *Moses and Monotheism* (London: Hogarth Press, 1939).
4. Sigmund Freud, *Totem and Taboo* (London: Hogarth Press, 1913)
5. Ibid., pp. 141–2.
6. Ibid., p. 145.
7. Freud's *Moses and Monotheism* was his last work, and there are those who have claimed
   that too much attention should not be attached to it. In fact, its extrapolations are
   embarrassing for some, for they are clearly based on Freud's fertile imagination and not on
   accepted texts. However, there is also clear evidence that Freud had always been intrigued
   by the figure of Moses and his final book may be seen as the real climax to which he had
   always been working. Thus, Paul Rozen writes that, 'It is well known that the figure of
   Moses had a special fascination for Freud', *Freud: Political and Social Thought* (New York:
   Knopf, 1970) p. 168; while David Bakan has written that, 'The primary key to the
   understanding of Freud is contained in his concern with Moses', *Sigmund Freud and the
   Jewish Mystical Tradition* (Princeton, NJ: Van Nostrand, 1958), p. 121. *See also* the
   biography of Freud by one of his disciples, Ernest Jones, who writes:

   > We cannot refrain from wondering how, when nearing his end, Freud came to be so
   > engrossed in [these] topics … and to devote to them all his intellectual interest during

the last five years of his life. To answer such questions we have to hark back to the earliest riddles of life that perplexed him.

The Life and Work of Sigmund Freud, Vol. 3
(New York: Basic Books, 1957), p. 367.

8. Freud, *Moses and Monotheism*, pp. 88–9.
9. Ibid., p. 50.
10. Ibid.
11. Freud, *Totem and Taboo*, p. 154.
12. Because of the brevity of the biblical text, especially the Old Testament, exegetical extrapolations are perfectly understandable, but they must retain some minimum fidelity to the text.
13. *See* Exodus, 18:2–4, as quoted in chapter 9:

> And Jethro, Moses' father-in-law, took Zipporah, Moses' wife, after he had sent her away, and her two sons, of whom the name of the one was Gershom; for he said: 'I have been a stranger in a strange land'; and the name of the other was Eliezer: For the God of my father was my help, and delivered me from the sword of Pharaoh.'

Ger means 'stranger' and *ezer* means 'help', while *Eli* is a reference to God.
14. Leviticus, 10:1–2:

> And Nadab and Abihu, the sons of Aaron, took each of them his censer, and put fire therein, and laid incense thereon, and offered strange fire before the Lord, which He had not commanded them. And there came forth fire from before the Lord, and devoured them, and they died before the Lord.

15. *See* Karl Mannheim, *Ideology and Utopia: An Introduction to the Sociology of Knowledge* (New York: Harcourt, Brace and World, 1936); *see also* his essay, 'The Social Problems of Generations', in Karl Mannheim, *Essays on the Sociology of Knowledge* (London: Routledge and Kegan Paul, 1959).
16. In a recent book, I have argued for the positive aspects of Eve's behavior in eating of the 'Tree of Knowledge of Good and Evil', the implication being that humans accept responsibility for their moral behavior: *see* Leon Sheleff, *Weeds in the Garden of Eden: Biblical Narratives and Israeli Chronicles* (Tel Aviv: Papyrus/Tel Aviv University, 2002), in Hebrew.
17. Sheleff, *Generations Apart*, 1, 'Who Speaks for the Young?' pp. 3–14.
18. These changes in Freud's thinking are expressed in his correspondence with Wilhelm Fliess; *see*, for example, Letter No. 69 to Fliess, 21 September 1897, *Extracts from the Fliess Papers, 1892–1897*, Vol. 1 of the *Standard Edition*.
19. *See* Sheleff, *Generations Apart*, pp. 309–10.
20. *See* Leon Sheleff, 'Behind Infanticide and Incest: Personal Aspects in the Formulation of the Oedipus Complex', *University of Dayton Law Review*, 18 (1987), p. 3.
21. Freud, *The Future of an Illusion* (1927) in the *Standard Edition*, Vol. 21. This book was written many years after the death of his father, but its preliminary ideas had quite likely already been formed.
22. Freud, *The Interpretation of Dreams* (1900), p. 262.
23. Freud, *The Future of an Illusion*.
24. *See*, for instance, Theodore Reik, *Ritual* (London: Hogarth Press, 1931); Erich Wellisch, *Isaac and Oedipus* (London: Routledge and Kegan Paul, 1954).
25. Erich Fromm, *The Dogma of Christ: And Other Essays on Religion, Psychology and Culture* (Garden City, NJ: Doubleday Anchor, 1966), p. 58.
26. Ibid., p. 59.
27. Ibid., for instance, even before Christianity became the official religion, according to Fromm:

> About the middle of the second century, Christianity began to win followers among the middle and higher classes of the Roman Empire ... By the end of the second century, Christianity had already ceased to be the religion of the poor artisans and slaves. And when under Constantine it became the state religion, it had already become the religion of larger circles of the ruling class in the Roman Empire. (p. 55)

28. *See* discussion in previous chapter.
29. Fromm, *The Dogma of Christ*, p. 65.
30. Ibid.
31. Ibid., p. 66.
32. Ibid.
33. Ibid. Fromm adds that:

> The actual possibility of identifying with a god who had suffered yet had from the beginning been in heaven, and at the same time of eliminating tendencies hostile to the father, is the basis of the victory of Christianity over the emperor cult. Moreover, the change in the attitude toward the real, existing father figures – the priests, the emperor, and especially the rulers – corresponded to this changed attitude toward the father-god. (p. 67)

34. Ibid., p. 67.
35. Ibid., p. 68.
36. Ibid.
37. Ibid., p. 80.
38. *See* discussion in chapter 7, 'Constantine'.
39. Fromm, *The Dogma of Christ*, p. 82.
40. Ibid., p. 94.
41. Ibid., p. 95.
42. Ibid., pp. 71–4. Fromm writes of a ' ... fantasy of the great pardoning mother' which was ...

> the optimal gratification which Catholic Christianity had to offer. The more the masses suffered, the more their real situation resembled that of the suffering Jesus, and the more the figure of the happy, suckling babe could, and must, appear alongside the figure of the suffering Jesus. But this meant also that men had to regress to a passive, infantile attitude. This position precluded active revolt. (p. 74)

43. *See* Ignez Maybaum, *Creation and Guilt: A Theological Assessment of Freud's Father-Son Conflict* (London: Vallentine Mitchell, 1969); *see also* Franklin H. Littell, *The Crucifixion of the Jews* (New York: Harper and Row, 1975); he writes:

> For a professing Christian, the red thread that ties a Justin Martyr or Chrysostom to Auschwitz and Treblinka raises issues far more serious than can be dealt with by conscious avoidance of vulgar anti-Jewish slur in speech or discrimination in practice. If we are, as we profess, linked in 'the communion of saints' across the generations with those who have died in the faith, we are also linked in a solidarity of guilt with those who taught falsely and with those who drew the logical consequences of false teaching. That false teaching has led in our own time to mass rebellion of the baptized against the God of Abraham, Isaac, and Jacob, and to wholesale apostasy. The cornerstone of Christian anti-Semitism is the superseding or displacement myth, which already rings with the genocidal note. This is the myth that the mission of the Jewish people was finished with the coming of Jesus Christ, that the 'old Israel' was written off with the appearance of 'the new Israel.' To teach that a people's mission in God's providence is finished, that they have been relegated to the limbo of history, has murderous implications which murderers will in time spell out. (pp. 1–2)

44. David Bakan, *Slaughter of the Innocents: A Study of the Battered Child Phenomenon* (San Francisco, CA: Jossey-Bass, 1971), p. xii.
45. Israel Charny, *Genocide: The Human Cancer* (New York: Hearst Books, 1982).
46. Zigmund Baumann, 'Sociology After the Holocaust', *British Journal of Sociology*, 39 (1988), p. 469; and *Modernity and the Holocaust* (Ithaca, NY: Cornell University Press, 1989).
47. Stephen Haynes, *Reluctant Witnesses: Jews and the Christian Imagination* (Louisville, KY: Westminster John Knox Press, 1955).
48. *See*, for instance, comments by Dan Cohn-Sherbok, *Modern Judaism* (London: Macmillan Press, 1996), where he writes that, 'Orthodox thinkers have ... failed to recognize the serious theological implications of the Holocaust – for many Jews the belief in an all-

powerful and benevolent Deity who lovingly watches over his chosen people is no longer credible.' He adds that, 'A ... difficulty with Hasidic theology concerns the concept of divine providence; to the modern Jewish mind it is inconceivable that human suffering, particularly during the Nazi period, could be a result of divine providence' (p. 213).

49. John Cuddhidy, *The Ordeal of Civility: Freud, Marx and Lévi-Strauss and the Jewish Struggle with Modernity* (New York: Basic Books, 1974).

50. Ibid., p. 6. Marx, of course, was only Jewish from an ethnic point of view, having been born of Jewish parents who had converted to Christianity when Marx himself was still a young boy – and it is within this religion that he was brought up. Marx himself had many critical comments to make about religion in general (the oft-quoted 'opium of the masses'), and about Judaism in particular in his essay on the Jewish question ('money is the jealous God of Israel'). Indeed, Marx has often been accused of anti-Semitism. See, for instance, M. Glickson, *The Jewish Complex of Karl Marx* (New York, 1961).

It is of some interest to note how the triumvirate of Lenin, Stalin and Trotsky culminated in the political leadership of the former two, and the excommunication, exile, and finally the extermination, of Trotsky the Jew. See, for instance, the fascinating discussion by Joseph Nedava, *Trotsky and the Jews* (Philadelphia, PA: The Jewish Publication Society of America, 1972). For instance, on p. 119, he writes:

> Trotsky's former Jewish name was to plague him for many years to come. Stalin saw to it, in his anti-Semitic campaign during his struggle against Trotsky and Trotskyism, that it was not forgotten. During the last years of his life Trotsky referred to the matter time and again. One case irritated him especially because it touched upon the fate of his son – a hostage in the hands of his enemy...on reading the press report about the arrest of his son, Trotsky issued a statement to the press entitled 'Methods of Anti-Semitism'. The method Trotsky was referring to was the manner in which the Soviet authorities – in accusing the son with (in Trotsky's words in an earlier article, 'Thermidor and Anti-Semitism')... 'the utterly incredible accusation of plotting to poison workers' – stressed the original family name – of Bronstein, thereby, of course, emphasizing Trotsky's '...Jewish origin and the half-Jewish origin of my son'.

For a general discussion of the impact of his Judaism on Trotsky, as well as the general role of Jews in revolutionary movements, the legend of Jewish Bolshevism, and the purges of most Jewish Bolshevik leaders, *see* Bertram D. Wolfe's discussion of the triumvirate, *Three Who Made a Revolution: A Biographical History* (New York: Dell Publishing, 1948), at pp. 178–86.

51. Arnold Toynbee, *A Study of History* (Oxford: Oxford University Press, 1946).

52. Ibid: as quoted in two-volume abridged version edited by D.C. Somervell, published by Dell Publishing (1965), Toynbee writes, 'Jewry, in the form in which it collided with Western Christendom, was an exceptional phenomenon. It was a fossilized relic of a civilization that was extinct in every other shape' (Vol. 2, p. 192).

53. Ibid., Vol. 1, p. 606.

54. Ibid.

55. Ibid., p. 607.

56. Ibid.

57. Ibid., pp. 607–22.

58. Ibid., p. 620.

59. Ibid., p. 621.

60. *See* previous chapter, 'Kierkegaard'.

61. Toynbee, *A Study of History*, Vol. 1, p. 622.

62. Ibid., p. 621.

63. As quoted in ibid., p. 621.

64. Ibid., p. 622.

65. Ibid.

66. Ibid.

67. Ibid.

68. Ibid.

69. Freud, *Civilization and its Discontents*

70. *See*, for instance, Maurice Samuel, *The Professor and the Fossil: Some Observations on Arnold J. Toynbee's 'A Study of History'* (New York: Knopf, 1956).

12
Moriah

The exact spot on which the *Akedah* took place is unknown. Mount Moriah is presumed to be a hillock in Jerusalem: the hillock on which King Solomon later chose to build the Temple, the hilltop on which today stand the Mosque of Omar (the Dome of the Rock) and the El Aksa Mosque.

The exact site is not known, since the Patriarchs and Matriarchs of the Israelites had little contact with the area which was to become, during the reign of King David, the capital city. Prior to the *Akedah*, Abraham had apparently made only one fleeting visit to the area.[1] Isaac was never to return there (and perhaps bore only traumatic memories of the site), while Jacob passed by fairly closely with his family, but made no detour in that direction. A few kilometers away, one of his wives, Rachel, died, and was buried on the outskirts of what is now Bethlehem.

The name Moriah has also disappeared from the geographical lexicon. What is presumed to be Mount Moriah is now referred to in Hebrew as the Temple Mount – in memory of and in acknowledgment of the two Temples that were built there, both being destroyed by invaders. The First Temple was built to specifications precisely and meticulously set out in the Bible.[2] The second was built within a few decades of the destruction of the first with the approval and the encouragement of the Persian King, Cyrus, when many of the Jews, who had taken refuge in Persia, returned. While it was presumed that, in the building of the Second Temple, efforts would be made to replicate, as far as possible, the contours of the First Temple, the two were vastly different, especially after King Herod expanded its dimensions many years later in line with his overall, ambitious building program.[3]

In one respect, there was a great difference in the two constructions. The centerpiece of the First Temple was the Holy of Holies, the Ark in which was kept the two tablets on which were inscribed the Ten Commandments. With the destruction of the Temple, the tablets themselves were lost. The other major functions of the Temple were as a place in which animal sacrifices could be offered to God, and where regular prayers were held, including the reading of psalms, to the accompaniment of music and dancing, with the members of the tribe of Levi being entrusted with the task of administering the Temple.

Within modern Jewish ritual, Orthodox Jewry retains memories of the Temple by occasional references in prayers, noted especially on the most solemn day of the annual calendar, the Day of Atonement, when a detailed description is given of the peak moment surrounding the entry of the High Priest into the Holy of Holies.[4] However, in Israel today, there are also fundamentalist groups who are preparing themselves for a possible building of a third temple, even making the priestly garments and holy artifacts that will be needed.[5] However, one of the major facets of the original Temple will always be lacking, namely the contents of the Holy Ark. Two questions arise. First, do these Jewish fundamentalist groups intend, if somehow a temple is ever re-built – no simple matter given the presence of the two mosques – to re-institute the practice of animal sacrifices? Apparently so, since there have been reports of an intensive search for a pure red heifer as required for part of the ritual, as described in the Bible, and even a rumor of a small, select group of children being kept from infanthood, in a state of quarantine, to preserve their purity and prepare them for sacred duties associated with temple rites. (Obviously, if this rumor is correct, it raises serious questions as to basic children's rights.) Second, a probing question of historic proportion: would the spiritual leaders of the Jewish people have been able to abolish the practice of animal sacrifice, if the Temple had survived over the centuries in all its glory; would they on their own have been able to creatively move ahead, in the realization that just as animal sacrifice replaced human sacrifice, so animal sacrifice could also eventually be abolished, with rituals and prayers as meaningful substitutes?

The fate of the Temple is closely bound up with the relations between Judaism and Christianity, since a significant part of Jesus' critique against the religious authorities of the time revolved around certain practices that had been allowed to penetrate into its sacred precincts: for instance, Jesus' references to the presence there of the money-changers, although he barely makes note of the sacrifices.[6] More specifically, the formal accusation lodged against Jesus was linked to his claim that the Temple would be destroyed and re-built three days later[7] (generally considered to be a metaphysical statement, which later took on added meaning for his followers in the light of Jesus' own resurrection three days after his crucifixion). Furthermore, Mark states that the 'veil of the Temple was rent in twain' almost simultaneously with the expiry of Jesus on the Cross.[8] In retrospect, it has been claimed by some Christian theologians, that from that moment, the Temple ceased to fulfill any sacred function.

As I have suggested in an earlier chapter, the destruction of the Temple about 40 years later was a crucial factor in the re-invigoration of the small community of Jesus' disciples, as it seemed to be a divine punishment for the rejection by the Jews of the Messiah. It was from this moment onwards that the episode of arrest, trial, execution, burial and resurrection became deeply imprinted in the minds of his followers; it was then that written affirmation (later declared canonical) was made of his virgin birth, his subtle claims to messianship, his proximity to God, the details of his Passion at Golgotha (Calvary) and his resurrection. Independent confirmation of what transpired (but only in reference to his ministry, the trial and Crucifixion, and not the virgin birth or Resurrection) is limited to passing comments by the Jewish historians, such as Joseph Flavius, and the Roman historian, Tacitus, or some writings that were later found in excavations, and about which there is in any case much controversy, such as the Dead Sea Scrolls or the Scrolls found in Egypt at Nag Hammadi.[9]

There is a more amorphous interconnection between the two religions relating to the issue of sacrifice. Moriah was where Isaac was to be sacrificed to God, and if this was indeed the site of the Temple, erected many centuries later, this was where animals were substituted for child sacrifice – which, according to much modern Jewish interpretation, was a momentous moment in human history. Jesus himself was crucified nearby at Golgotha, partly because of his severe critique of temple practices. The demand originally made upon Abraham, and then rescinded, was now consummated in inverse fashion, with God Himself making the sacrifice on behalf of humanity. The pain, humiliation and suffering of Jesus during those hours on the Cross are an integral part of Christian theology and an essential aspect of Christian belief. Judaism, however, also has its figures who, because of their belief in one God, were subjected to an excruciating death. Yet the two religions differ in their approach to commemorating such events.

On the Day of Atonement (Yom Kippur), a reading takes place of the tragic demise of the Ten Martyrs, with the ritual incorporating a few sentences on the cruelty imposed on them (burning, beating), stressing the manner in which they retained, to the end, their absolute faith in God.[10] These are important, but not dominant, figures in Jewish history. Their martyrdom was surely as great a test as that to which Abraham was subjected; their suffering was surely no less than that of Jesus. They are all post-biblical, and, like Jesus, the victims, in the following centuries of Roman cruelty. In the liturgy of Yom Kippur they are known as the Ten Martyrs. It is a one-time reference, adding to the solemnity of this special day, with its 24-hour fast and total involvement in prayers of repentance from sundown to sundown the following day. No further reference is made, at any stage of the year's ritual, to the suffering of these martyred persons. As for the destruction of the Temple, a fast day is set aside once a year, with a special reading from the Book of Lamentations, because it is believed that both Temples were destroyed on the same day (the ninth of Ab in the Hebrew Calendar), and that on this self-same date, other tragedies befell the Jewish people.

The issue of sacrifice is of paramount significance, and the interpretations placed upon this phenomenon are critically important, even today, when the actual practice of sacrifice is non-existent. Two Jewish writers have, in recent years, made notable contributions to an understanding of the historical meaning of sacrifice within the context of the impact of the *Akedah*. Erich Wellisch has claimed that, given the prevalence of child sacrifice at the time when Abraham was tested, the climax of this eisode – the saving of Isaac[11] – marked a turning-point in history. David Bakan has added an extra dimension by linking the two events of the *Akedah* and the Crucifixion in practical terms.[12] According to him, the intention of the *Akedah* was to present the message that child sacrifice was an abomination to be abolished: hence the need to actually act it out up to its potential climax, in order for the message to be fully appreciated. However, according to Bakan, the message was neither understood, nor incorporated into practice; child sacrifice was still practiced in various parts of the Roman Empire, and thus there was a need for a full sacrifice to be made, the sacrifice of a divine son, to act in a cathartic manner, and to finally achieve the desired goal.[13]

In practical terms, it is doubtful if this second attempt to convey a humanitarian message was fully understood; indeed, it is only now that research is enabling mankind to begin to comprehend the enormity of child abuse at all times – from the extreme act of infanticide to the more subtle expressions, such as verbal humiliation.[14] No less serious and sad is the fact that the presumed sacrifice of a divine son did not provide any cathartic release, but served rather as a catalytic and causative factor in the centuries-long oppression of the Children of Israel – from the individualized and sporadic blood-libel, to the organized sophistication and massive dimensions of the Holocaust. Neither the direct message of kindness and humanness verbalized in the Sermon on the Mount, nor the identification of Christians with the Passion of Jesus, have, in a broad historical vista, had the desired effect, whether in the internecine struggles within the Church, or as between different movements in Christianity with its religious wars, or in its attitude to the people to whom Jesus belonged.

The Crucifixion may or may not have served (in terms of the claims

of Christian theology) as a redemption for humanity, but for the Jews, it
has served mainly as a focal point of their own suffering, since it is a
reminder to Christians of the punishment necessary for their presumed
obstinacy in refusing to acknowledge the Messiah.[15] For some Christians,
it is also a cause of frustration and anger, since the ongoing refusal of
Jews to change their historical decision is a hindrance to a second
coming of the Messiah. Much fundamentalist Christian theology to this
day predicates a second advent on the admission of the Jews of their
error and their conversion to Christianity.

These are deep theological issues, but they do not remain in the realm
of divinity – they have direct, practical implications for Christian–Jewish
relations. Suffering is an inevitable part of the human experience, but
just as medical advances may help to alleviate some of the physical pain
of illness, or aggressive and intrusive surgery may help restore a patient's
health, so ruthless honesty is required in inter-faith discussion for human
tragedies to be avoided. As already mentioned, it is fortunately possible
in the modern world to raise controversial issues that in earlier times
might have had fatal consequences for their authors.

Indeed, the issue of sacrifice may not be as remote from modern
concerns as it may superficially seem. If some Jews (Orthodox and Ultra-
Orthodox) are prepared to contemplate the possibility of re-instituting
animal sacrifice in a rebuilt temple on Mount Moriah (a utopian fantasy
that one can only hope will remain in that dimension, given the
empirical fact of two mosques that occupy the site), then outlandish
ideas of this type cannot be ignored, neither in practical politics nor in
academic discourse. In any event, a significant part of Catholic ritual
involves a mimetic acting out of the sacrifice of Jesus. As described by
Hyman Maccoby, a Jewish scholar of early Christianity:

> The Eucharist signifies the mystical incorporation of the initiate
> into the godhead by eating the body and drinking the blood of
> Christ. Such a ceremony implies the deification of Jesus and it is
> quite impossible to reconcile with a view of Jesus as a Messiah in
> the Jewish sense. Moreover, the Eucharist...implies a doctrine of
> the sacrifice of Jesus as an atonement for mankind; the worshipper
> partakes of the body of the sacrificed Jesus much as the Jewish
> worshippers used to eat the Paschal lamb (to which Jesus is linked
> in Corinthians 5:7). Such a concept of the death of Jesus cannot be
> reconciled with any variety of Judaism, for it amounts to the re-
> instatement of human sacrifice, which for Judaism was anathema –
> indeed a large part of the Hebrew Bible constitutes a campaign
> against human sacrifice. The institution of animal sacrifice was

understood to entail the complete supersession of human sacrifice,
and the story of the *Akedah* or Binding of Isaac which finally
renounces human sacrifice in favor of animal sacrifice is the validat-
ing myth of this advance.[16]

A Christian writer, Frances Young, has, in a thoughtful book,
acknowledged the importance of coming to terms with what she calls, in
the book's title, *Sacrifice and the Death of Christ*.[17] In fact, she states
specifically at the outset that 'Sacrificial images are hardly those which
arrest the attention of most people today' and that, 'It might well seem
that the subject ... is irrelevant in the context of modern culture and the
twentieth-century Church.'[18] However, she argues that ignoring the issue
'has unfortunate consequences', as '... it makes it more difficult for the
average churchgoer to understand the religious language he uses in
worship' or to guarantee 'continuity of his responses and religious
experiences with those of Christians of the past'.[19] She claims that Jesus
himself, for all his critique of temple practices, did not repudiate
'Temple-worship and the sacrificial system'.[20] However, as the Church
distanced itself from Judaism, 'sacrificial language' came to be used 'to
describe the worship and service of Christians',[21] similar to what the
Jews were doing outside of Jerusalem (especially after the destruction of
the Temple). But, for Christians, an added factor – especially in the work
of Paul – was the use of 'sacrifice as a means of understanding the death
of Christ'.[22] Indeed, one of the reasons for the Christian rejection of
animal sacrifice was specifically its replacement by the sacrifice of Jesus
– Paul's approach:

> ... was an assertion that *Christ's sacrifice had replaced them*.
> Sacrifice should no longer be offered by Christians, not because
> Christ's message was in conflict with Old Testament revelation of
> the past, but because he had so fulfilled it as to make it meaning-
> less.[23]

This is a crucial factor in terms of Paul's activities: both the sacrifices and
the law could be disregarded because of the fulfillment of such ritual
aspects of the Jewish religion by the sacrifice of Jesus; his death 'was the
one perfect sacrifice rendering all others unnecessary'.[24] Indeed, from a
Christian point of view, as presented by Paul, there was no need for any
aspirations to re-build a temple, as any such re-building was understood
in spiritual terms, both in the constitution of a communion of believers
and 'the resurrection of the Body of Christ' (John 2:21).[25] Sacrifice
becomes a spiritual endeavor; if necessary, the willingness to suffer, as

indeed Jesus had, becomes a factor that creates also a willingness for martyrdom, in terms of religious (or even ideological) belief.

An insight into the larger social context of sacrifice, but with religious overtones, may be gleaned from a recent, interesting attempt to understand the nature of martyrdom by Lacey Baldwin Smith.[26] His book opens with a discussion of Socrates as a prototype; he then discusses Jewish martyrdom, as expressed a few hundred years before Jesus in the struggle of the Maccabeans against the Greeks, who were determined to eliminate Jewish monotheistic beliefs and practices.[27] Then follows an analysis of the martyrdom of Jesus, before the author moves on to other instances, including those of Jews and Christians who willingly underwent suffering in order to retain fidelity to their faith.

The opening chapter on Socrates is sub-titled 'The Genesis of Martyrdom'. What is of particular interest to note is that Socrates was tried for his corruption of youth. In modern times of youth protest movements and student revolt, inspiration has also been derived from the writings of authors of an older generation: for instance, see the impact of Herbert Marcuse on the youth movement of the 1960s.[28] However, while Socrates is seen mainly in secular terms, as a philosopher dealing with social and political matters, Smith stresses the religious framework of his writing. He notes the challenge that Socrates posed for atheists and religious people alike. As for the latter, Smith writes that:

> His religious views were profoundly disturbing, for, as he confessed, he dared inquire 'into things under the earth and in heaven', which exposed him to the accusation that he was 'a god-maker', who disbelieved in the old deities and was bent on 'producing new ones'. He rejected the anthropomorphic and unreliable gods of the Homeric past, believing instead in the existence of a divinely inspired and ultimately purposeful universe, in which humanity played a vital, if extremely difficult, role. Religion for Socrates was not 'the art of commercial exchanges between gods and men' whereby the deities in an outrageously unbalanced transaction were expected to perform miracles on behalf of their worshippers in return for trifling sacrificial offerings which the gods could not possibly need. He rejected as unacceptable the traditional behavior of the gods, who were blind to the moral chaos that their irresponsible actions produced on both Olympus and earth. Instead, he predicated a single morality for god and man.[29]

For Smith, Socrates was a martyr, because he was prepared to die for his beliefs, and because he also presumed that his ideas would be given even greater credence by his death and have even greater effect. Scholars have debated whether his challenge to the authorities was basically political in nature or philosophical and theological. A similar debate has revolved around Jesus, as to whether the threat he posed was as a religious leader or as a political rebel.[30]

The next example of martyrdom that Smith provides is of the Jewish Maccabees, some two and a half centuries later, who were determined to fend off the inroads being made against the Jewish religion by Hellenic culture. Smith explains that:

> The Jews may not have invented Western martyrdom – that credit goes to Socrates and Plato – but they were certainly the first to use it as means of national inspiration and to endow its hideous suffering with eschatological purpose.[31]

The Maccabees were led by a group of five brothers under Judah; their opponent was the Greek emperor, Antiochus, whose full title was Antiochus IV Epiphanes. The word Epiphanes means 'god manifest', a term that in itself was liable to arouse the ire of monotheistic Jews and was, of course, to become some 200 years later a mark of contention between the Jewish authorities and the followers of Jesus.

Smith describes not only the valiant battle of the Maccabees, but also the fate that, in particular, befell one woman and her seven sons, who were all cruelly killed for refusing to foreswear their faith: an event recorded in the Book of Maccabees. The victory of the Maccabees is commemorated by Jews in the minor holiday of Chanukah, normally celebrated (by the lunar calendar) a few weeks or days before Christmas. Both holidays, in the depths of winter, accentuate light; in the case of Chanukah, candles are lit for eight days to commemorate the re-capture of the Temple from the Greeks and the fact that the amount of holy oil found on the site, which was sufficient to burn for only one day, lasted for eight, until more holy oil could be prepared. (This story, incidentally, does not appear in any of the Books of Maccabees, which are apocryphal books in the Jewish Bible, but was incorporated later into the collective memory of the event.) The Temple itself had been defiled, and a thorough purification was required in order to have its traditional functions re-instated.

Smith claims that neither Socrates nor the Maccabees were perfect examples of the phenomenon of martyrdom: Socrates, because his character made his motives suspect (perhaps he really wanted to commit suicide), and in any event, 'He is too logical, too much the product of the philosophical mind – brittle, without love, passion or compassion';[32]

the Maccabees, because they carried it out 'on such a heroic scale' with 'such lavish hyperbole, that all sense of reality dissolves'.[33] Whereas in the case of Socrates, there is no real suffering (he drinks the hemlock voluntarily and dies shortly afterwards), in the case of the Maccabees, 'They suffer hideously, but their pain is uncommunicable. We feel for them in the abstract but do not know them as people who lived as well as died. Even the mother's agony seems stylized and stagey.'[34] He then ends his two chapters on Socrates and the Maccabees with an explanation of what was required for a more effective and meaningful martyrdom. He writes:

> Before the martyr – Platonic or Hebraic – could break out of the prison of the faceless inhumanity and sterile unreality of a philosophic or heroic ideal, he had had to be assigned narrators who possessed the literary artistry and ideological desire to portray the whole man, his history, his frailties, his frustrations as well as his purpose.[35]

These factors, according to Smith, come together in the crucifixion of Jesus.

Part of the reason for this is that, unlike the other examples, where death was a peripheral aspect of their life-work, in the case of Jesus, his death is of the essence. Smith writes: 'Remove the hemlock and Socrates remains a formidable figure, still ... the hero of unfettered inquiry. Remove the instruments of torture – the mutilations and the stench of burning flesh – from the story of the Maccabees and nothing much happens'[36] – the outcome of their battle might well have been the same, or others may have achieved a similar goal.

However, in the case of Jesus, the situation is totally different. Basically, without the Cross – the symbol of the martyrdom – the entire personal history of Jesus becomes problematical. In Smith's words, 'Remove Golgotha ... and Jesus in a sense is annihilated and history reconstructed. Never was the style of a man's death so essential to the understanding and recounting of his life or so important to human history.'[37] Focusing on the content of what took place at the Crucifixion, in the context of the importance of martyrdom, Smith argues that:

> If death must be an integral part of a martyr's purpose; if suffering is the ingredient that gives validity to his determination; if free choice is necessary to the drama of self-sacrifice; if staging, self-control, and the cooperation of the persecution are essential to the desired end; and, finally, if belated recognition and comprehension

are the ultimate signatures that translate an ordinary public
execution into a historic – some might argue cosmic – event, then
the crucifixion of Jesus of Nazareth stands almost alone in the
annals of time. Certainly no other death has been so crucial in
establishing the concept of Western martyrdom or, for that matter,
in shaping the course of history. But no other death is so difficult
to the church in time, place and circumstance.[38]

Thus, whereas the death of Socrates is merely the end to a creative life,
a basis at the most for discussions on issues of justice, punishment,
choice, even suicide and euthanasia (Socrates may have willed his death
for motives that are not completely clear); and whereas the Maccabees
and their supporters died in the course of a difficult struggle (which in
the end turned out successfully, if at a heavy price); 'with Jesus ... death
controls the plot; it becomes the purpose of his life, the instrument by
which God reveals His ultimate plan'.[39] And in order for the story to be
complete, 'Death had to be the most violent, painful, prolonged, humiliating, and public that could be devised.'[40] More than hemlock (as for
Socrates) and more than 'grisly torture'[41] (as for the Maccabees), ' ... the
sight of the Crucifixion was sufficient to prove Jesus' credentials as a
martyr and validate the truth of his message'.[42] However, even this was
apparently not sufficient; amongst other reasons, because so many other
people, Jews and later even Christians, were exposed to the same
punishment. Thus, according to Smith, the story of Jesus' trial and
execution needed an additional element – that of betrayal; however, not
merely by an individual, since Judas was only peripheral, in a sense a
mere symbol or reminder of a far greater failure. Smith explains that:

> The Gospel writers were insistent that the focus of evil resided not
> in the actions of a simple traitor but in the betrayal of God's truth
> by all Israel, especially its religious leaders. The evangelists had
> excellent and historically compelling reasons to blacken the priests
> of the temple and the elders of the Sanhedria.[43]

On the one hand, the tragedy of the Crucifixion became the triumph
of the Cross; on the other hand, the image of a divine son being put to
death became not a cathartic release from temptation to evil acts –
toward the young or to the Jewish people – but a stimulus for similar
acts as proven by the history of abuse against children and Jews.[44] The
process of substituting animal sacrifices (in the Temple) for child
sacrifice (as in the *Akedah*, with all its powerful symbolism) was
thwarted, as vengeful actions continued to be focused on the Children

of Israel throughout the generations, from fabricated trials of blood-libels, through the mob violence of pogroms, to the meticulously planned, scientifically executed murder of millions in the Holocaust.

The paternal hand was withdrawn in the nick of time to save the sacrificed son at Moriah, but other parents and adults, in different ways, at different places and through the years, were not bound by similar inhibitions and used their power – parental, physical, authoritative – to exploit the young and to harm them.[45] The love bestowed on humanity by God's willingness to sacrifice his only-begotten son (as understood in Christian theology) was not echoed by a similar benevolence toward the people who were considered His children. Their exposure to suffering was not always mitigated by a last-minute intervention, as had saved Isaac on Mount Moriah. Abraham's faith was not always available with its redemptive power.

Two imposing mosques now stand on the hillock in the center of Jerusalem, presumed to be Moriah where the Temple once stood. Several plans have been made by underground Israeli groups to damage these buildings;[46] and on one occasion, a Christian tourist actually succeeded in setting fire to the El Aksa Mosque.[47] The name of this mosque has more recently been used to refer to the uprising of Palestinians against continued Israeli occupation of the West Bank (*Intifadah El-Aksa*),[48] because the violence that erupted in October 2000 was a response to what was seen as a provocative visit to the site by the then leader of the opposition in the Israeli Knesset, Arik Sharon. On this visit, Sharon was accompanied by almost half of the members of his party in the Knesset and protected by several hundred policemen (possibly even more if the surrounding area is taken into consideration) – all of this, ostensibly, in order to prove that Israel possessed sovereignty over the site, but, more pragmatically, for internal political purposes. His presence at the site (in terms of the ostensible claim of sovereignty) was really a sort of mimesis: a wishful hope, by Sharon and his supporters, that out of the symbolism would emerge reality, that out of a demonstrative act, legal issues of sovereignty could be claimed.[49] On the following day, a Friday, at the conclusion of prayers on the Muslim holy day, five worshippers were killed by Israeli police during demonstrations against the visit. This violence took place on the eve of the Jewish New Year, the holiday when, on two consecutive days, the morning services include readings on the incidents of the expulsion of Ishmael and the *Akedah* of Isaac.

This book deals only with Christian–Jewish relations, but Mount Moriah has strong historical connections with all three monotheistic religions. Religious interpretations of what transpired on this place, when Abraham prepared to sacrifice his son (in Muslim tradition, the son is believed to be Ishmael), see this as proof of absolute, unquestioning faith in God, to the extent of a willingness to sacrifice a beloved son. In a modern, secular world, however – where biblical themes and stories are still well remembered – this story can well become one, not of religious faith, but of human love, not of obsessive obedience to God but of concerned consideration for the meaning of behavior, including a challenge to the implementation of immoral demands, such as the gratuitous sacrifice of a child.

In a modern, secular world, where the Oedipus Complex has provided a framework for understanding generational contacts in terms that favor the parental and adult generation, there is a need also to be aware of the Rustum Complex, with its description of parental and adult hostility towards children.[50] And in a modern, secular world, where religion still has an important role to play, there is a need to balance the ostensibly straightforward story of the Crucifixion (a Heavenly Father willingly sacrificing His son) with the more complex story of the *Akedah* – focusing not on the sacrifice of Isaac, but on his binding; not on his death, but on his survival; not on a test of faith for his father, but on a probing of the latter's sensitivity and wisdom.

If such a re-interpretation could be made of the *Akedah* by all three religions then a similar re-interpretation could be made of the Crucifixion: not as a vicious cry for blood by a crowd of Jewish onlookers, but as an authoritative decision by a Roman court; not as a lesson of suffering on the Cross as an invitation to endless vengeance, but as a mimetic identification with suffering, by all. The problem of the present attitude to the Crucifixion is that by focusing on the suffering of Jesus, a divine son, there is a danger of a psychological displacement which allows for the present suffering of humanity to be too easily ignored. Perhaps an inkling of the kind of re-assessment needed is found in a footnote at the end of a learned analysis of Mark's Gospel by a committed Christian writer. Susan Garrett acknowledges the possible problems of presenting God, as she does in her book, 'as a testing God':[51]   namely as a God who imposes tests or, more specifically, 'temptations' on his son, Jesus. She admits that:

> Some contemporary theologians may object to the aloofness of a God who would permit the testing/suffering of Jesus on the cross, preferring instead to see God as one who through Jesus *enters into* the human condition of sin and suffering, healing us from within.[52]

At this stage, on the penultimate page of her text, Garrett notes reservations being expressed as to the Crucifixion by feminist scholars who :

> ... have objected to the implication of atonement theories that God willed for the Son to suffer, arguing that such a stance by God amounts to divine child abuse and that such notions of atonement have long functioned (and continue to function) to reinforce patriarchal structures in which the weak, especially women, must submit to violent abuse by men.[53]

I do not wish to confront the feminist assertion of the patriarchal structures, which is in my opinion a separate (yet substantially correct) issue, although related only indirectly to the suffering of Jesus. The direct issue is of course that of child abuse, that of a suffering son, that of a complacent Father witnessing yet not intervening, but most of all, that of a theology developed by men as their interpretation of what transpired on that fateful day, for all humanity, nearly two millenia ago.

Nevertheless, from the shadow of the Cross may yet emerge a glimmer of light, through the story of the *Akedah*, with its subtle meaning – perhaps also, and hopefully so, its true meaning. If the *Akedah* can be seen in terms of its climax – the saving of Isaac, the ending of child sacrifice, the warning of a possible Rustum Complex, of potential adult hostility to the young, then, from the initial binding of Isaac, it is possible to visualize his ultimate bonding with Abraham. And if there is indeed a link between the *Akedah* and the Crucifixion, then this potentiality may help to lighten the burden of the Cross that lies so heavily on Jew and Christian alike, both Children, according to their respective monotheistic ideologies, of the same Heavenly Father.

'Lay not thy hand upon the lad',[54] were the words that Abraham heard as he prepared to consummate the sacrifice of his son. For Jesus, there was no such last-minute reprieve. Nor for those who, over the years, have been the victims of child abuse in the family and in society. Nor for those Jews who have borne the brunt of Christian anger and vengeance.

Both the *Akedah* and the Crucifixion are momentous historical events and powerful symbolic images. They have been the subject of endless explanations, but they are still in need of further interpretation, based not just on respect for religious traditions, but also on an awareness of the harsh truths of social reality, of the exciting progress of scientific thought, and of the divine gift of human sensitivity.

NOTES

1. *See* the reference in Genesis, 14:15 to Melchizedek King of Salem. There is a presumption that the reference to Salem indicates the area where later Jerusalem was situated.
2. *See* description in I Kings, 6–7.
3. *See* discussion in Joel Carmichael, *The Death of Jesus* (New York: Macmillan, 1962); he writes:

> The Jewish Temple, celebrated in antiquity as the most splendid shrine in the world, was a vast edifice … It was restored on a still more magnificent scale by Herod the Great; more than 200 yards wide and 450 yards long, its rebuilding began in 20–19 BC. The work was so extensive that by the time of Jesus – 46 years later, according to John (2:20) – it was not yet completed. Actually the work on the outbuildings and the courts was to go on for 80 years altogether; it was not finished until AD 62–64 (pp. 135–6).

Carmichael goes on to explain that the Temple Hill was altogether a

> Huge complex of all sorts of administrative buildings, houses for attendants, offices, stables and a number of great courtyards. The Temple … also had a gigantic staff of attendants, supposed to number as many as 20,000, for a great variety of functions. (p.136)

He indicates that in its variety of functions, including commercial activities, it was, 'like other shrines in the Oriental world' (p. 136). The size and complexity of the total compound is then used by Carmichael to suggest that if Jesus had arrived there and made an impact on its activities, especially during the crowds that would have gathered for Passover, he would have had to have done so with a considerable group of supporters, possibly armed (since the Temple itself was protected by a force of several hundred troops) (p. 137). His description of such a confrontation seems far-fetched, but his description of the actual size of the Temple, and the nature of the compound, is of interest (see also p. 135 for a sketch plan of the Temple 'showing the immense courtyards and complex of buildings').
4. See Philip Goodman, *The Yom Kippur Anthology* (Philadelphia, PA: The Jewish Publication Society of America, 1971), p. 5, 'The Temple Ritual on the Day of Atonement'.
5. See Ph.D. dissertation by Ronen Friedman (Tel Aviv University, Department of Sociology and Anthropology – in progress).
6. *See* Matthew, 21:12–13:

> And Jesus went into the temple of God, and cast out all them that sold and brought in the temple, and overthrew the tables of the moneychangers, and the seats of them that sold doves. And said unto them, It is written, My house shall be called the house of prayer; but ye have made it a den of thieves.

7. *See* Mark, 14:57–8: 'And there arose certain, and bare false witness against him, saying, we heard him say, I will destroy this temple that is made with hands, and in three days I will build another made without hands.' However, as to the possibility that Jesus had actually said something to this effect, see Susan Garrett, *The Temptations of Jesus in Mark's Gospel* (Grand Rapids, MI: William Eerdmans Publishing, 1998), pp. 119–24, 'The Sanctuary Charge'.
8. Mark, 15:38. At 15:39, it is written that when the centurion saw that Jesus was dead, 'he said, "Truly this man was the Son of God"'. In this context, see comment by Bart Ehrman, *The Orthodox Corruption of Scripture: The Effect of Early Christological Controversies on the Text of the New Testament* (Oxford: Oxford University Press, 1993) who asserts that:

> The confession of the centurion represents the first (and only) instance of a person in Mark's gospel fully recognizing who Jesus is: he is the son of God who had to die, whose death was not alien to his divine sonship but was instead constitutive of it. In short, the ripping of the curtain and the confession of the centurion represents

> Mark's understanding of Jesus' death as an atoning sacrifice ... as the key to salvation. (p. 201)

9. *See*, for instance, Jonathan Campbell, *Deciphering the Dead Sea Scrolls* (London: Fontana Press, 1996), especially at pp. 136–41, under the sub-title of 'Was Jesus an Essene?', and pp. 141–53, under the sub-title of 'The Dead Sea Scrolls and Early Christianity'; *see also* Neil Asher Silberman, *The Hidden Scrolls: Christianity, Judaism and the War for the Dead Sea Scrolls* (London: Heinemann, 1995). Of particular interest is Silberman's reference to Josephus Flavius and:

> ... his grim anecdotes of charismatic prophets and messiah figures, public hysteria, and the customary cruel execution of would-be saviors in first-century Judea ... Simon, Athronges, Judas, John the Baptist, Jesus of Nazareth, Theudas ... were just some of the leaders and preachers mentioned by Josephus who ended up beheaded or nailed to a cross. (p. 6)

Later, again relying on Josephus, Silberman adds, 'The fact is that Jesus of Nazareth was but one of a long line of working-class prophets and would-be saviors who ended up in Roman custody' (p. 117).

10. *See* Goodman, *The Yom Kippur Anthology*, 'The Martyrdom of the Ten Sages', with commentary by Louis Jacobs, p. 72 – as originally published in *A Guide to Yom Kippur* (London: Jewish Chronicle Publications, 1951). *See also* Elaine Pagels, *The Gnostic Gospels* (London: Weidenfeld and Nicolson, 1979). Referring to two of the best-known individuals amongst the ten, Jacobs writes:

> Among the ten martyrs were Akiba, who died with a smile on his lips in obedience to the verse, 'And thou shalt love they God with all they life' ... and Hananiah ben Teradyon who was burned at the stake with a Sefer Torah wrapped round his body and who said that he saw 'the parchments burning but the letters of the Torah flying aloft'. (pp. 52–3)

See also S. Zeitlin, 'The Legend of the Ten Martyrs and its Apocalyptic Origin', *Jewish Quarterly Review*, 36 (1945), p. 1. He notes that there is no unanimity as to the identity of all ten, stating, 'Students differ as to who they actually were ... nevertheless they did not question the historicity of the Ten Martyrs' (p. 1).

11. Erich Wellisch, *Isaac and Oedipus: A Study in Biblical Psychology of the Sacrifice of Isaac – the Akedah* (London: Routledge and Kegan Paul, 1954).

12. *See* Bakan, 'Paternity in the Judeo-Christian Tradition', *The Human Condition* 4 (1972), p. 354. Bakan claims that, 'The essence of Judaism and Christianity is the management of the infanticidal impulse ... and a binding of the father against acting out the impulse.'

13. David Bakan, *The Quality of Human Existence: An Essay on Psychology and Religion* (Chicago, IL: Rand McNally, 1996). In discussing what he terms 'The Infanticidal Impulse', he explains the main ways in which Jewish law, custom and ritual were oriented to 'preventing the acting out of the infanticidal impulse. But by the time of the birth of Jesus, it no longer appeared to be sufficiently effective, as witness especially the holocaust of infant slaughter under Herod.' Referring to such rituals and rules, including the circumcision, the redemption of children by money, the substitution of animals for children, they 'did not seem to be effective any longer ... The rituals associated with the Mosaic Law were becoming perfunctory and empty. What, according to my interpretation, was their major function, the prevention of infanticide, was no longer being effectively performed' (p. 224). Drawing on his psychological approach, Bakan suggests that:

> We may interpret the Christianity of Jesus as an 'insight' into the nature of a repressed wish ... It took the repressed wish out of the deep unconscious and made it at least partially conscious, providing also a kind of fantasy satisfaction of this repressed wish in the image of the crucifixion of Jesus and the Pauline Eucharist. (p. 226)

He concludes that, 'one of the most significant features of the Christian doctrine is that it tended to lift the infanticidal impulse closer to consciousness' (p. 227).

14. In general, *see Leon* Sheleff, *Generations Apart: Adult Hostility to Youth* (New York: McGraw-Hill, 1981).

15. *See*, for instance, Dagobert Runes, *The Jew and the Cross* (New York: Philosophical Library, 1965). He writes: 'For some, the Roman cross is a symbol of charity, of supreme love and devotion. To the Jew it is a reminder of perennial persecution. The Cross to the Jew is the symbol of pogrom' (p. 67).

16. Hyman Maccoby, *The Mythmaker: Paul and the Invention of Christianity* (London: Weidenfeld and Nicolson, 1988), p. 110.

17. Frances Young, *Sacrifice and the Death of Christ* (London: SCM Press, 1983). *See also* Bruce Chilton, *The Temple of Jesus: His Sacrificial Program Within a Cultural History of Sacrifice* (University Park, PA: Pennsylvania State University Press, 1992). The larger issue of sacrifice, within a religious framework, has been addressed by a number of writers, most especially René Girard, *Violence and the Sacred* (Baltimore, MD: Johns Hopkins University, 1977); and Walter Burkett, *Homo Necans: The Anthropology of Ancient Greek Sacrificial Ritual and Myth* (Berkeley, CA: University of California, 1983). They both stress the role of violent acts as an underlying aspect of religious ritual. Their joint contributions are succinctly discussed in *Violent Origins: Ritual Killing and Cultural Formation* (Stanford, CA: Stanford University Press, 1987), edited by Robert G. Hamerton-Kelly, and based on a special conference devoted to their work held in California in 1983. The editor explains that, 'René Girard and Walter Burkett present analyses of human culture and its origins that focus on the role of violence.' Yet, while clearly focusing on the connection between the nadir of violence and the uplifting of religion, they basically ignore two of the major acts of violence in the religious traditions of the western world: the *Akedah* and the Crucifixion.

Burkett has no index reference to either of these events or to the key characters of Isaac and Jesus, but he does make one passing reference to the fact that, 'The death of God's son is the one-time and perfect sacrifice, although it is still repeated in the celebration of the Lord's Supper in breaking the bread and drinking the wine' (p. 8). This statement appears immediately after his contention that:

> Judaism in the Diaspora spread more easily because cult practices had become consecrated in one temple in Jerusalem, thus virtually making Judaism outside of Jerusalem a religion without animal-sacrifice. This also helped form Christian practice which could thus take up the tradition of Greek philosophy. On the other hand it gave the idea of sacrifice a central significance and raised it to a higher status than ever before.

In Girard's book, there is no mention of either Jesus or the Crucifixion, but there is a reference to Isaac; however, this is made in an incorrect context, with reference to Muslim ritual, whereas, in the latter religion, the son to be sacrificed by Abraham is Ishmael. In his book, Girard deals with Greek mythology, and makes many references to the Oedipus story (*see*, especially, chapter 7, 'Freud and the Oedipus Complex'). He notes that Oedipus 'has no monopoly on anger' and that his anger 'is never without antecedents' (p. 69), and that 'The whole of psychoanalysis seems to be summed up in the patricide-incest theme.' He also stresses that 'It is this theme that has won psychoanalysis its glory', but he fails to make any acknowledgment of filicidal aspects in the story: namely that the antecedent anger (which he mentions) stems mainly from a parental source.

It might also be mentioned that in *Violent Origins*, most of the participants in the conference made only peripheral mention of the critical fact that the defining moment of the Christian religion is of the sacrifice of a divine son. Indeed, Girard's reference to this fact is made not in his prepared lecture, but in the course of the subsequent discussion, where he states:

> Fraser says that a proof of the nonspecial nature of the Bible is that the centrality of the death of Jesus Christ makes the New Testament just like many other religious

> sources that have a dying savior at their core … The Crucifixion is the same event as in the myths. (p. 141)

See pp. 142–5 for a continuation of the discussion, but again there is no reference to the filicidal nature of the sacrificial act in Christian theology.

18. Young, *Sacrifice and the Death of Christ*, p. 3.
19. Ibid.
20. Ibid., p. 48.
21. Ibid., p. 49.
22. Ibid., p. 50.
23. Ibid.
24. Ibid., p. 51.
25. Ibid.
26. Lacey Baldwin Smith, *Fools, Martyrs, Traitors: The Story of Martyrdom in the Western World* (New York: Knopf, 1997).
27. Ibid., chapter 2, 'Socrates: The Genesis of Martyrdom', p. 23; and chapter 3, 'The Maccabees and the Doctrine of Suffering', p. 41. For a discussion of the role of martyrdom in Jewish tradition, stemming not from the Maccabees, but the *Akedah, see* Aharon Agus, *The Binding of Isaac and Messiah: Law, Martyrdom and the Deliverance in Early Rabbinic Religosity* (Albany, NY: State University of New York, 1988).
28. *See*, for instance, the discussion in Sydney Lipshires, *Herbert Marcuse: From Marx to Freud and Beyond* (Cambridge, MA: Schenkman, 1974).
29. Smith, *Fools, Martyrs, Traitors*, pp. 26–7.
30. *See*, for instance, Richard A. Horsely, *Jesus and the Spiral of Violence: Popular Jewish Resistance in Roman Palestine* (Minneapolis, MN: Fortress Press, 1993).
31. Smith, *Fools, Martyrs, Traitors*, p. 45.
32. Ibid., p. 61.
33. Ibid.
34. Ibid.
35. Ibid.
36. Ibid., p. 63.
37. Ibid.
38. Ibid., pp. 63–4.
39. Ibid., p. 71.
40. Ibid., p. 72.
41. Ibid., p. 86.
42. Ibid.
43. Ibid., p. 85.
44. *See*, for instance, *History of Childhood Quarterly*, for articles documenting abuse of children at different periods of history.
45. *See* Loyd de Mouse, *The History of Childhood* (New York: Harper Torchbooks, 1975).
46. *See*, for instance, reference in Jeurgensmeyer, *Terror in the Mind of God: The Global Rise of Religious Violence* (Berekely, CA: University of California Press, 2000), chapter 3, 'Zion Betrayed', especially at p. 46, where he describes the view that, 'the prophesized Messiah will come to earth only after the temple is rebuilt and made ready for him. Thus the issue of the temple was not only a matter of cultural nostalgia but also one of pressing religious importance.'
47. A governmental commission was appointed to investigate this incident. Juergensmeyer, ibid., explains that 'The location of the biblical temple is often described as directly beneath the holy Muslim shrine, the Dome of the Rock' (p. 46). *See also* Roger Friedland and Richard Hecht, 'Divisions at the Center: The Organization of Political Violence at Jerusalem's Temple Mount/al-Haram al-Sharif – 1929 and 1990', in Paul Brass (ed.), *Riots and Pogroms: The Nation State and Violence* (New York: Macmillan, 1996).
48. Because of the number of child victims of the violence, a Working Group was established in Israel by the initiative of the Defence of Children International to make representations to the authorities on both sides to make every effort to avoid harm caused to children.
49. *See* Leon Sheleff, *The Thin Green Line: Intractable Problems and Feasible Solutions to*

Israeli–Palestinian Conflict (in manuscript). chapter 8, 'Commissions – and Omissions – of Enquiry'.

50. Ibid., part 3, 'The Rustum Complex'.
51. Susan R. Garrett, *The Temptations of Jesus in Mark's Gospel*.
52. Ibid., p. 180.
53. Ibid., fn 12. Garrett makes reference to a summary article by L. Van Dyk, 'Do Theories of Atonement Foster Abuse?', *Perspectives*, 12 (1997), pp. 11–13.
54. Genesis, 22:12.

Index